HARVARD ECONOMIC STUDIES

VOLUME LXXXIII

LONDON : GEOFFREY CUMBERLEGE

OXFORD UNIVERSITY PRESS

HAWAII

A Century of Economic Change
1778–1876

By

THEODORE MORGAN
ASSOCIATE PROFESSOR OF ECONOMICS
UNIVERSITY OF WISCONSIN

HARVARD UNIVERSITY PRESS
CAMBRIDGE, MASSACHUSETTS
·1948·

PRINTED AND BOUND BY
THE COLONIAL PRESS INC.
CLINTON, MASSACHUSETTS, U.S.A.

To

MY FATHER AND MOTHER

PREFACE

THE FOLLOWING study was begun at Honolulu in 1937–1938, and completed at Cambridge, Massachusetts, through work done at intervals between 1940 and 1947. The period of Hawaiian economic history which it covers can be briefly defined as that of the transition between the native feudalism and an agricultural and commercial private enterprise system. The chronological limits are defined as 1778, the date of Cook's first visit, and 1876, when the Reciprocity Treaty with the United States was signed and the framework of the present economic organization fixed.

When Captain Cook made his landfall at Kauai in 1778, he initiated a contact with western civilization which ended more than a thousand years of nearly complete isolation. Before this, the forms of social organization had evolved primarily from internal causation. Afterwards, economic and social evolution was determined by external forces—the need of fur traders bound from the northwest coast to oriental harbors for fresh provisions and water; the demand in the temples of China for sandalwood, growing unvalued on the slopes of the Island mountains; the desire of New England churches to spread the Gospel; the requirement of New England whalers (forced around the Horn by the shrinking quantity of game in the Atlantic) for safe anchorage, repairs, and provisions; and, finally, the external demand, varying with political and economic circumstance, for agricultural produce growable in the Island valleys. Each of these has risen to its noon of influence, and, save the last, has declined; and all together have bound Hawaii tightly to western civilization. They have made its development since 1778 as fully a theme of adaptation as social adjustments earlier represented effects of internal causes.

The development of Hawaii since discovery gains significance through its being representative: it is a special case of what has been going on generally in the last several centuries, as Europe has expanded upon less technically developed societies. Hawaii's smallness of size, its strategic position, and its useful resources have resulted in a more rapid and total transformation than generally occurred elsewhere; but in a number of essential ways the same kind of events took place. Native economies crumbled beneath the impact of the white man, whether he came with peace or violence, preaching the Gospel or swearing lustily that "There is no God west of the Horn"—or both, as in Hawaii. There succeeds an intervening period of rapid transformation, of shifting, precarious short-term interests on the part of the whites, of loss of morale and decline in numbers and power on the part of the natives; until the area finds a place in the interdependent relationships of the regional or world economy.

I am indebted to Mr. R. J. Baker and Dr. A. L. Dean, both of Honolulu, for information and suggestions; and to Professor Chester W. Wright of the University of Chicago for criticism of emphasis and organization. Dr. William H. Taylor, then of the University of Hawaii, generously put his notes on the Hawaiian sugar industry at my disposal. I remember gratefully also the assistance of the staff of the Archives of Hawaii. And to Professor A. P. Usher, of Harvard University, I owe my sincere thanks for his continuing interest and helpfulness.

T. M.

April 20, 1948

CONTENTS

SECTION I

THE ECONOMIC STATUS OF THE HAWAIIANS IN 1778

SECTION II

THE DECAY OF FEUDALISM, 1778–1844

SECTION IV

POSTSCRIPT ON RECIPROCITY

CHARTS

SECTION I

THE ECONOMIC STATUS OF THE HAWAIIANS IN 1778

CHAPTER I

THE ISLANDS AND THEIR PEOPLE

The Islands

The Hawaiian Islands are placed centrally in the Pacific Ocean, at the northern edge of the Tropic Zone. The group as a whole extends nearly 2000 miles in a northwest-southeast direction, along the great fault in the earth's surface running from Japan to California; but the extreme limit of the eight main islands, Niihau, Kauai, Oahu, Molokai, Maui, Lanai, Kahoolawe, and Hawaii,[1] is only 388 land miles.

The isolation of the Islands is striking. The nearest land mass of size is the Pacific Coast of the United States, over 2000 miles away. Next nearest are the inhabited islands of the South Seas, Tahiti, Samoa, and Fiji, from some of which the Hawaiians came originally, approximately 2300 to 2800 miles distant. It is 3400 miles to the coast of Japan, and 3800 to the nearest ports of New Zealand and Australia. Manila, the Coast of China, and the west coast of South America are 4700 or more miles away. But this same isolation, which led to Hawaii's being one of the last livable parts of the globe to be inhabited by man, has led to the Island's becoming a center in later days, an advertised Pacific Crossroads. Sailing ship, steamship, and plane alike have been grateful for a mid-voyage stopping place in the vast expanse of the Pacific.

The Islands aggregate 6407 square miles in area, almost exactly that of Connecticut plus Rhode Island. Four of them preëmpt attention as being largest, most productive, and most populous: Kauai, Oahu, Maui, and Hawaii. All are of volcanic origin, formed of successive layers of basaltic lava, oozing out on the ocean floor, and building up to the peaks above the ocean which are the Islands. The process still goes on in the largest island,

[1] Hawaiian words are spelled phonetically. The pronunciation is roughly that of Spanish, with accent on the penultimate syllable. For a detailed guide to pronunciation see Lorrin Andrews and Henry H. Parker, *A Dictionary of the Hawaiian Language* (Honolulu: 1922), pp. xix–xx.

Hawaii, where Mauna Loa Volcano and Kilauea on the flank of Mauna Loa erupt their flows toward the sea every few years, and where Hualalai erupted during the nineteenth century. North on Maui, Haleakala is thought to have had its last eruption 250 years ago, only a moment distant in geologic time.

But the older portions of these islands, and the other islands, have seen thousands of years since the last eruption; and the original stark volcanic domes have been generally obliterated by decay and erosion. Desolate lava fields have been sculptured deep by water courses from the central heights, and valleys and alluvial plains have replaced the lava. Growth of coral over centuries has added to land area along the coast and reshaped the water line.

To windward, that is to east and northeast from which the trade winds blow over four-fifths of the time, headlands rise precipitously from the sea, channeled by streams, and covered thick with vegetation. Rainfall is heaviest along the slopes and summits of the eastern ranges where the trades are first intercepted. Annual rainfalls of over 500 inches have been recorded: jungle swamps cover the summit of Waialeale on Kauai, which has an average of over 476 inches, and that of Kaala on Oahu. The leeward sides of the Islands usually slope more gradually to the sea, and rainfall diminishes. Where the ranges to the east are high, desert conditions may be found, with total annual rainfall under ten inches.

In contrast with the variance of rainfall, temperature at given altitudes is very stable, due to the effect of the immense surrounding area of water. Winter is experienced mainly as a rainy season. Two typical temperatures may be given: at Honolulu an average for August, the warmest month, is 78.4°; for the coldest month, January, 70.1°. At Kailua on Maui, with an elevation of 700 feet, the range is from 73.2° (September) to 67.6° (February). The mean difference for four locations between the averages for the coldest and warmest months is 6.8°.

Such few species of plants grew, before the coming of the Hawaiians, as had their seeds transported by waves, wind, or migratory birds. The earliest comers doubtless found the pandanus (*lauhala,* or *hala*) there before them, a plant whose fruit could be prepared in several ways for eating. Among other edible plants might have been a kind of coconut, a yam, and several plants whose leaves or roots could be eaten (such as the *ki ieie*), starchy tree ferns, and sea weeds. There were probably a few berries and a native apple. Of animals there were only birds, insects, and snails; and of course fish in abundance.

Original Colonization

The Polynesians came in remote times from India and Asia Minor. Early migrations brought them south into the island groups between Sumatra and Luzon. From these islands organized expeditions took place into the Pacific Ocean during the first few centuries of the Christian era. By this time they were a thoroughly mixed race. Hawaii was reached, probably by way of Tahiti and perhaps the Marquesas, in or before the sixth century A.D.

After the first migratory period there was a cessation of intercourse with the south for some centuries, but starting with the eleventh and twelfth centuries many voyages were made between the southern islands and Hawaii. "The Polynesian folklore in all the principal groups becomes replete with the legends and songs of a number of remarkable men, stirring adventures, and voyages undertaken to far-off lands." [2] Voyages might have been easier in those days through the existence of islands and shoals which do not now exist, intermediate between Hawaii and the South Pacific. The Hawaiians possessed a considerable knowledge of navigation, and there is reason to believe that they possessed more seaworthy canoes then than later.

These voyagers, and the earlier immigrants, brought to Hawaii a number of useful plants and animals. Among the former were taro,[3] sugar cane, certain greens and roots, and probably varieties of sweet potatoes and bananas. Of animals, they brought the pig, dog, a kind of common fowl, and probably the *iole*, or rat.[4]

The period of great voyages ended at the close of the fourteenth century or beginning of the fifteenth, having brought north a large influx of new people, among them the ancestors of most of the Hawaiian *alii*, or chieftain class. From then until Cook's visit

[2] Abraham Fornander, *The Polynesian Race, its Origin and Migrations* (London: 1880), II, p. 6.

[3] A low growing plant (*Arum esculentum*) looking something like a thrifty rhubarb, whose bulbous root, when macerated, mixed with water, and (usually) fermented, was *poi*, a chief food of the Islanders.

[4] *Hawaiian Historical Society Report* (Honolulu: 1916), p. 52.

in 1778, the Islands were without significant contact with the outer world. Hawaiian legend mentions three minor visits. It is fairly sure from Spanish records that Juan Gaetano came on the group in 1555, as he was sailing from New Spain to the Spice Islands; but nothing came of his discovery.[5]

THE POPULATION SUPPORTED AT THE TIME OF COOK'S VISIT

The population of the Islands was in 1779 estimated to be 400,-000. The estimate, made by Captain King who took command of the Cook expedition after the death of the great explorer, was a generalization based on the supposed population of the Kealake-kua region in Hawaii:

> The Bay of Karakakooa in Owhyhee [Kealakekua, Hawaii] is three miles in extent, and contains four villages of about eighty houses each; upon an average in all three hundred and twenty; besides a number of straggling houses, which make the whole amount to three hundred and fifty. From the frequent opportunities I had of informing myself on this head, I am convinced that six persons to a house is a very moderate allowance; so that on this calculation, the country about the Bay contains two thousand one hundred souls. To these may be added fifty families, or three hundred persons, which I conceive to be nearly the number employed in the interior parts of the country among their plantations, making in all two thousand four hundred. If therefore this number be applied to the whole extent of the coast round the island, deducting a quarter for uninhabited parts, it will be found to contain one hundred and fifty thousand.[6]

The population of seven other islands was estimated similarly.

It is evident that the figures resulting are too high. Captain Cook's previous estimate[7] for Kauai is 30,000, as compared with 54,000 in King's estimate, though his method is the same, a generalization on the basis of accepting the village of Waimea, Kauai, as a standard, and estimating sixty such villages on that island. Likewise Cook had judged Niihau[8] to have only one-twentieth of what King estimated, 500 as against 10,000.

[5] See Fornander, *op. cit.*, II, 359–364.

[6] (Captain) N. King, *A Voyage to the Pacific Ocean in the Years 1776–1780* (London: 1784), III, 128–129. (Volumes I and II were written by Captain Cook.)

Professor Adams reproduces a less careful estimate by Bligh, master on Cook's ship, of 242,000. The original source of this is given as penciled notes on the margin of page 129 of Bligh's copy of volume III of the 1784 edition of Cook's voyages, a volume now in the possession of the Admiralty library. Romanzo Adams, *Interracial Marriage in Hawaii* (New York: 1937), p. 1.

[7] Captain James Cook, *op. cit.*, II, 230.

[8] Cook, *op. cit.*, II, 218.

King's figures are biased upward for several reasons. Although one small island, Kahoolawe, is omitted from the list, one other is included, Lehua, with 4000 people credited to it, which could hardly have had any permanent population, because of lack of water supply. Further, the area taken as a sample—the Kealakekua region of Kona, Hawaii—was able to support a far heavier concentration of population than were the Islands generally. Its rainfall is adequate, the soil is productive, the topography not too rough, and the fishing opportunities excellent. Elsewhere the possibilities of support were often much poorer because of rough terrain (northeast Hawaii and Maui, north Molokai, and northwest Kauai), or inadequate water supply (Lanai and Niihau, Kahoolawe, west Oahu), or poor fishing. And, finally, to the extent that wars were an important depopulating influence, Kealakekua was favored through the stability implied in its being under a powerful chieftain, well able to protect his domains. It was the stronghold of Kamehameha I, who at the end of the eighteenth century was able to conquer all the islands and unite them under his rule.

Two recent students have accepted 300,000 as a reasonable figure for the population of Cook's time.[9]

In the four to five centuries intervening between the end of the great Polynesian voyages and Cook's visit, the population had time to stabilize itself at a level approaching the maximum which the land and sea resources of the Islands could sustain with the given social organization and stone age techniques and economy of the Hawaiians. Early navigators were generally impressed with the intensive and effective use made of available land. About 1793, Menzies, a surgeon with Vancouver, reports of the region above Kealakekua Bay: "For several miles around us there was not a spot that would admit of it but was with great labor and industry cleared of the loose stones, and planted with esculent roots, or some useful vegetables or other." [10]

In the valley of Kalalau on Kauai as elsewhere "the ancient Hawaiians had terraced the land far up the hillsides. Small

[9] Adams, *Interracial Marriage in Hawaii*, p. 2; Andrew W. Lind, *An Island Community* (Chicago: 1938), p. 90.

[10] Archibald Menzies, "Hawaii Nei 128 Years Ago," in the *Hawaiian Annual* (Honolulu: 1908), p. 76.

terraces no larger than one-tenth the size of a class room were watered and made to produce food. Great irrigation ditches were dug, and the land was extremely productive." [11]

Fishing resources were utilized to the full: "We have often been surprized to find the desolate coasts more thickly inhabited than some of the fertile tracts in the interior; a circumstance which we can only account for by supposing that the facilities which the former afford for fishing induce the natives to prefer them." [12]

The primary orientation of the population was toward the productive resources of the sea and the rich bottom land, from which their staple foodstuffs of fish, taro, and sweet potatoes could be obtained. Scattered or compact villages grew up along the seacoast, their size proportionate to the quantity of adjacent food supply; and the scarcer resources from the island uplands—wood, plants, and game—were carried down to the villages. It is notable that King's estimate of population distribution at Kealakekua, a region with an extensive and productive hinterland, nevertheless ascribes seven-eighths of the population to the coast.

The aim of security was, however, equally important with that of food supply. In the decades before discovery, wars had become such a menace to stable life that unproductive but inaccessible valleys were often thickly populated, while certain near-by rich plains would be without inhabitants because they were more open to marauding.[13] When the alien civilization of the *haole*[14] disrupted adjustment between the Hawaiian people and their resources, the population abruptly declined; and it was not for 150 years, or until about 1925, that the supposed original population of 300,000 was again achieved on the material basis of a capitalist economy.[15]

[11] Thomas B. Vance, "Industrial Hawaii," MS. in University of Hawaii Library pp. 7–8.

[12] Journal of William Ellis, *Narrative of a Tour Around Hawaii in 1823* (Honolulu: 1917), p. 203.

[13] There doubtless was some decline of population below the maximum as a result of disorders and wars, for temporary periods at any rate. Probably such a decline had taken place in the decades just before Cook's visit.

[14] "White," that is, foreigner.

[15] Lind, *An Island Community*, pp. 93–94.

Social Classes and the Tabu

The population was sharply divided into social ranks. A complex and precise hierarchy had grown up, especially after the two centuries of the great voyages; and around its feudal structure distribution and production, too, were essentially organized.

As in Europe, the feudal organization grew up during an epoch of disorder. The hardening of its divisions and tightening of its form took place especially during the several centuries before discovery. Ambitions and jealousies between chieftain families, rapacity and avarice on the part of chiefs of all ranks, and population pressure led to frequent wars within as well as between islands. Legend reports heavy slaughter in such struggles, of battle where two alone escaped to tell, and of rivers and sea red with blood.

As custom gave way to the blunt authority of social rank, the chieftain (*alii*) and priest (*kahuna*) class became more and more tyrannically dominant and aristocratic, and the commoners (*makaainana*) increasingly degraded and defenseless. Turnbull gives us a portrait of chiefly manners in the early days after Cook:

> After some time appeared one of the deputy chiefs of the island . . . whose approach occasioned no small alarm among the other islanders in their endeavoring to open a passage for him. But as many of their canoes were crowded and tangled together, they were in a hurry run down by the canoe of this great man, who took not the least notice of the disasters he had so wantonly occasioned . . . The poor natives, recovering their canoes, cleared them of the water without expressing the slightest dissatisfaction or complaint . . . He commanded the canoes to remove to a greater distance . . . For as many of his countrymen as were in any degree tardy in obeying his mandate, he saluted with stones from our ballast, which maimed not a few. . . Philosophers are most mistaken who build systems of natural liberty. Rousseau's savages exist nowhere but in his writings.[16]

During this turbulent period for the first time kings were recognized on each island. In previous times no chief had possessed authority beyond his own proper lands, though the largest landholder among the chiefs might claim to be "first among equals."

Any aspirant to the status of chiefhood had to show that he was descended through either parent from one or more of the undisputed ancestors of the Hawaiian nobility in order to gain

[16] John Turnbull, *Voyages round the World* (London: 1805), II, 16–19.

admission to the *Aha-Alii*, the "congregation of chiefs," or Herald's College. Once admitted, no crime, no offense, could affect his status; nor could loss of his possessions decrease his rank. His parentage once and for all placed him in the hierarchy.[17] Hence sometimes the hierarchy based on social rank came into conflict with that based on possessions; and a chief superior in the Aha-Alii might hold lands from an inferior. Allegiance and fealty were given to a chief socially superior only for other than social reasons: personal interest (as tenure of land), family attachment, or predominant force. Allegiance might be ended abruptly by a fancied slight or by caprice, with the inferior maintaining himself by war if he could, or fleeing for refuge to another island.

The priesthood grew during this era to be a separate and immune group. After a time in which they measured wills on equal terms with the chiefs, the two came to be closely interrelated in their policies, joined in what takes on the aspect, from one point of view, of a continuous conspiracy against the makaainana. With the growing rigidity of social divisions, human sacrifice was introduced into ceremonies, or at least was more generally performed; and the *kapus* (tabus) were enforced with growing rigor.

Of the tabus, some were specifically religious. At the building of a temple (*heiau*), or during ceremonial times, a strict general tabu might be promulgated: all people stopped their usual occupations and stayed indoors, all fires were put out, and all animals and poultry were muzzled so that they could make no noise. Often there was a mixture of religious and political implications, as a "strict" or an "ordinary" tabu (one in which regulations were milder) might be proclaimed before a war, or during a chief's sickness.

In contrast with these general tabus, denoting periods of time in which all activities were affected, there were numerous tabus which were specific regulations. "If a man made his idol of an apple tree, or of a hen, or hog, or taro, that was henceforth tabu to him." [18] Some special regulations had a primarily political significance. Commoners had to prostrate themselves before the sacred chiefs, nor might the shadow of a commoner fall on such

[17] Abraham Fornander, *The Polynesian Race*, II, 28–29.

[18] Rev. Sheldon Dibble, *A History of the Sandwich Islands* (Lahainaluna: 1843), p. 80.

a chief, nor on his canoe, nor on any of his possessions. A commoner was not allowed to sit or stand at a higher level than such a chief,[19] and areas which the high chiefs or priests frequented were often tabu to commoners.

Many of the ordinary economic activities such as planting and harvesting of crops, and (more emphatically) fishing, canoe building, and house building were restricted with prohibitions and required ritual, to an extent which significantly increased the necessary outlay of effort in production.

But the tabus evoked extra labor mainly as a by-product of their prohibitions to women.[20] It was forbidden for a woman to eat pork, bananas, and some kinds of fish. Preparation of food, and eating were entirely separate for men and women. A man had to heat one oven and bake for his wife, then heat another and bake for himself. Their taro was pounded separately.[21]

> A man had to thatch a house for himself to eat in, and another house as a sanctuary (*heiau*) in which to worship his idols . . . He had to prepare a third house for himself and his wife to sleep in. After that he must build and thatch an eating place for his wife, and lastly he had to prepare a *hale kua,* a place for his wife to beat tapa in [as well as engage in other domestic occupations].[22]

Any violation, intended or not, of the tabu was punishable severely, generally with death, though enforcement was not rigorous against the higher *alii.*

The all-pervading authority of the tabu was the primary defense of the customary Hawaiian "way of life" in its widest sense: it protected and sanctified the political order and enconomic procedures, furthering stability in return for its heavy burden on production and social relationships.

One can analyze the social classes more in detail. In the top rank, after the uniting of the Islands, was the king (*moi*), the

[19] A high (*kapu*) chief could put aside for a spell his dread exclusiveness, bothersome alike to himself and his subjects, by smudging himself with the smoke from the fire of a given kind of wood. Then he could mingle with the commoners on equal terms.

[20] "They fall very far short of the other islanders in the respect shown women . . . In their domestic life they live almost entirely by themselves; and though we did not observe any instances of personal ill-treatment, yet it is evident that they had little regard or attention paid them." Captain King, *ibid,* III, 130.

[21] Dibble, *History of the Sandwich Islands,* pp. 80–81.

[22] David Malo, *Hawaiian Antiquities* (Honolulu: 1903), p. 51.

queen, and all the members of the royal family. The king owned all land and all property, and held power of life and death over all the people. Ranking with him was his chief counselor, or *Kalaimoku* (Island-carver), who might have risen by merit from a much lower station among the chiefs. He was always a man of mature judgment, skilled in war and government, whose task was to oversee the complex details of administering the kingdom, with especial emphasis on the collection of taxes and the dispensing of land among the loyal followers of the king.

In the second rank were the governors of the several islands, and the major chiefs who held a *moku* (or principal section of an island), which usually covered several valleys and ran from the seashore to or near the central mountains. These, after the conquest of the Islands, were the principal followers of Kamehameha or their descendants; or descendants of those of the original ruling chiefs who had pledged their allegiance to the new regime. Their tenure was conditional on military support and transmission of taxes, in a fashion to be described later.

Next were the chiefs who held *ahupuaas,* or large estates, typically a valley running from shore to mountain; and under them those lesser chiefs who held *ilis,* a segment of the ahupuaa. These two groups of chiefs were by far the most numerous of the chieftain class, and might be considered plantation proprietors, cultivating the land with their own retainers, or hiring it out to commoners. As we descend the scale of land sizes, compensation for tenure comes to be not so much the obligation of military service as payment of taxes. These taxes were feudal dues in the form of produce of the soil, forest, and sea.

At this level of the social scale are most of the priests, powerful because of their cordial relationship with the gods, and their expert knowledge in many technical activities. They reported on signs and omens, established tabus, and liquidated those who broke them; and supervised and gave ghostly sanction to canoe building, house construction, fishing, navigation, and the like. They were recognized as doctors and paid in advance.

The executive agents of the king and chiefs were called *konohiki.* One major concern of theirs was the execution of orders, such as the procurement of men for fighting in wartime, and for public works construction in peacetime (the digging and maintenance of irrigation channels, and the building of paths, temples, and fleets of canoes). No less important were their duties with respect to the smooth functioning of the tax collection system. They saw to it that a regular flow of food, *tapa* (native cloth), mats, utensils, and other needed supplies came to the royal household, and that the main taxes, due annually at the time of the Makahiki, were properly gathered.[23]

The *ilamuku* were police and sheriffs, "guardians of the law," looking to the enforcement of regulations and tabus. They seem not to have been a permanently separate class.

The commoners, or *makaainana,* included canoe and house builders and other craftsmen, fishermen, hunters, and farmers. Among the latter were those who rented small plots of ten to thirty acres, and landless persons who attached themselves to some small landholder in return for food and clothing. The division of labor indicated above implies that barter was fairly well developed: craftsmen often spent their whole time on their specialty, and were paid in articles which they did not themselves produce.[24] The commoners were by far the most numerous of the classes.

Several other groups stand out sufficiently to deserve special mention. About the residence of the king and foremost chiefs there collected a group of courtiers, either commoners or lower chiefs. Their description by the native historian Malo has a familiar ring:

> The people about court were not timid or easily abashed; they were not rough or muscular in physique, but they were bold and impudent in speech . . . There was hardly anyone about court who did not practice robbery, and who was not a thief, embezzler, extortionist, and shameless beggar . . . The court of a king offered great attractions to the lazy and shiftless.[25]

In an easier position than most of the commoners were the servants of the high chiefs and of the king. They generally worked "much less than the people who occupy the lands, or cultivate them." It was a life of careless improvidence, of much pretense at work but little protracted effort, of gormandizing when food was plentiful and of going without for days when it was scarce, of moving along to another chief when prospects seemed

[23] E. H. Bryan, "Government and Society," number 18 in a series in the *Honolulu Advertiser,* February 21, 1938.

[24] See below, pp. 46–48.

[25] Malo, *Hawaiian Antiquities,* p. 94.

better with him. At Lahaina, Maui, where Ellis interrogated a group during his 1823 tour, they told him that they worked on the plantations three or four days in a week, sometimes from daylight till nine or ten o'clock in the forenoon; that preparing an oven of food took an hour; and that when they went for sandalwood, which was not very often, they were gone three or four days, and sometimes as many weeks. After their work time, and on the days they did not work, "they ate poë,[26] lay down to sleep, or *kamailio no* (just talked for amusement)." [27]

Malo speaks of the existence of a class of beggars, *noi* (vociferous) and *makilo* (silent), and of genuine tramps *kuewa,* who "wheedled their way from place to place." [28]

Then there were the group of hereditary pariahs, the *kuawa,* who were slaves from generation to generation to corresponding generations of masters. They had lost right to land and personal possessions.[29]

In summary, the population in Hawaii can hardly be classed as "savages"; nor was their social system a feudal structure that can rightly be called primitive. It was evolved and well articulated. The blunt term "stone age culture" is inadequately appreciative of the complexity of their development: the fact that they smelted no metals may have been due to the lack of mineral resources in the islands, rather than to any inability to make use of metallic ores had they been available.

Authority radiated from its source, the king, through several collinear channels: through the hierarchy of chiefs; through the priests; and through the administrative officials, from the Kalai-

[26] An old spelling of *poi.*

[27] Ellis, *Journal,* p. 64.

[28] Malo, *Hawaiian Antiquities,* p. 86.

[29] Malo, *ibid.,* p. 99. Lind argues that the *kuawa* were the remnants of a slave class once important in the economy, when population was sparse in relation to resources; but that as in other parts of Oceania, when population increased to the biologic limit, the utility of the institution disappeared with the rise of a surplus labor force seeking subsistence (*An Island Community,* pp. 31–32).

Another, social, factor must be in any case added to this, that the compulsions of the tabu and landownership systems were sufficient to supply needed consumption goods to the *alii.* Since produce was mostly perishable, there were limits on what the chiefs had any incentive to exact.

The anthropologist E. H. Bryan says merely: "It is not known how persons came to be in this class. They might have broken laws or *kapus,* have been those conquered in wars, or in some sections have been even the remnant of another, perhaps aboriginal, stock of people." (*Ibid.*)

moku, down through the Konohiki and Ilamuku. Settled specialization existed among the commoners in many crafts.

The complexity of the relationships suggests a long period of social stability. These relationships existed in part despite the epoch of wars; in part no doubt because of them, since the need for security demanded an effective organization. There is suggested too the fundamental character of a feudal structure, which "naturally" arises at a given stage of social evolution from internal reasons, under widely varying external circumstances of climate, topography, and details of culture.

CHAPTER II

LAND DIVISIONS, LAND TENURE, AND TAXES

Land Divisions

The typical land division of an island can be represented graphically, as shown in the accompanying drawing. Here the island is assumed to be circular, and to have one central dome.[1] One *moku* only is shown divided.

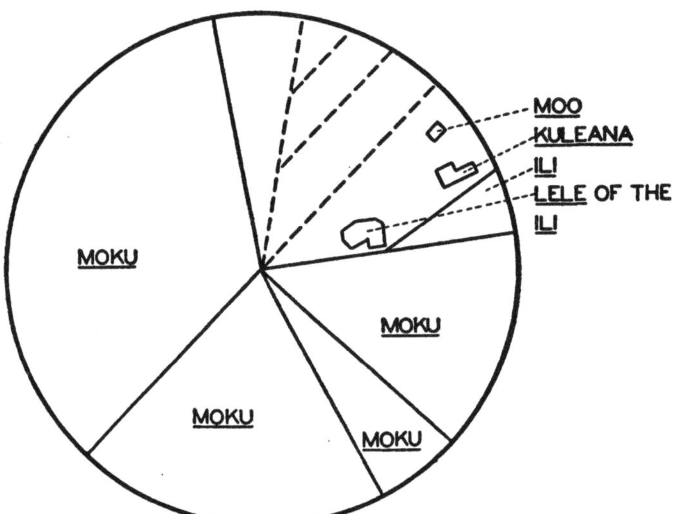

Borders of the *ahupuaas* are indicated by broken lines.
All of them together make up the fifth *moku*.

I. The largest unit was the island, in charge of a major chieftain, the *alii nui*. When the islands were still independent, the chieftain was a king in his own right; after they were united he was a governor, a chief deputy under the king of all the islands. To emphasize the island's separateness from others, it was called

[1] Following, in general, John H. Wise, *Ancient Hawaiian Civilization*, pp. 88–89.

maku-puni (cut-off); and to emphasize its being a stable dwelling place of men, it was called *aina* (land, place of food).[2]

II. Within the island the largest unit was the *moku*. This appears to have been an administrative unit, for there was no chieftain over it.[3]

The moku generally ran in wedge-shaped fashion from the shore to a conspicuous point on the crest of a mountain range, or to the summit of the central mountain of the island or of a major region of the island. Its boundaries might be very irregular as they followed natural boundaries such as main ridges. Mokus were relatively large, though varying in size: there were six on Oahu, an island of over a hundred miles in circumference; and six also on Maui, which is somewhat larger.

III. The typical and most important unit for the alii class was the *ahupuaa*,[4] into which the moku was divided for landholding purposes. The ahupuaa was a complete estate, running from the sea to the mountains, and hence providing a share of all the different products of soil and sea: fish at the seashore; taro, yams, sugar cane, breadfruit, and bananas in the fertile area of the lowlands; and further up in the forest belt, firewood, poles for houses, logs for canoes, bark for tapa cloth,[5] *oloana* and other plant fiber for cord and rope, and feathers.[6]

The ahupuaa was by no means an area of given size. Ellis speaks of it as a district or village, which sometimes extended five or six miles along the coast, at other times not more than half a mile.[7] Lyons, a land surveyor of the mid-nineteenth century, found the area to vary from 100 acres to as much as 100,000 acres, and even more in the wastes of interior Hawaii. On that island he found the typical ahupuaa to be a strip of about a thousand feet

[2] Malo, *Hawaiian Antiquities*, p. 37.

[3] Board of Commissioners to Quiet Land Titles, *Indices of Awards* (Honolulu: 1929), pp. x, xi, lx.

[4] Its name is derived from the *Ahu*, or altar, which was erected at the point where the boundary of the land intersected the main road which ran around the island. Upon this altar was deposited the yearly tax paid for the land whose boundary it marked; and also the image of a hog, *puaa*, carved of kukui wood, symbolic of articles paid as tax. (C. J. Lyons, "Land Matters in Hawaii," in *The Islander*, July 2, 1875.)

[5] A kind of paper cloth, used by the Islanders for clothing. It was pounded out from the inner bark of (chiefly) the paper mulberry tree. See pp. 61–63.

[6] Certain feathers were prized by the chiefs for helmets and cloaks. See pp. 82–84.

[7] *Journal*, p. 314.

wide, running from the seashore not by any means to the top of the mountains, but a half-mile or a mile into the zone of timber land that usually covers the expanse between the 1700-foot and 5000-foot line of elevation.

Then there are the larger ahupuaas, which are wider in the open country than the others, and on entering the woods expand laterally so as to cut off all the smaller ones, and extend toward the mountains until they emerge in the open interior, not however to emerge at the tops of the respective mountains. Only a few reach those elevations, sweeping past the upper limits of all the others, and by virtue of some privilege in bird catching or some analogous right, taking in the whole mountain to themselves. Thus Mauna Loa, a major volcanic peak on the island of Hawaii, is shared by three great lands, Kapapa and Kahuku from Kau, and Humuula from Hilo. The whole body of Mauna Kea belongs to one land from Hamakua . . . to whose owners belonged the sole privilege of capturing the *ua'u,* a mountain inhabiting bird. High on its eastern flank, however, stretched the already mentioned land of Humuula, whose upper limits coincided with those of the *Mamane,* a valuable mountain acacia, which, starting from the shore, . . . extends along the upper limits of all other Hilo lands to the crater of Mauna Loa.[8]

As indicated above, the extension of the territory of the ahupuaa normally took place by gaining the exclusive right to gather some product of the land, or to catch some bird or animal. Further examples of such rights are the privilege of cutting down large koa logs, used for canoe making, or of cutting *wauke,* a source of tapa cloth, or of gathering *oloana,* from which cord and rope were made.

The larger ahupuaas likewise had more extended sea privileges. Where the smaller ones often had fishing rights only out to the depth where one could just touch with his toes, the largest arrogated to themselves the main sea fisheries.

On east Maui the principal lands radiated to the sea from a rock on the edge of the crater of the volcano Haleakala. An uncommon situation existed there in the district of Kola: powerful chiefs from Wailuku and Waikapu had been able to extend their ahupuaas so as to cut off a very long stretch of other lands from the sea. On west Maui the abrupt ridges furnished natural divisions.

On the windward side of Oahu where valleys are also sharply separated by high ridges, the valley idea again dominated. Lyons mentions Waimanalo, Kailua, Kaneohe, and Heeia as names there

[8] C. J. Lyons, "Land Matters in Hawaii," in *The Islander,* July 9, 1875, p. 111.

of ahupuaas and valleys alike. So too with Nuuanu, Moanalua, Halawa, and Kalihi on the west of the Koolau range. But across the broad, even stretch of the south and middle of the island (Ewa), the long narrow strip common in Hawaii prevailed. The ahupuaa of Waianae was an exceptional case, sweeping across the ridge of the Waianae range, then in a broad strip across the center of the island, up to the crest of the Koolau mountains to the east. Several on Oahu were more extended: Waikiki for example stretched along the coast over a number of valleys, nearly to the east point of the island.[9]

On Lanai, much smaller than these islands, and on Molokai, narrow in the northeast-southwest direction, some lands extended directly across the island from sea to sea.

Boundaries were "definitely marked, well-understood, and permanent," a sure indication of population pressure. Land and its resources had attained a scarcity value as a result of increasing demand for them: this alone could explain that it was justified to delimit precisely rights and ownership, and so allow use of wood, productive land, or fishing resources to some, and forbid them to others who might also have need. This pressure had, we remember, existed long before Cook's time. Five centuries before, so the legendary account goes, the king of Oahu, Mailikukuahi, had that island carefully surveyed, and the boundaries marked, to eliminate disputes between adjoining chiefs and other landholders.[10]

Watercourses, ridges, and gulches were often dividing lines. Where a dispute had arisen between hillside (*kewalo*) and valley (*kaimuohena*) property, a conventional procedure was followed, still in use as late as 1848: "The dividing line between them is where a stone will stop when rolled down the ridge. Kewalo is any place above where a stone running down will stop; below where it will stop is Kaimuohena. This is a general rule for the division of land in the same position." [11] Where boundaries were artificial, a stone wall, a line of stones, or a path might serve.

IV. Next in size to the ahupuaa, though its area too varied greatly, was the *ili* or smaller estate of the chiefs. Sometimes most of the area of the ahupuaa was absorbed by several of them.

[9] Lyons, "Land Matters in Hawaii," *The Islander*, July 1, 1875, p. 111.
[10] Fornander, *The Polynesian Race*, II, 89.
[11] *Hawaiian Annual* for 1890, p. 65.

Nine-tenths of the area of Waimea ahupuaa in Hawaii was taken up by two independent ili, Puukapu and Waikoloa.[12]

Very often, and especially on Oahu, the ili consisted of several separate tracts of land,

> one for instance on the seashore, another on dry, open land or *kula,* and another in the regularly terraced and watered [taro] patch or *aina loa* district, and another still in the forest, thus carrying out the equitable division we have seen in the ahupuaa . . . Punahou (in Honolulu) had anciently a lot on the beach . . . then the large lot with the spring and [taro] patches where the school now is, and again a forest patch on the steep sides of Manoa Valley. Kewalo had its sea coast adjoining Waikiki, its continuous kula on the plain and one-half of Punch Bowl Hill, and its [taro] land in Pauoa Valley . . . These different pieces were called either by their individual names, or by that of the entire *ili,* thus puzzling one sadly when attempting to obtain information with respect to them.[13]

These separate patches were referred to generally as *lele,* or "jumps."

Most of the ili were integral portions of the ahupuaa in which they were placed, and were fiefs of the chief of the ahupuaa. Tenure on them was at the will of that chief, and feudal dues were paid to him. But in contrast to these "ili of the ahupuaa," there were also others, *ili kuponos,* held without any condition of allegiance or dues to the holder of the ahupuaa, subject to claims only of the king for taxes and service. Transfer of ownership of the ahupuaa had no effect on tenure of the ili kupono. These ili were probably given originally in payment for special service to the king. Their existence was a conspicuous assertion of royal authority, and the royal power was strengthened wherever there were such ili, with holders dependent upon and giving allegiance directly to the king. They might have been maintained for such purpose alone where in isolated portions of distant islands the central power was felt weakly and fitfully.

Some ili seem not to have been included in any ahupuaa at all. Very likely they were ili kuponos whose relationship to the ahupuaa in which they were originally included had been forgotten.

V. Next come several less important land units, named on the basis of the special use to which the land was put. The *moo,* next

[12] W. D. Alexander, *Appendix to the Surveyor General's Report* (Honolulu, 1882).

[13] C. J. Lyons, "Land Matters in Hawaii," *The Islander,* July 16, 1875, pp. 118–119.

to the ili in size, was a small tract or field in the arable portion of the ili, named separately and cultivated. It usually did not extend to the sea.

The *pauku* was next in size to the moo. Smaller yet was the *kihapai*, "a field, potato patch, or garden belonging to and cultivated by the tenants or common people for themselves." The *koele* was a like area cultivated by the common people for their landlords, and belonging to the chief or landlord. *Poalimas* were patches which were in later years worked on by tenants for the chiefs on Friday only, poalima being the Hawaiian word for Friday.[14]

It is clear that these were not alternative names, but often overlapped: two or more might be applied to the same area.

VI. The basic land unit of the common people was the *kuleana*, or individual tenant's holding. (The word itself means "rights," that is, a right to use and possession pertaining to an individual.) It was an improved and cultivated tract, used by the people for growing their crops, taro, yams, and sweet potatoes, and to which they could substantiate their claim.

The boundaries of the kuleana were by no means so clear as those of the larger land divisions, a fact made obvious in the surveys of the late 1840's and 1850's. In the upland kuleanas each tenant cultivated two to three acres during a given year; and then the flat was let lie fallow for two to three years. On this basis, and adding a bit for waste land, some of the surveyors turned in reports of from six to twelve acres for an ordinary kuleana.[15] Kuleanas were smaller in the well-watered and richer bottom lands.

The kuleana was the functional unit in soil cultivation, corresponding to the peasant's holding in Europe, as the ahupuaa corresponds to the large estate of the nobility, and the ili to a small estate, or "gentleman's farm."

Tenure of the Land, Taxes, and Property Rights

Of fundamental importance in considering tenure is recognition of the rights of the king. When Kamehameha I had united the Islands under him by conquest at the end of the eighteenth century, he, like lesser conquering chieftains before him, divided the

[14] Board of Commissioners to Quiet Land Titles, *op. cit.*, pp. ix, x, xi.
[15] See p. 134.

subjected lands among his followers.[16] The king was acknowledged in every island as the lord or proprietor of the soil, either by hereditary right, or by right of conquest.

The chief (alii nui) whom the king had appointed in charge of an island distributed rights to hold ahupuaas to lesser chiefs, and they to lower ranks successively, down to the commoner with his kuleana. A "chain of command" existed, with authority from the top down, duties from the bottom up.

In the "Principles adopted by the Board of Land Commissioners to Quiet Land Titles" during the land reform of the 1840's is a brief statement of the system of land holding:

> The tenures were in one sense feudal, but they were not military, for the claims of the superior on the inferior were mainly either for the produce of the land or for labor, military service being rarely or never required of the lower orders. All persons possessing landed property, whether superior tenants or subtenants, owed and paid the king not only a head tax, which he assessed at pleasure, but also service, which was called for at discretion on all the grades from the highest down . . . They also owed and paid some portion of the production of the land, in addition to the yearly taxes. They owed obedience at all times.[17]

More concisely, lands were held by all persons on condition of obedience and payment of taxes.[18] Military service was a potential obligation of the alii group, seldom required of the commoners as an explicit condition of tenure. The analogy between the European feudal system and the Hawaiian social organization is a close one.[19]

Obedience cannot be measured concretely. But no matter how conscientious the tenant, he could not (especially if he were a commoner) secure more than a very doubtful holding, terminable at the will of the alii.

As to taxes, though sometimes agreements might specify payment for a given quantity of land, there was not in general a fixed amount due. Taxes were regulated by the necessities or caprice

[16] As indicated above, the king continued to hold a few districts personally on most of the islands.

[17] *Statute Laws of Hawaii,* 1845–1847 (Honolulu: 1847), II, 81.

[18] Another fundamental requirement might be mentioned, though it was not a condition only for holding land: observance of the customs and laws, a restriction heaviest for the commoners.

[19] These dues and claims were rendered not only by natives but also, after discovery, by foreigners who came to hold land. *Statute Laws,* 1845–1847, II, 81.

of the rulers: "There was no dividing line by which the tenant might know or hold anything his own." [20] However in time certain amounts of goods and of labor came to be recognized as roughly normal taxes for a given area. So, in the letter of information which William Richards, one of the missionary group, wrote to Wilkes, Commander of the United States Exploring Expedition which visited the Islands in 1841, he gave the annual royal tax laid on the ili as having amounted pretty regularly to about:

> A hog, a dog, a fishnet, a fishline, a cluster of feathers, 20 *tapas*, a part of which were square for bed clothes, and a part long and narrow for female dress. The size of the hog, dog, net, etc., varied somewhat according to the size of the ili.[21]

According to a statement of the 1842 laws:

> Formerly the royal tax of a common size farm was 1 fathom swine, 40 *tapas*, 40 *paus* [a skirt-like covering for women made of tapa], 1 dog, 80 fathoms of fish line, and a fish net 800 meshes in length.[22]

Though these taxes were levied on the ili, the alii in charge of course collected the amount from the commoners on his land. In addition to the annual (rent) taxes, the people were expected to make presents to their chiefs, such as the first fish of the season and the first produce of the soil.

The governor of the island laid an additional impost on the commoners; and petty chiefs exacted further but smaller levies.[23]

[20] Rev. Sheldon Dibble, *History of the Sandwich Islands*, p. 74.

[21] MS. letter dated March 15, 1841 (Archives of Hawaii), p. 19.

[22] *Fundamental Law of Hawaii* (Honolulu: 1842), p. 133.

[23] The overseer-of-finances of Kamehameha I, Ka-lani-moku, had charge of all the immense detail of taxes of the kingdom. "All taxes and revenues were collected under his supervision. One of the methods of keeping account is . . . almost the only thing of the past showing artificial aid to the memory. When taxes were called for, a place was designated where all kinds of produce would be brought. Each family was to send its quota. Some of the overseers trusted to memory; and sometimes a few of the people thought they could stay away without being noticed. To remedy this a long line of plant fibre would be held by the collectors, and a knot tied for each person bringing in his quota . . . Some brought pigs, dogs, sweet potatoes, mats, calabashes, and like products of home industry. Hunters brought rare feathers and birds; and the fishermen brought fish. Woe to the family who failed to have the knot tied in the fibre cord. A heavy conscription, and frequently an entire confiscation of all the personal property, and even death, was the result." W. D. Westervelt, in *Hawaiian Historical Society Papers for 1921* (Honolulu: 1922), p. 30.

[A time] . . . is appointed annually for receiving the rent, when the people repair to the governor's with what they have to pay. If the required amount is furnished, they return . . . to enter again on their land. But if unable to pay the required sum, and if the landlords are dissatisfied with the presents they have received or think the tenants have neglected their farm,[24] they are forbidden to return, and the land is offered to another.[25]

With respect to the labor tax, the king had the unqualified right to call out everyone in the community to perform any kind of work he wished. There were no limits on the quantity which could be required.

Usually the king gave his orders to a chief of rank, and he communicated his orders to the next rank of chiefs, and they onward to the lowest tenants. If the work was one of magnificence, then the king gave his orders to each of the chiefs of the first rank, and through them they were extended through all the different classes of people.[26]

One day of labor out of five was normally required by the immediate landlord, as part of the rent for the land. The work was generally on the cultivated patches belonging directly to the alii. Also other services might be exacted.[27]

Aside from these fairly regular land taxes or rents, more nearly arbitrary demands were made on the commoners. One polite mode of oppression, which showed power of persistence into the days of white dominance, was that of *traveling*,[28] either for some "business" purpose, or for pleasure:

On such occasions chiefs . . . of rank might take large trains with them, proceed slowly, and lay the hospitality of the whole country through which they pass under enormous contribution . . . A few chiefish companies passing in quick succession through a poor and remote district act like swarms of

[24] This "right conditioned on use" was emphasized as late as 1842, when negligence and slovenly cultivation was an acute problem. An edict threatened the eviction of tenants from all poorly cultivated farms. (Fundamental Law of Hawaii, 1842, pp. 133–135.)

[25] Ellis, *Journal*, p. 316.

[26] *Letter of William Richards to Commander Wilkes*, pp. 20–21.

[27] John H. Wise, *Ancient Hawaiian Civilization*, p. 88.

[28] But a limitation lay on this right in that a lower chief, who held only a section of land, could not require labor or supplies from those who occupied the land of another without permission. This was definite limitation on the prerogatives of the alii, and a long step in the direction of social orderliness.

locusts, devouring all substance, and leaving famine and starvation behind them.[29]

A further method of taxation was that of "requiring gifts" on the completion of a house of the king or of a high chief. All persons holding lands or authority under him were expected to come to the new house, bringing with them a present in proportion to their means.

Or produce might simply be seized. The chiefs were supposed to own everything, the people nothing: further exactions were justified by the sanction of custom. The king or high chief could send his men to nationalize the potatoes or taro of near-by farmers without compensation. If the aggrieved person ventured to protest, he could easily be liquidated.

Estimates were made, not long after primitive Hawaiian days, of the proportion of the fruits of their labors which the commoners paid in one or another form of tax. Richards and Dibble agree that the commoners did not retain for their own use more than one-third of their produce,[30] the remaining two-thirds being divided among the various orders of chiefs and priests. This may be compared with the reported one-sixth to one-fourth of the gross product paid to the proprietors of land on share-tenure leases in Italy in the eighteenth and nineteenth centuries;[31] or with the half-and-half agreement for share tenants common now in mid-west United States. But in the latter cases a greater or lesser share in the outlay for equipment, buildings, and taxes is borne by the landlord; in Hawaii the service of the chieftain class amounted to no more than permission to use the land, plus a varying degree of protection against marauding expeditions of other chiefs.

One limitation to demands of the chiefs lay in their interest in

[29] The Reverend Titus Coan, in *Answers to Questions Proposed by R. C. Wyllie* (Honolulu: 1848), pp. 67–68.

Dibble reports a special trick (the original source was Richards' letter to Wilkes): "There are many oppressive impositions, as a report circulates that the King is about to visit, so houses are built, hogs and other articles collected. The King does not come, the report being a mere fabrication of the landlord, who is not slow to turn the preparations to his own advantage." *History of the Sandwich Islands*, p. 74.

[30] Richards' MS. Letter to Wilkes, p. 14; Dibble, *History of the Sandwich Islands*, p. 74.

[31] Bowden, Karpovich, and Usher, *Economic History of Europe* (New York: 1937), p. 268.

keeping the social system, and especially their corner of it, strong. There grew up in addition a suggestion of ethical restriction. Malo later wrote:

One thing which the *kalaimoku* impressed on the king was to protect the property of the common people as well as that of the chiefs; not to rob them, not to appropriate wantonly the crops of the common people. If the king made a tour about the island . . . it was not right for him to enter the house of a commoner to pass the night . . . The wrong lay in the fact that when the king entered the house of a common man, his men entered with him. They ate of the commoner's food, helped themselves to his goods, seduced or ravished the females, and raised the devil generally. Their counsel to the king was that when, in traveling along the *alaloa* [main road], he came to a branch road, he was not to follow the branch, because that was a bad practise . . . The evil lay in the fact that when the king left the beaten way, the people followed along with him. The path probably led to a little farm . . . and as soon as the king's men saw it they pulled the crops, helping themselves to the sugar cane, etc., and the blame for the outrage fell upon the king.[32]

For the sake of the safety and welfare of the alii themselves, their demands needed to be moderate enough to keep the commoners fairly well satisfied, to insure not only their effectiveness in peacetime but also their loyalty in war.[33]

Another limit lay in the freedom of the commoner to leave one chief if his burdens proved too heavy, and seek a kuleana from another. Seldom was such a refugee commoner (or chief) turned away when he sought protection and place in another district or island. The tradition of hospitality was deep . . . The commoner was not bound to the soil. But he was dependent in any case on the alii as a class; and in pre-white days, the social pressure lay all in the other direction. The alii did not fear losing their tenants: on the contrary the tenants often insured themselves against being dispossessed of all their holdings, and hence of their

[32] Malo, *Hawaiian Antiquities,* p. 255.

[33] Their demands were further restricted by the perishableness of much of the produce (fish, bananas, sweet potatoes, poi); and in the circumstance that there was no reason for the chiefs to take more than they could themselves use. (Cf. Lind, *An Island Community,* p. 35.) And although the alii prided themselves justly upon their fatness and stature—the women especially were proud of their bulk—there was a limit to their power of consumption.

Only later, when the white traders learned of the quantities of valuable sandalwood in the forests, and tempted the chiefs with appealing foreign goods—textiles, looking glasses, furniture, firearms—did the chiefs levy labor burdens on the commoners far out of proportion to their ability to use the goods which that labor brought them.

substance, by taking up several small pieces of land, each under a different chief. Then if one alii ejected them, they would still hold land under the others.[34]

Universally up to the time of Kamehameha I, and to some extent up to 1825,[35] the land of the chief at his death reverted to the king, or to the governor of the island. Any nomination, as his son or wife, which he might have made for his successor, had to be confirmed by the king or governor. Likewise upon the death of the king of an island it had been the custom for some generations for the lands of the island to be divided anew and redistributed among the chiefs and friends of the new ruler.

> This division was generally in a grand council of chiefs, and those who were dissatisfied had either to submit, or take their chances of a revolt if their means and connections made it judicious to attempt it . . . The great business of state on the accession of a new monarch was . . . to adjust and accommodate the ever-clashing claims [of proud and demanding chiefs].[36]

If previous owners of lands were of the court party, or too powerful to be interfered with in safety, they were left undisturbed.

This reversion of all landholdings to the new chief upon the death of a previous lord was a powerful influence in the direction of maintaining the authority and prestige of the kings and higher chiefs.

Tenants were likely to lose their lands sooner or later from the death of some superior chief; and they might lose them at any time through his favoritism, jealousy, or fickleness of character. All these uncertainties caused the lower ranks of landholders to ridicule the idea of making improvements from which they themselves were not likely to profit. And usually when a man was dispossessed of his lands his personal property was also confiscated. Sudden insecurity of all possessions, and conventional grief and emotion at the chief's death, were made the excuse for a saturnalia. License was without limit: houses were burned, property plundered, and all variety of criminal enterprises embarked upon.

To some extent the full rigor of customary law was tempered "among all the better classes" by the feeling that it was "im-

[34] Richards' letter to Commander Wilkes, p. 15.

[35] Sanford B. Dole, "Evolution of Land Tenure in Hawaii," *Hawaiian Historical Society Papers,* December 5, 1892.

[36] Fornander, *The Polynesian Race,* II, 300.

proper" to eject the direct cultivators of the soil; and hence it was often the case that all the different ranks of chiefs were dispossessed, while the last dependents, the cultivators of the soil, were continued in their tenures.[37]

The unlimited rights of the chiefs to levy taxes for whatever appealed to them had a natural result. There was a powerful pressure on the commoners not to exceed a certain maximum of well-being, even something of a competition in the direction of poverty.

> No valuable article was secure in the hands of the lower classes, for if it were not directly plundered, some form of taxation would be devised, or some mode of suffering invented until it was obtained. Hence none of the lower orders dared to live in a large house, cook a large hog, fish with a large net, or appear well-dressed.[38]

He who appeared most miserable was safest from exactions. The extraordinary extent of the authority of chiefs over commoners gives an aspect a little too capricious and arbitrary to the social relations of the islanders. There existed the softening influence of custom where the chieftain-commoner relations was not a factor. A considerable body of customary rights resulted, indefinite it is true, and administered often arbitrarily and with favoritism; but still they existed. The land tenure and taxation procedures which we have already mentioned might be cited under this head. Rights to irrigation water, once work had been done on the project, were also well established. These will be discussed below. But there were others: "criminal laws directed against murder, robbery, theft, and adultery," and "laws relating to personal property, personal security, domestic relations, and barter." Two types of primitive courts existed, those held by the king and chiefs, and those maintained by the priests. Decisions might be arbitrary; judgments varied with the character of the chief or priest; punishments were of great variety and sometimes bitterly cruel. Appeals could be taken to a higher chief or king.[39]

[37] Richards' letter to Commander Wilkes, pp. 16–17.

[38] Dibble, *History of the Sandwich Islands*, p. 76. Statements by missionaries, or by others reflecting missionary influence (Richards, Coan, Malo, Dibble), as to the lot of the natives in pre-white days ought to be accepted with some degree of caution; for these writers did not underestimate the advances resulting from their efforts and from the spread of Christianity.

[39] W. F. Frear, in *Hawaiian Historical Society Papers for 1906* (Honolulu: 1907), pp. 17–18.

The very legal phrasing in which a description of this must be put suggests a more regularized system than existed: actually the relations were such as must in some degree evolve whenever men achieve organization of their activities within a hierarchy of rank. "Law" and "courts" were implicit, not explicit; were far from the conscious existence which our terms, with their connotations, imply to us. One can perhaps best depict the situation as William Richards did in his report to Commander Wilkes, that government was by a union of law, custom, and will. There were, first, definite laws, or tabus. Then there were the established customs, of which we have been speaking here, and which even a chief could not violate persistently over a long period, since he would become unpopular, and eventually be supplanted. Finally there was rule by will, since "despite many restraints upon such a person as the king, powerful influences imposed by fear, custom . . . still a bad man found means to break many of the rules." [40]

With respect to property rights—theft was, under settled social conditions, a recognized offense and was severely punished, always with reasonable qualification as to who had done the thieving and from whom. If the robbers were discovered, the injured person could go to the robbers' house and take whatever he found. Even if the guilty persons were the strongest, Ellis reports, they would not dare to resist the recapture, "for in the event of their making any opposition, the people of the whole district would support those who were thus punishing the individuals by whom theft had been committed." [41] There was, at least on Oahu, a law of the land providing that such malefactors should be sacrificed, and their bones scraped for fishhooks and arrowheads; but it was by no means always observed. If the robbery had been of a great amount, or had been against the property of a chief, the offender was sometimes executed by being bound tightly, and turned adrift at sea in a leaking canoe.[42]

[40] Richards' letter to Wilkes, pp. 35–36.

[41] Ellis, *Journal*, p. 318.

[42] Fornander gives an account of the judgment in a case of theft of the mild king Lupekapu, on Oahu, just before the time of Kamehameha: "Once a native stole a hog from the chief. When the theft was found out, Lupekapu went to the house of the thief and asked, 'Did you steal my hog?' The native answered trembling 'Yes.' Lupekapu then ordered the thief to prepare an oven and bake the hog. When that was done he was told to sit down and eat. The thief fell to with a light heart, but on attempting to rise when his natural appetite was satisfied, he was sternly told to continue eating until he was told to desist. When nearly suf-

On the other hand the natives who treacherously killed two of Vancouver's men in order to steal their weapons are reported to have gone unpunished for their act.

Treachery was a commonplace among themselves, as well as in dealing with foreigners in the early years after discovery. In times of disorder, and in places where regular authority was weak, no rules held. Lawless bands arose, pursuing their immediate interest, owing allegiance to no chief. "What they wanted, they went and took." When wars of conquest were going on, "the kings of several islands . . . paid little attention to the affairs of distant portions of their own kingdoms, consequently a general license prevailed, and petty squabbles, robberies, and murders were of frequent occurrence." [43]

But if during quiet times it was not the best policy to go in for persistent thieving, it was still true that disguised methods of graft and bribery were the rule rather than the exception. It was customary to curry favor with the chiefs by offering them gifts. Colcord, another early arrival, complains that "This seems to be the case more or less all over the world, but in the Sandwich Islands it is more prevalent than any place I ever knew." [44] In fact the system of taxation was to some extent merely a regularization of this practice, and the chain method of collecting taxes—that is, passing them up rank by rank to successive superiors—gave the opportunity for quietly withholding a discreet amount at each step. The total of such losses must have compared impressively with the final total of the taxes.

No customary protection was given to lenders: apparently willingness to lend was assumed to imply willingness to bear the risk of the debtor's not repaying. "Only by the good will of the debtor, not by the operation of any law regulating such matters could the lender recover or obtain justice." [45]

In barter, the bargain was considered complete only when the

---

focated with food, the poor wretch was told to get up." Lupekapu then warned him that he would be executed as indicated above if he again stole (II, 269–270).

In later times, to the native law of retaliation the scriptural specification of fourfold indemnity might be added, as Governor Kekuanaoa enforced payment to the Bishop family of 120 goats for 30 stolen. (S. E. Bishop, *Reminiscences of Old Hawaii* (Honolulu: 1916), p. 43.)

[43] J. J. Jarves, *History of the Hawaiian or Sandwich Islands* (Boston: 1843), p. 157.

[44] Colcord's "Journal," Hawaiian Historical Society MS., p. 113.

[45] Malo, *Hawaiian Antiquities*, p. 84.

goods were actually exchanged and each side was satisfied. After that there was no withdrawing, though one had received much the worse of the deal, and had thought better of his decision.[46] Workmen were hired either through a personal bargain or through an arrangement with a lower chief. They were generally paid in advance; and if they did not then perform the work, their possessions could be seized.[47]

Several of the rights generally recognized have been mentioned above: the right to an equitable share of irrigation water, when the requisite work had been done; the right to shift to another chief's land; the right to appeal for justice to a higher chief. A further right was the absolute right of ownership over one's children, and to some extent over wives, though the chieftain rank of women was recognized and there are even reports of female sovereigns. But any disposition could be made of children, without interference by a chief; and infanticide was in fact a settled custom, to the horror of the missionaries, into the nineteenth century. As the result of a siege of bad luck at betting, a man might become desperate and stake his wife and children, and perhaps lose them. Children might be bartered for a specified time, or sold.[48]

[46] See p. 49, below.
[47] Ellis, *Journal,* p. 319.
[48] Colcord, "Journal," p. 113.

CHAPTER III

THE ORGANIZATION OF PRODUCTION

Irrigation

The distribution of rainfall in Hawaii encourages irrigation practices. Heavy rainfall about the mountain tops provides abundant stream flow; while moderate rain to leeward of the mountains and in low altitudes generally gives incentive to use effectively the available stream flow. As soon as population growth provided a sufficient demand to give a scarcity value to the richest and best watered lands, it became justified and increasingly economic to irrigate and improve poorer areas.[1]

Natural spring water was on occasion conserved by throwing up high water-tight dikes. Campbell, one of the early visitors to the Islands, speaks of such patches being something under a hundred feet on a side, with levees about six feet high. Paths, and even roads, ran along the embankments.

More often dams were thrown up in streams, and trenches (*auwai*) dug to carry water to the cultivated areas. The settled rule was that no dam should divert more than half the stream flow, the remainder being allowed to continue to lower plots. The dams were temporary, of stones and earth, and probably often were carried away by flood water. There was drastic penalty for willful damage or destruction of a dam: the offender could be killed and his body used in repairs as a warning to others who might be tempted. There was no reprisal for this punishment—"unless the culprit was of consequence."

There are small indications today of the old ditches: they would have been quickly overgrown when abandoned, and probably

[1] The importance of irrigation in ancient Hawaii is indicated etymologically. *Wai* meant water; *kanawai*, "water rules" came to be the generic name for all laws. "A literal translation of the Old Testament in early Hawaiian would list the ten water laws of Moses in place of the familiar Ten Commandments." *Waiwai* meant goods or wealth. H. A. Wadsworth, *A Historical Summary of Irrigation in Hawaii* (Honolulu), p. 125.

most of them were small and short. However there is a report of several tunnels and shafts through lava rock that seem to date back to the native period.[2]

Dams and channels of any size were authorized by the king, or by one or more chiefs or konohikis whose lands were to be watered. Authority over the construction went to the chief who provided the most men; and the water supply resulting was distributed, first to each chief in proportion to his contribution of men, and secondly to each tenant in proportion to the labor he had furnished. The latter might himself only have helped, or brought also his relatives. The procedure encouraged industry, it may be noted, by apportioning reward according to effort.

There were three methods of water distribution to the cultivated patches. The least careful of the methods was simply to water successive lower patches by overflow from neighboring higher patches, and not directly from any auwai. Two difficulties suggest themselves, and go to explain why this was the rarest type of distribution: first, an excess of water must be available, else the lower patches would remain dry. In addition, the holder of the lower patch was dependent to a real degree on the good will of the tenants above him, for it often would have been necessary to put an excess of water on the upper plots before any water reached the lower ones.

This system served best where the number of patches was small. Its existence is probably to be explained by a topographic reason, the labor cost in given terrain of constructing an auwai; or by a social reason, joint interest on the part of cultivators of the higher and lower patches.

A second arrangement, adapted to conditions of fairly abundant supply of water, was for each plot to take in succession from an auwai all the water needed without regard to time. When the last had received its share, the auwai was opened again on the first, and the process repeated.

The most common arrangement was by time. The channel was opened to a given plot on alternative weeks, or on given days of each week, or for given hours of the day or night, time being kept track of by position of the sun or stars. This method of allocating supply must have developed late, when demand had

[2] J. N. S. Williams, "A Little Known Engineering Work in Hawaii," *Hawaiian Annual* for 1919, pp. 121–126; also Ellis, *Journal*, p. 289.

increased sharply or supply sharply diminished. Only a high scarcity value for water would have justified the effort of making a precise division.[3]

Every irrigation project of importance had over it a *luna wai* (water master), a chief, or chief's konohiki, or a designated agent, who had general authority. He had charge of distribution of water, of the maintenance of dam and channels, and of the adjudication of disputes. In dry seasons a right of need was recognized: the luna wai could divert water from those having more than they really required to those in distress.

Also the water master could at any time call up the users of water to do maintenance work on the system, "the penalty for failure to come being a withholding of water from the delinquent. The rapid deterioration of the kuleana in such case might lead to eviction by the chief." [4]

Water rights were obscure where streams crossed two or more ahupuaas on their way to the sea—a problem that would not have arisen had all ahupuaas been valleys, bounded by ridges and mountain spurs. It was customary that where two or more chiefs combined to develop water canals that the konohiki of him who had provided the most men to labor on the project should be in charge of the completed dams and canals—but the basic right to the water has not been settled even now.[5]

But Judge Perry reports, from his acquaintance with water-right cases in latter-day court actions, that testimony of *kamaainas* (old residents) makes it clear that "under the Ancient Hawaiian system disputes concerning water were extremely rare." [6]

[3] Cf. Antonio Perry, in the *Hawaiian Annual* for 1913, p. 92.

[4] H. A. Wadsworth, *A Historical Summary of Irrigation,* p. 131.

[5] Wadsworth, *op. cit.*, p. 140.

[6] Perry, *Hawaiian Annual* for 1913, p. 95. There is doubt about the reasons for this absence of conflict. Justice Perry says that "land tenures were so precarious as to be conducive to abstention from unjustifiable or otherwise irritating claims by the tillers of the soil." But precariousness of tenure would equally tend toward extension of claims by those who felt themselves stronger, able to overbalance the weakness of their case by strength of arm or influence; unless it is argued that the commoners, the class immediately concerned with water problems, were too meek and cowed to squabble.

Also persuasive is the notion that "the desire for wealth, as the term is used now, did not exist." Most produce was perishable; prestige had to be gained perforce not by heaping up quantities of goods but in political and social ways.

TECHNIQUES AND PRODUCTS

FOODS

Before discovery the Hawaiians cultivated taro, sweet potatoes, bananas, sugar cane, breadfruit, plantains, and a few greens and other roots. Coconuts and mountain apples (*ohia ai*) grew more or less without care. Pigs of a lean husky variety, dogs, and domestic fowls furnished meat. Wild geese too, were eaten when they could be captured, and a few small birds besides.[7] From the sea came oysters, and a variety of fish. The preferred and basic foods of the islanders were their sweet potatoes, "poe," and fish.

In the rich wet bottom lands or irrigated terraces taro was the favorite plant, since it thrived with plenty of water.[8] The irregular plots within embankments were laid under water from the adjoining aqueduct, and cultivation was carried on with the workers continuously up to the middle in mud. The ground was dug, leveled, and worked into a muck with a wooden spade, the *o-o,* "a long stick of hardwood with a flattened point, held paddle fashion by the squatting laborer, who would rapidly clean the ground of weeds, and break up the soil two or three inches deep . . . The Hawaiian preferred to dig on his haunches."[9]

In the dryer upland (kula) section, the naturally aquatic taro required different treatment. Two or three taro plants were planted in a hole some nine inches below the general ground level:

> These holes are about four feet apart, and as the plants grow up, the earth is gathered around their stems in the form of a basin to retain the water, either from rain or otherwise, around their roots. The whole field is generally covered with a thick layer of hay, made from long, coarse grass, or the tops

[7] Cook, *A Voyage to the Pacific Ocean,* II, 211, 213, 227, 228, 234, 235, 244, 245, 535, 541.

[8] William Ladd, one of the first plantation managers, estimated that one square mile planted with taro would support 15,151 individuals; and that not more than 1/25th of the number would be required to cultivate it. *Hawaiian Spectator* (periodical), January 30, 1838.

This estimate is repeated by G. W. Bates, *Sandwich Island Notes* (New York: 1854), p. 122. It has been doubted by others, in that it assumes unusually favorable conditions of cultivation, and overlooks the heavy drain on the fertility of land that taro causes.

[9] S. E. Bishop, *Reminiscences of Old Hawaii* (Honolulu, 1916), p. 27.

of sugar cane, which continually preserves a certain degree of moisture in the soil.[10]

Water supply for sweet potatoes was less critical, even in the upland section. The potatoes were planted "three or four feet apart, and earthed up around their stems in much the same manner as the common potatoes are treated in England. When they dig any . . . after stripping off the potatoes, they carefully put the old plant back again in the ground for the ensuing crop." [11]

Level terraces were often built far up on the hillsides.[12] But where sloping irrigated plots were used, taro was planted farthest down the slope in the muckiest portion; yams and sugar cane higher up where they secured water in accord with their lesser needs; and bananas, needing least moisture, were planted on the tops of embankments—as they were also on the levees of level plots.[13]

Breadfruit was cultivated in the upland region. Menzies reported them planted "a good distance apart, so as to give room to their boughs to spread out vigorously on all sides, which was not the case in the crowded groves of Tahiti . . . The space between the trees did not lie idle. It was planted chiefly with sweet potatoes and rows of cloth plant *wauke,* or paper mulberry." [14]

Foods cooked before eating, were usually baked in an oven (*imu*). A pit was dug, several feet in diameter and about a foot deep, and lined with stones. The fire was kindled by rubbing briskly together two dry sticks of hibiscus wood, and let burn until the stones were very hot, when the ashes were thrown out and swept cleanly away. Food wrapped neatly in leaves, often banana or *ti* leaves, was then laid on the hot bottom stones, the top stones placed back, and the whole covered some inches deep with earth and leaves. In about half an hour the food—fish, fowl, dog, pig, sweet potatoes, breadfruit, or taro—was well cooked, to a succulence that boiled foods lack.

Taro was not usually eaten at this stage, but pealed, macerated

[10] Archibald Menzies, *Hawaii Nei 128 Years Ago* (MS. Department of British Museum), p. 76. Reported first printing in the *Hawaiian Annual* for 1908, p. 104.

[11] *Ibid.,* p. 76.

[12] See pp. 7–8.

[13] H. A. Wadsworth, *A Historical Summary of Irrigation,* p. 134.

[14] Menzies, *Hawaii Nei 128 Years Ago,* p. 76.

through beating with a stone pestle in a wooden trough, mixed with water, and let ferment for several days. Whether fermented or not, it was now poi, a carbohydrous, viscous, gray mass looking like soft dough, one of the three Hawaiian staple foods. *Aipai,* or hard food, was poi pounded without admixture of water: it could be kept for several months without spoiling.

From another plant, *awa,* an intoxicant—or more accurately a stupefying drink—was brewed. The root and stalk of the awa, a kind of pepper, were macerated, and let steep in water. The drink is reported satisfactory save that it made the skin crack and the hair fall out. It was tabu to any but the chiefs, and not often used even before the white men came. After the latter had introduced the art of distilling alcoholic drinks, it was scarcely used at all.

Among the land animals which furnished food, dogs were of primary importance, as also in islands farther south. Quantities of small sized dogs, somewhat of the terrier variety, were raised each year. They were kept in yards, fed on vegetables and refuse, and eaten at an early age. As many as two to four hundred dogs were killed at a single major feast.[15] Often they made up part of the rent for land.

Pigs were also common, a small variety with "long heads and small erect ears." They were, like dogs, often made pets of, but seem to have been less prominent as an article of food. They were used rather more often as sacrifices in the temples (*heiaus*). The flesh was preserved by "taking out the bones, and rubbing it well with salt, after which it was made up into rolls and dried." [16] Pork was tabu to women.

A large type of rat was the only other quadruped found on the Islands. It was sometimes eaten, being hunted with the small kind of bow and arrow of the Hawaiians.

Domestic poultry were cared for, and many wild birds were

[15] Ellis, *Journal,* pp. 260–261.

[16] Archibald Campbell, *A Voyage round the World* (Roxbury, Massachusetts: 1825), p. 182.

"The pans in which they make their salt are formed of earth lined with clay: they are commonly about six or eight feet square and two thirds of a foot deep. They are elevated on a bank of stones near the high water mark, whence the salt water is conducted to the bottom of them in trenches, out of which they are filled, and in a short time the sun performs the process of evaporation. The salt obtained at Karakakooa [Kealakekua] is the best, and is also obtained in great quantities." Anonymous, *History of the Otaheitan Islands* (Edinburgh: 1800).

eaten when they could be caught. Malo enumerates a considerable list used for food, among them the *nene* (goose), *pueo* (owl), the *moho, o-o, mamo,* and *ama-kihi.*[17]

The waters around Hawaii were not so productive of fish as those farther south, among the islands of the southern Pacific. But fish were sufficiently abundant to make up a fundamental part of the food supply. Fishing techniques were elaborate, and specific for different varieties. Before any significant fishing expedition, detailed religious observances were carried out at the shrine of the fish god, with sacrifice and perhaps a night-long vigil; and on return an offering from the catch was left at the altar.

Near shore the dart was used,[18] and the throw net: the Hawaiians were expert in deducing the presence of fish from ripples on the surface of the water. At night they fished along the shallow reefs by the light of torches made from *kukui* nuts and lauhala leaves, or from coconut husks. Fish were trapped in hand nets or the *hina'i* (basket) and the octopus and bonito were captured through the fascination exerted by the careful manipulation before them of the *leho,* or cowry. The hook and line[19] were also used. In the *k'oi* method a baited hook attached to a strong line and pole was drawn slowly back and forth over the water to attract the prey.[20] Sometimes fish were poisoned, the appropriate plant being bruised and put into rock crevices. The sickened fish floated to the surface where they were easily picked up. The simplest technique was that of simply scooping up fish marooned

[17] Malo, *Hawaiian Antiquities,* pp. 62–65.

[18] Cook, *A Voyage to the Pacific Ocean,* II, 234, 247. The dart was the only means for catching fish which Cook saw used.

[19] Hooks were made of bone (sometimes human bone, a motive for the secretive burial habits of the Hawaiians), or mother-of-pearl, or tortoise shell. For fishlines and for fishnets the best of native fibers, and one remarkably strong by any standard, was used. It came from the oloana, a branch of the nettle family, growing in the damp forest valleys. The plant was given some partial cultivation by the natives. "The bark was carefully stripped from straight stems about six feet long, rolled into coils, and carried to the lowlands. Here it was stretched out in running water and allowed to soak until the pulp could be scraped from the tough bast fibers upon a long narrow board (*papa olona*), using the scraper of pearl shell or turtle rib. After bleaching in the sun, the fibers were twisted on the thigh, and rolled into cord of various sizes." (E. H. Bryan, number 9 of the series on "Ancient Hawaiian Life," in the *Honolulu Advertiser,* December 20, 1937. See also Joseph Emerson, *Hawaiian Historical Society Papers for 1915* (Honolulu: 1916), p. 52.

[20] Malo, *Hawaiian Antiquities,* p. 274.

in tidal pools, or catching them by thrusting one's hand into holes in the coral reef.

Farther out from shore the *pa* or troll hook might be used. More frequently the Hawaiian utilized a net made out of strong *oloana* fiber—sometimes a small hand net, often a very large one.

A small type of oyster thrived in the Pearl river, and "a handsome speckled clam, of delicate flavor." [21]

The Islanders also resorted to fish growing by artificial means. Fish ponds of from less than an acre to several hundreds of acres extent were built, in which favorite varieties of fish, especially mullet, could thrive and fatten in safety from their enemies and be easily captured when needed. Their limits were determined by the available area of shallow water protected from heavy wave action, and by the amount of labor available for throwing up the stone, or earth and stone, dikes.

The building of a large fish pond took on the character of a major public works project, and ancient kings and queens were remembered for the fish ponds they had built. Kalaimanuia of Oahu was remembered for Kapaakea, Opu, and Paaiau ponds.[22] Kamehameha enclosed a bay half a mile wide at Kiholo on Hawaii by a sturdy stone wall twenty feet wide and at times six feet high. The total area must have been between a half and one square mile. In several arches in the wall verticle stakes were driven close together to form a sieve, permitting the water to flow in and out with the tides, but not permitting the fish to escape.[23] It is said that some of the ponds were so ancient that their construction was ascribed to the legendary predecessors of the Hawaiians, the Menehunes. The diked taro patches also served on occasion, when flooded with water, for the growing of fish.

Fish were eaten raw, or were broiled, or were baked in the imu, or oven, described above. They were preserved by drying, or by being well rubbed with salt and then dried. Preserved in such fashion, they were a main article in intra- and inter-island trade.

[21] S. E. Bishop, *Reminiscences*, p. 46.
[22] Fornander, *The Polynesian Race*, II, 269.
[23] Ellis, *Journal*, p. 308.

CLOTHING

Had the Islands been much farther north, the problem of clothing would have been a serious one, in view of the scarcity of materials for warm clothing, especially the absence of animals bearing furs of any quality. But the climate around the seacoast was moderate and even, and little clothing was needed.

Their cloth, or tapa, was made from the wauke, or paper mulberry plant. The wauke was cultivated along with food plants, trimmed of side-branches as it grew, and sometimes budded. After a year or two of growth it was cut, the bark stripped off the sticks in strips of three inches or less wide and six to ten feet long, and rolled flat into coils. After a time, when the natural curve of the bark had been flattened out, the coarse outer bark was scraped off by a sharp shell. The inner bark might then be soaked in water for a time to extract its resinous gum before beating, or it might be beaten immediately—placed on a long and flat plank and hammered out with a mallet until six inches, a foot, or even several feet in width.[24]

Tapa was decorated by regular colored patterns. The dye, usually red, yellow, or black, came from red or red-brown ferruginous earth, or from the berries, leaves, bark, or roots of certain plants. The pattern was cut into the inside of a flat piece of bamboo. The worker dipped the bamboo into a bowl of pigment, then pressed it tight against the fresh tapa, shifting the bamboo precisely after each impression so that the pattern extended evenly along.

Clothing could hardly have attained a greater degree of simplicity. Men wore the *malo,* a strip of tapa wound round the waist and passed between the legs. Chiefs in addition could wear the *kihei,* or mantel tied diagonally across one shoulder and under the other arm. The *pau* of women, made of five thicknesses of tapa, was a section of tapa cloth a yard wide and several yards long.[25] It was wrapped about the waist, extending to the knees.

Tapa was also made up in broad sections, successive strips being cemented together by prolonged beating, for use as bed clothing.

Tapa came in varied quality and thickness, some kinds heavy

[24] See further in Ellis, *Journal,* pp. 82–84.

[25] For origin, see Fornander, *The Polynesian Race,* II, 62.

like leather, some thin and light, depending on the number of layers and the extent of the pounding. Sometimes vegetable oil, such as the oil from the coconut, was spread on it to cause it to shed water, and perhaps wear longer. If so impregnated, it could be washed. Generally it was not washed, but worn till it was in shreds—which was not long. The best tapa lasted only several weeks.[26] The wants of the population for clothing could hardly be supplied, in view of the length of time wauke took for growing, the labor of making the cloth, and the speed with which the finished product wore out.

HOUSES

A few of the Hawaiians had as dwelling places caves, hollows of trees, or overhanging cliffs; and some sponged on those who had houses. "But people of respectability put up houses of their own." [27]

The first step in house construction was to plant two parallel lines of stout posts in the ground, three to four feet apart, to make up the basic frame of the side walls. The height of the posts varied from three or four feet high for commoners' houses to twelve or fourteen for chiefs'. At the middle of each a tall post was driven to support the ridgepole of the roof. Rafters were then laid, resting on the ridgepole at one end, and at the other end on a wall-plate lying in grooves cut in the tops of the vertical wall beams. The ends were then filled in, as the sides had been, with more vertical posts three or more feet apart. In the smaller houses these posts were put up in rough fashion with the bark still on them; but in the houses of the chiefs they were straight and smooth, and carefully cleaned of bark. Tough vegetable fiber, generally that of *ie,* bound together all joints.

Next, horizontal sticks, an inch or two thick and three to six inches apart, were tied to wall posts and rafters. To these sticks was fastened the thatched external covering, whatever that might be. The leaves of the *lauhala,* or pandanus, sometimes served, the tips of the leaves hanging outside and down, and the base woven neatly over the horizontal sticks, "resembling a coarse matting on the inside." Plantain leaves, and the broad ti leaves,

[26] Reverend Ephraim Eveleth, *History of the Sandwich Islands* (Philadelphia: 1831), p. 41.

[27] Malo, *Hawaiian Antiquities,* p. 158.

were used in like fashion; and, as the most durable thatch, covered the best houses.[28] But most houses were covered with grass, tied to the sticks in small bundles.

There were two chief types of these buildings, the dwelling house (*hale noho*), and a long structure (*halau*), which though lived in was designed for building and storing canoes. Dwelling houses varied considerably in size. The typical commoner's house was five or six feet high, and ten feet square. A chieftain's house might be three times as high, and forty or even seventy feet long. The houses of the chiefs were neatly kept; those of the commoners were damp, and usually filthy inside and out.

A village looked much like a group of haystacks, the more so since there was only one opening in a building, the door, which was so low that one had to stoop to enter, or even crawl on hands and knees. In large dwellings a windhole was sometimes left in the wall near the sleeping places for ventilation at night. There was never any internal partition.

The commoners built their own houses, ordinarily without benefit of any division of labor; but a chief called on all his tenants to work in unison when he wanted a house built for himself—a procedure suggesting the "house-raising" of pioneer days in midwest United States. Several scores of people worked at one time, with specific tasks allotted to different divisions. One group cut and transported wood from the upland forests, a burdensome task where, as might be the case, the forest was eight or ten miles distant. Another gathered and braided into twine or rope the fiber of the *ie* root, or of the coconut husk. A third collected leaves or grass for thatching. With such numbers construction went along quickly, and in several days the people could again return to their own lands.

The durability of houses, as of clothing, was not great: the most poorly constructed lasted from two to three years, a commoner's fairly well built house perhaps five years, and a chief's dwelling as much as ten years. The weakest point about a house was its ability to withstand rain, especially since in some regions there

[28] Ti is a low growing plant, with heavy leaves up to three inches wide and two feet long. Ti thatch was likewise preferred for tents in time of war, and for making temporary shelters. Also, the leaves were woven into a coase matting and worn as a cloak in inland journeys.

were during the late winter up to four months of nearly continuous wet weather. A poor house leaked freely within a year.[29]

House furnishings were simple. Sometimes the floor was covered only with pebbles or small fragments of lava, for the sake of dryness and to discourage the growth of vermin; or grass was scattered as a rug cushion, and mats woven of *lauhala* leaves laid down. Several mats were piled up for sleeping on: in the king's house twenty or thirty were piled one on the other for use as a couch, as well as a bed.[30] Wooden pillows were used.

There were often wicker baskets for holding tapa or dry objects; and wooden dishes. Always there were gourds, shaped into calabashes and jugs. Some even served as trunks, closets, and musical instruments. They were shaped usefully by bandages tied over them as they were growing. Some were open and flat, like a dish, to hold poi and other foods; others were of cylindrical form, to contain fishing tackle. Both of these types had close fitting covers of the same material. Still others, used for holding water, were shaped like a long-necked bottle, the largest being of about twelve gallons' capacity. They were decorated by lines and geometric patterns. First the gourds were filled with the same dyes used for coloring tapa; then the outer skin was bruised in the design chosen. After the dye had been in for several days, the gourds were baked in an oven, coming out colored their natural yellow where they had not been bruised, but in the bruised places brown or black. The dye was then emptied out, and they were dried in the sun.[31]

OTHER PRODUCTS

Fiber work was used extensively. Lauhala leaves, scraped clean of the spines along their edges and central stem, and dried, were plaited into many other forms than the house mats mentioned above, into mat sails for canoes and into fans, pillows, sandals, and baskets.

The finest type of mat came from Niihau, and was "made of the

[29] See further in: Bishop, *Reminiscences*, p. 42; Ellis, *Journal*, pp. 236–239; Campbell, *A Voyage round the World*, p. 180; Eveleth, *History of the Sandwich Islands*, p. 41; E. H. Bryan, *Ancient Hawaiian Life* (Honolulu: 1938).

[30] *Diary of Andrew Bloxam* (MS. in Archives of Hawaii), pp. 25–26.

[31] Anonymous, *History of the Otaheitan Islands* (Edinburgh: 1800).

stem of a sedge (*ahuawa*), which grows along the edge of streams and brackish swamps . . . The mats were made with a diagonal plait or twill, and some have as many as a dozen or twenty strands to the inch. The largest makaloa mat in the Bishop Museum measures 19 by 6½ feet." [32]

From the aerial roots of the *ieie* vine came "coiled baskets, fish traps, coverings for gourds, clothing containers or traveling trunks, and the framework of helmets and feather images." [33]

Feathers were utilized for covering helmets and images, and for royal and chieftains' cloaks and capes. Some feathers were specifically tabu to commoners, and all articles so covered had about them the suggestion of conspicuous consumption. Feathers made a decidedly wasteful kind of clothing—a great deal of effort was required to gain only a few.[34] Some of the birds whose feathers were used were very rare, like the *mamo* and the *oo,* obtainable on Hawaii with near relatives in a few other places. Both of these birds were mainly black, with a few tufts of yellow feathers which alone were actually used. Feathers of certain other endemic birds were also utilized: those of the *iiwi, apapane, ou,* and *amakihi;* and sometimes those of the *iwa,* or frigate bird, and the *koae,* or tropic bird.

Birds were caught even by the bare hands, being enticed by calls or tame decoys; or by nooses or nets woven of light fiber. Most often birdlime was used, gummy substances from the sap of certain trees being smeared on well-baited poles or on branches on which the birds were accustomed to light. Seldom were they killed: the feathers wanted were plucked and they were again released.

Capes and cloaks were fashioned by tying feathers to a fine net of oloana fiber, the tip being bent over and lashed securely. Generally yellow feathers were reserved for the royal cloaks. The feather helmets worn with them were of a framework of strong fiber, with a raised central crest. The standard or banner of a high chieftain was the *kahili,* a pattern of feathers arranged at the end of a pole, unique for each so that he could be

[32] E. H. Bryan, "Fibrework," number 9 of his series on "Ancient Hawaiian Life," in the *Honolulu Advertiser,* December 20, 1937.

[33] *Ibid.*

[34] The golden war-cloak of Kamehameha I is supposed to have taken nine generations of kings in making. J. J. Jarves, *History of the Hawaiian or Sandwich Islands,* p. 63.

recognized by it. Cloaks, helmets, and kahilis were symbols of events of state. They were worn or carried during state ceremonies and during battle;[35] and were among the most prized of native possessions.

The canoe of the Hawaiian was his masterwork. The chief tool for hewing it into form, and in fact for shaping nearly any wood article, was a stone adz. Specially hard stone was obtained from quarries, sharpened and lashed tightly to a hardwood handle —a small branch with a piece of the tree stem attached to it. With such an adz, the native craftsman hewed and carved away at lumber, fashioning it into any shape he desired.

Around the time of Cook's voyages and after, canoes were always made from a single tree, though large vessels of plank construction are reported in an earlier period.[36] The later canoes were from twelve to fifty or more feet in length, one or two feet across, and up to three feet deep. The sides were about an inch thick: to obtain this thickness with rude tools must have been a task of much labor and unremitting care. Usually boards were fitted above the sides to ward off water from splashing in.

The outside of the canoe was painted black with a compound made of earthy materials and the oil, burnt nuts, and bark of the *kukui* tree. Most of the canoes, the smaller ones and those of the commoners, were "single," and steadied against rough water and surf by outriggers. Double canoes, intended for longer voyages and for war, were tightly lashed together by curved poles. In the center between the canoes a raised platform was built upon which provisions, hogs, and vegetables were put and on which chiefs sat while the commoners paddled below in the body of each canoe. The double canoe was more stable than the single; but if in a storm the two canoes were torn apart, all aboard would probably be lost.

Propulsion was either by the mat sails already mentioned, or by paddles. The latter were stout and large, made of hardwood (*koa*), with oval blades and handles. They were five feet or a little less in length, and rather heavy.

In addition to its use in torches,[37] the nut of the kukui tree was

[35] E. H. Bryan, "Featherwork," number 10 of his series on "Ancient Hawaiian Life," in the *Honolulu Advertiser,* December 27, 1937.

[36] Fornander, *The Polynesian Race,* II, 8.

[37] P. 38.

also a means of lighting the inside of houses at night. With the husk on, the nut looks something like a small walnut. Sound nuts, that is, those which sank when thrown into water, were baked in an oven and their shells broken off. "When used as candles, they string twenty or thirty up on a slit of bamboo, each of which will burn five or six minutes; but they require constant trimming, and it is necessary to reverse the torch whenever a nut is consumed that the one under it may catch fire." [38] Hence someone had to be specially detailed to look after it.

Among their implements of war were daggers, small swords, and clubs, spears up to twenty feet in length, javelins of twelve feet. Bows and arrows were not built sturdily enough to be very useful. Slings were made to throw small stones forcefully and well.[39]

Extent of Specialization and of Trade

A number of the professional occupations have been spoken of in connection with social classes. There was doctoring in which some of the kahunas claimed proficiency and practiced after inherited tradition.[40] They also monopolized soothsaying and sorcery. There were the konohiki, or executive agents of the king and main chiefs, a tolerably well-recognized professional group, in effect the business managers of districts and plantations. Less distinct and permanent a group were the ilamuku, or agents entrusted with seeing to the enforcement of the laws and will of the chief: often instead of members of a fixed group any individuals trusted by the chief were sent.

In addition, and on a high level of repute, were the professions of orator and bard. The former pleaded causes before high chiefs, though in general individuals spoke for themselves. The orators also spoke to general assemblies in negotiations between hostile chiefs or parties. The great honor in which the bards were held was due to absence of written communication among the Hawaiians. Their only duty was to remember accurately chants

[38] Archibald Campbell, *A Voyage round the World, 1806–12* (Roxbury, Massachusetts: 1825), p. 184.

[39] J. J. Jarves, *History of the Hawaiian or Sandwich Islands*, p. 62.

[40] They used herb compounds, of both crushed and cooked plants, often with powerful cathartic effect. Patients were steamed over ovens, or held in the smoke of fires in which certain green herbs were smoking away. Friction and massaging were used for pain, and simple fractures set successfully. But we should class much of their treatments as sorcery and superstition. See J. J. Jarves, *op. cit.*, p. 80.

and songs recording the racial history and traditions: for this purpose "they commenced repeating them by rote from an early age, until they were indelibly fixed in their memories." [41] Often these songs were on a high artistic level with moving language and memorable imagery . . . Strolling musicians were a less fixed group, and on a lower social level.

The higher chiefs maintained a group of runners, men specially inured to the fatigue and exposure of long and rapid journeys. This was often a hereditary function, as was the likewise honorable post of herald. Both offices implied the trust and confidence of the chief. Also, kings maintained a select band of men to row canoes.[42] There was no permanent warrior class, men usually being conscripted from their peacetime occupations.

But these professions and official posts took up only a small proportion of the total population. Nearly all the people are to be classed in the skilled or unskilled manual occupations. Farmers and fishermen made up the two largest divisions; and the latter especially developed individualized skills within the general occupation, as the list of techniques of fishing indicates.[43] The trade of bird-catcher stands out in the general occupation of hunting as a distinct pursuit, certain men being skilled in the arts of liming and snaring, and hence valuable to chiefs desiring to complete their cloaks and helmets.

The trade of adz-maker was an honored one, the art of shaping and sharpening the stone and tying it securely to the handle being handed down from remote times. Canoe-builders were recognized experts. Skill was needed for effective designing, and for neat hewing with the stone adz according to plan to realize the design. There was also the danger of ruining many days of work by splitting or stoving in a side through a careless blow. Other men were expert in carving wood generally; or in framing houses. "To finish thatching the corners, or the roofs of houses, properly and handsomely, was a difficult art, and understood but by a few." [44]

[41] Jarves, *op. cit.*, p. 68.

[42] *Letter of William Richards to Commander Wilkes*, p. 58.

[43] Richards, pp. 70–73; above, p. 38.

[44] Jarves, *History of the Hawaiian or Sandwich Islands*, p. 75.

The Menzies manuscript gives a portrait of division of labor in native Hawaii: "The men were differently engaged in a forest on the slope of Mauna Loa, some in felling of large timber for various purposes; others in hollowing out and forming

But most of these skilled trades were in an incipient stage, rather than permanent occupations.

A division of labor existed between men and women, women taking care of children, the making of tapa, and the weaving of mats; men doing the fishing, hunting, cooking, and the heavy work. As the inferior status of women implies, they were excused from no work they were physically capable of doing, even entering into war along with their husbands. Men's preparation of food was a restriction of the tabus, not a courtesy.

Because of the development of special skills, or of locally favorable conditions of supply, or a combination of the two, portions of the Islands became identified with special commodities. Incentive existed for regular exchange between areas, just as individual specialization led to exchange between inhabitants of the same area. Niihau, for example, being small and dry, had no wood supply for canoes, but grew yams in abundance,[45] and wove its fine *makaloa* mats which could be exchanged for the needed wood.

A settled commerce grew up between Kauai and Oahu: "With the inhabitants of Atooi [Kauai] the natives carry on considerable trade. The inhabitants of Wahoo [Oahu] excell in making taper [tapa] or cloth; whilst those of Atooi excell in canoes, paddles and spears, and they very often make exchanges in these articles."[46]

In Hawaii a durable tapa made at Kapapala called *mamake* was famous. Dried fish from the Kona coast and other sections com-

canoes and planks in the rough, which after laying some time in the wood to season, were dragged down in that state to the seashore, to be finished by canoe builders, who are distinct persons from those who thus form them in the rough; while a third set seems to have no other occupation than that of catching small birds for the sake of their feathers, especially those of a red, yellow, or black color; it is with them that a large part of the rents are annually paid to the chiefs by the lower class of people, who thus employ themselves by catching the birds with bird lime. The women are no less assiduous in collecting and manufacturing the bark of a shrubby species of nettle, which grows wild in the woods, for making a kind of coarse russet cloth." (From the *Hawaiian Annual* for 1908, pp. 107–108. The original manuscript is in the British Museum. Menzies was in Vancouver's 1790–1794 voyage.)

[45] "Life and Adventures of John Nicol" (typed copy of the original manuscript in the Archives of Hawaii), p. 76. Nicol's ship stood in to Niihau in 1785 for yams. He wrote that Niihau "grows . . . scarce anything else."

[46] Campbell, *A Voyage round the World,* p. 200.

monly entered into barter for this and other tapas, and for vegetable produce from the fertile and damp Hamakua coast.[47]

Exchange had become so regularized on Hawaii (much the largest island both in population and area) that regular market fairs were held beside the bank of the Wailuku river near Hilo—an institution marking a high point of economic development in the Islands before Cook's visit. Peddlers from all parts of the island brought goods produced abundantly in their own districts to barter for other commodities. Tapas of different sorts, mats, baskets, pigs and dogs, dried fish, poi, and hard food (ai pai) were exhibited on each side of the stream, arranged and shown according to rule. When a bargain seemed likely to be struck between two traders, the goods they were considering exchanging were taken to a broad rock in the middle of the shallow stream. There they were examined in the presence of inspectors, who saw to the observance of fair play and good order, and arbitrated any disputes that arose.[48] The inspectors received a small commission from each transaction.[49]

This market had been held during the reigns of several generations of kings before Kamehameha; and continued to 1819.

No commodity had attained the status of a medium of exchange, or money: probably dried salted fish was closer to that status than any other, being of fairly uniform quality and not very perishable.

Social Attitudes with Respect to Production and Consumption

It is clear there was heavy weight of discouragement to economic effort from the lack of security of personal property, the doubtful tenure of land, and the unlimited dominance generally of the chieftain class. But the discouragement was not sufficient in the native economy to lead to idle and careless habits of life. Early voyagers are unanimous in praising the industrious habits of the natives. Even the preëminent conqueror Kamehameha I is reported in mud up to his middle among his taro. Campbell writes from about 1810:

[47] Ellis, *Journal*, p. 203.

[48] Pp. 30–31.

[49] Jarves, *History*, pp. 77–78; Ellis, *Journal*, p. 242. A toll was charged at all times for crossing the river at this point, the amount collected being proportional to the rank of the person who passed over.

I have often seen the king working hard in a taro patch. I know not whether this was done with a view of setting an example of industry to his subjects . . . Such exertion could scarcely be thought necessary among these islanders, who are certainly the most industrious people I ever saw.[50]

And Menzies, from Vancouver's expedition 1790–1794, concludes: "They possess ingenuity, industry, and abilities to an eminent degree, and the only thing wanting is mildly to guide these into a proper channel."

But there was some feeling among the chiefs that labor was menial, properly to be associated with commoners. However, when public work was being carried on, such as "building temples in honor of their gods, or performing some labor in honor of the dead, the highest chiefs of the nation, both male and female, were often seen carrying stones on their shoulders, or engaged in some other kind of manual labor." On such occasions one high chief of tabu rank was kept aside to remain uncontaminated by menial labor, so as to preside at purificatory ceremonies for the others when the project was complete.

A heavy bar to effective utilization of resources lay in the psychological immaturity of the natives, or what we could call in a well worn phrasing "weakness of will and want of imagination," leading to astonishing lack of provision against future wants.[51] "One reason why people soon ran out of food was that they planted it all at once, so that when it ripened it ripened all at one time. While they were eating of one part, another part was also ripe, so they invited their neighbors to help themselves" [52]—and thereafter were in want. But not all were so improvident.

Lack of foresight in planning production was paralleled by lack of restraint in consuming: just as the former led to a smaller useful output than the input of effort could have resulted in, so the latter occasioned a lower level of "welfare" than the available quantity of consumption goods might have provided.

[50] Campbell, *A Voyage round the World*, p. 163.

[51] The naïveté of their emotions struck early reporters. So Jarves wrote: "Their joys and griefs were equally ephemeral; tears of sorrow could follow in quick succession peals of laughter, and both give way to an almost immovable apathy" (*History*, p. 97). He speaks of mourners, "at one moment buried apparently in deepest affliction, and in another reveling in boisterous mirth about their food, while their places . . . were supplied by a fresh set" (p. 69).

[52] Malo, *Hawaiian Antiquities*, p. 272.

> Those who had a supply of vegetable food and fish often ate six or eight times in the twenty-four hours. It was a frequent practise to rise in the night to eat. This was especially true of those who had fish brought in at the evening . . . When they had less . . . they ate perhaps only once a day; and not infrequently went without eating anything for two or three days, then on succeeding days ate proportionately more.[53]

Custom sanctioned long visits to families who had an abundance of food: people often left their own fields for several months, while their own taro and sweet potatoes were growing, to visit some distant friend whose crops were ripe; and judged it foolish to leave their friend so long as his food supply held out.[54] Though the custom increased welfare by spreading already produced supplies to those who needed them, it diminished incentive to produce anew.

The customary hospitality was consonant with a total lack of social conscience in matters subject to other mores. Eveleth reports from as late as 1825 that when four grass houses were burning down, the neighbors made no slightest effort to put out the fire, but instead pilfered whatever they could put their hands on.[55]

The Level of Welfare

The net picture of the welfare of the Hawaiians is an uneven one. In good times the food supply was adequate in quantity and variety;[56] when the harvesting and fishing were poor, there was "more or less of *wi,* or famine." Two of the chief foods, taro and sweet potatoes, grew best on lower and warmer ground, where they were more likely to be stricken with drought.[57]

[53] Dibble, *History of the Sandwich Islands,* p. 104.

[54] John Nicol, having left his ship to reside in the Islands at the turn of the century, writes that when he married a Hawaiian woman his bride's whole family, to his consternation, moved in to share his house and table. They were shocked at being asked to do any work; and the desperate man had finally to drive them out with a club. (*Life and Adventures of John Nicol,* manuscript in the Archives of Hawaii.)

[55] "The destitute families were more the objects of ridicule than of pity . . . When I gave them taros, the people were astonished . . . Some said, 'What a fool this foreigner is!'" (Reverend Mr. Eveleth, *History of the Sandwich Islands,* p. 92.)

[56] For an evaluation by a present-day nutritionist of the merit of articles of the Hawaiian diet, see C. D. Miller, *Food Values of Poi, Taro, and Limu, Bernice P. Bishop Museum Bulletin* (Honolulu: 1927).

[57] Bishop, *Reminiscences,* p. 14. "The village was a place of great and squalid

To the extent that it is valid to argue that "utility" increases as goods are more nearly equally distributed [58]—a concept our sense of humanity is much in favor of though economists may partly doubt—the feudal order with its sharp division of classes and their disparate privileges of consumption diminished the general welfare. Accounts from early days contrast the proud bearing, commanding stature, and astonishing fatness—a variety of "conspicuous consumption"—of the alii with the timorous manner and meager and squalid appearance of the makaainana. Wrote the missionary Bishop:

> Governor Kuakini . . . was an enormous man of great stature . . . His weight was estimated at 500 pounds . . . His wife was a royal chief of the highest rank and not quite equally ponderous. I remember seeing the princely pair lolling on their own pile of rich Niihau mats, with many attendants busy kneeding their bodies and limbs (*lomi-lomi*). The relative ranks of other natives could be approximately estimated by their stature and corpulence. But the great crowd of common people were miserably lean and often very squalid in appearance . . .[59]

When we ask whether there was perceptible improvement in social welfare in the centuries before discovery, we find our answer clouded by the meagerness and doubtfulness of ancient tradition. In so far as it can be trusted, we should conclude that after first colonization and for several centuries there was continuous growth and technical and economic progress. This was a period of small population and unutilized resources, with no basis for rigorous competition toward means of subsistence. In such a pioneering society it is unlikely that class divisions cut deep or that class privileges were important.

---

poverty . . . It was infested by miserably lean pigs, whose scant food came from scavengering. Occasionally a pig was fattened in a pen. But the eye of the chief's retainer was usually on such pigs, and it was likely to be snatched away even after being cooked . . . The chief causes of destitution were the ceaseless oppression of the chiefs, and the attendant shiftlessness of the people."

[58] The argument is based on the (Marshallian) declining utility curve, which indicates diminishing significance to a person of an additional unit of a good, as the number of the units increases. If we can make the further courageous assumption that tastes of all individuals are alike, then "utility" will be at a maximum when each person has the same quantity of every good. For if in such case a unit of a good is given from one individual to another, the one who now has less than the average had lost more than the other, who now has more than the average, has gained.

[59] Bishop, *op. cit.*, p. 13. See also Reverend Mr. Eveleth, *op. cit.*, p. 35.

But before the great voyages of the early eleventh to early fifteenth centuries, population was pressing on resources. For from this period date some of the great engineering projects, like "the irrigating systems of Wahiawa, Kapaa, and Kilauea on the Island of Kauai, and great sea walls, bays and reefs for fish ponds as the one at Huleia on Kauai . . . The antiquity of some of these is so great that even tradition fails to account for their origin." [60]

We have spoken of the traditions of the centuries following the epoch of migration, in which there is evidence of a deepening and confirming of the divisions of society. The even course of productive activity was interrupted, probably increasingly, through forays, insurrections, and wars. Finally, at the beginning of the nineteenth century, Kamehameha, with the help of the white man's guns and equipment, succeeded in imposing his rule—and peace—over all the Islands.

Techniques of utilizing Island resources improved decidedly at the beginning of the period through the introduction of new plants and animals from the South Seas. It is not likely that these introductions led to any rise in average real income, but simply, after a time for adjustment, to a larger population at the old level.

But the tendency to a larger population would have been opposed by hardening class divisions and a parallel increase in inequality of consumption, tending toward a smaller population maintained at a higher *average* real income.

[60] Sanford B. Dole, in *Report of Committee of Senate on Foreign Relations for 1894* (Washington: Government Printing Office, 1894), p. 94.

SECTION II

THE DECAY OF FEUDALISM, 1778–1844

CHAPTER IV

THE FUR AND SANDALWOOD TRADE

After Cook's expedition, the Islands remained unvisited for seven years.

But the intelligence which the published reports of Cook's voyages[1] gave to the world about the resources of the Northwest Coast (what is now British Columbia, Oregon, and Washington)[2] was an effective incentive toward the exploitation of the virgin resources of fur in that region. For England the incentive was especially strong: in so far as her statesmen were yet under the dominance of mercantilist beliefs, an opportunity was here suggested of paying for the immense quantities of tea which she annually imported from China, not by specie but by furs, which sold there at a good price. And the fur need not be obtained from the distant areas of Hudson Bay and eastern Canada, to be transported round the Horn, but was relatively near at hand on the Northwest Coast.

Captain King had suggested a route for the new trade: a fur trader might leave China with the April monsoon, go north to the coast of America along Japan, the Kurile Islands, and the Aleutian Islands, arriving in June. He could spend three months gathering fur along the coast, leaving for China direct in October.[3] Hawaii had no place in this route.

King's route was actually followed by Captain James Hanna, who made two trips from China to the Northwest, one in 1785,

[1] The first edition was published in London in 1784.

[2] Americans were generous in their recognition of Cook's services, even while at war with England. Benjamin Franklin wrote in a letter of instructions to captains of American cruisers that, "In whatever part of the sea they might meet the great discoverer, Captain Cook, they were to forget the temporary quarrel in which they were then fighting, and not merely suffer him to pass unmolested, but offer him every aid in their power, since it would ill beseem Americans to lift their hands against one who had earned the reverence and gratitude of all mankind." Quoted in pp. 6, 7 of *Official Papers of the Captain Cook Sesquicentennial Celebration* (Honolulu: 1928), by Dr. Herbert Gregory.

[3] N. King, vol. III of Cook's *Voyages,* 1784 edition, pp. 438 f.

one in 1786; and also by two other ships under command of Captain Strange.[4]

But promptly vessels entering into fur trade began to stop at the Islands for "refreshments." There were no provisions on the Coast in the quantities needed for provisioning vessels; but they could be obtained in abundance in Hawaii and at first at extraordinarily low prices, due to the high valuation the wondering Islanders put on simple iron objects and other commodities. For a second reason, the natives on the Coast were backward, and could give no intelligent help in navigating vessels; whereas the Hawaiians were excellent seamen, and hence were valued hands on foreign ships. Third, scurvy was still a terror of the sea, and early vessels frequently put in with their men disabled from it.[5] The need of quantities of fresh provisions became greater since after the first few years vessels were unable to complete their cargoes of fur and sea otter skins in the summer months, and had to stay over more than one season. Accordingly a voyage out of Boston came to extend not to one year and something over, but up to three years. The Islands seemed invaluable to the traders. One of them wrote:

> What a happy discovery these islands were! What would the American fur trade be without them to winter at and get every refreshment? A vessel going to that trade will only need sufficient provisions to carry her to these islands, where there is plenty of pork, and salt to cure it, and yams as a substitute for bread.[6]

Captains Dixon and Portlock, first to reach the Islands (Oahu) after Cook, were English traders,[7] bound for the Northwest Coast for furs and sea otter skins. The Frenchman La Pérouse touched at Maui about the same time. The competitive spirit stirred also in India, from which Meares left in 1786 to make several trips to the Islands. American ships, later nearly to monopolize Island trade, soon entered into competition: two and perhaps

[4] The ships were *The Captain Cook* and *The Experiment*. Hanna's voyage was the pioneer venture in fur trade between China and America. John Meares, *Voyages* (London: 1791), is the sole source for this information.

[5] The first two ships after Cook's expedition, the *King George* and the *Queen Charlotte*, under Captains Portlock and Dixon, put in for this reason in May of 1786.

[6] Bell's *Journal*, p. 35, manuscript copy in Archives of Hawaii.

[7] Captain Portlock had been with the Cook expedition.

three American ships had wintered in the Islands before 1800.[8] Two vessels in the trade, the *Columbia* and the *Washington,* had wintered on the Coast. When Vancouver came to Kauai in 1791, about thirty different visits had been made to the Islands, by the same or different vessels.

Supplies obtained at the Islands during these early years were pigs, fowls, yams, fruits and vegetables, water, and firewood. Salt too was obtained for the curing of furs on the Coast, and it seems likely to have been the first article of export. Turnbull, by 1802, complains of the scarcity and dearness of salt.[9] In exchange the natives took iron in any form, utensils, guns and ammunition, and tools, such as knives, chisels, and axes.

The evolution of rates of exchange is interesting. Two groups ignorant of each other's scale of valuation were entering into continuing commercial contact. At first both sides felt they were doing wonderfully well. Taking iron as an example, the value of iron nails and scraps was nearly indefinitely low to the haole compared to the value of provisions: just the reverse held as to the native valuation of the iron, and of the effort required to supply provisions. As a consequence the bargaining range within which exchange was advantageous to both sides was very wide; though probably transactions tended to take place in an area relatively favorable to the haole due to his greater sophistication, and hence acuter perception of the other's standards of valuation.

John Nicol, who had shipped with Captain Portlock, describes trade on Hawaii in 1785:

> The natives came on board in crowds, and were happy to see us . . . Our decks were soon crowded with hogs, breadfruit, yams and potatoes . . . Our deck . . . resembled a shambles; our butcher had fourteen assistants . . . I was as busy and fatigued as I could be cutting iron hoops into lengths of eight and nine inches, which the carpenter ground sharp. These are the most valuable commodity in the eyes of the natives. I was stationed down in the hold of the vessel, and the ladders were removed to prevent the natives from coming down to the treasury. The King of Owhyhee[10] (Kamehameha) looked to my occupation with a wistful eye; he thought me the happiest man on board, to be among such vast heaps of treasure.[11]

[8] Out of six, or perhaps seven, in all. Frederick Howay, in *Papers of the Captain Cook Sesquicentennial Celebration* (Honolulu: 1928), p. 31.

[9] *Voyage round the World,* p. 199.

[10] Old spelling of Hawaii.

[11] Nicol continues: "Captain Portlock called to me to place the ladder, and allow the king to come down and give him a good long piece. When the king

Eight years later iron was still estimated as of high value: "The natives . . . go up to the woods . . . to fetch water for our vessels. One of these natives, going down under a heavy load of calabashes, showed us three small iron nails he got for his labor, with which he seems very well satisfied." [12]

But the golden days were passing: the natives were heaping in a supply of iron, and hence valuing it less.[13] By 1795 a "Muskett" was required in one case to purchase nine large hogs; and a "few chissels" to buy six pigs.[14]

With increasing quantity within the Islands of the most valued foreign products, and with identical experience by each side of market conditions, the bargaining range lessened. And the natives in time became more adept at bargaining; that is, able to conclude transactions within the bargaining range closer to the maximum offer obtainable from the haole.

Turnbull by 1802 complained of the high price of provisions compared with former rates.[15] Lisianski reports from the summer of 1804 that iron which in any form had formerly been considered of the highest value was now little regarded, unless in bars; and that their rusty hoops brought them in nothing. The bay of "Caracacooa" (Kealakekua) had during the preceding year been visited by eighteen different ships; and in consequence everything was dear:

> For four large hogs, I gave a piece of thin canvass; for three others, I gave a bar and a half of iron; for a middling sized one, two iron axes; for a small one, a single iron axe; for a suckling pig, a piece of printed linen, measuring nearly three yards, but cut in two lengthwise . . . The same for

---

descended he held up his hands and looked astonishment personified. When I gave him a piece of hoop twenty inches long, he retired a little from below the hatch into the shade, undid his girdle, bent the iron into his body, and adjusting his belt with the greatest haste, concealed it. I could not but laugh to see the king concealing what he took to be stolen goods." *Life and Adventures of John Nicol, Mariner* (Edinburgh: 1822), pp. 71–72.

[12] A. Menzies, in the *Hawaiian Annual* for 1908, p. 106. Menzies was encouraged to contemplate the possibility of starting sugar plantations, with such cheap and docile labor abundant.

[13] Honolulu harbor was discovered by about this time, 1794, by a Captain Brown. Safe anchorage and a sure welcome from Kamehameha made it the leading Island harbor within two or three years.

[14] Boit, *Journal of the Union*. Typed copy of a photostat of the original in Archives of Hawaii.

[15] *Voyage round the World* (Philadelphia: 1810), p. 199.

six or eight bunches of sweet potatoes, or a hundred weight of yams; and lastly a small knife for a fowl.[16]

Lisianski pays tribute to the sharp bargaining of the natives:

They are certainly very difficult in bargaining, and know how to keep up the price of whatever they have to sell; and if it happened that we purchased anything at a dear rate, it was immediately known to the whole throng, and the article could not afterwards be obtained cheaper. They would even let a day or two pass, in the hope of bringing us to their terms; but aware of this, and as unbending as themselves, we generally obtained what we wanted reasonably.[17]

Campbell from 1809 to 1810 reports that by that time exchange had settled down to the following rates:

A pig is estimated by its length; the largest size, called . . . fathom pig, measures that length from snout to rump, and is valued at two axes, a junket of the thickest part of a sea horse tooth, a yard and a half of blue cloth, or five dollars . . . A pig that measures from the elbow to the opposite hand, is valued at one axe, or about half the price of the larger size. A sheep or goat may be had for a smaller piece of ivory; a *maro* or pair of fowls, for a knife, a pair of scissors, or a small mirror.[18]

Already by this time the fur trade had led to, and was merging into, a new kind of commerce, that revolving around sandalwood.[19] The demand for the wood came from China where incense made from it was burned in the temples.

In 1791 two ship captains had discovered the existence of what they thought to be sandalwood. Captain William Douglas seems probably to have been first: he left two men on Maui before May of 1791 to collect a shipload of the wood, "which wood he had

[16] *Voyage round the World* (London: 1814), pp. 125–126.

[17] *Ibid.*, p. 125.

[18] Archibald Campbell, *A Voyage round the World* (Edinburgh: 1816), p. 201.

[19] The shift in type of trade was correlated fairly well with a shift in nationality of traders. Where up to 1791 ships touching the Islands were largely British fur traders, afterwards American sandalwood (or sandalwood and fur) traders came to carry on the traffic nearly exclusively. One main reason for American preëminence was the East India Company's monopoly of the China trade, which compelled English venturers not of the Company to ship their goods in foreign bottoms. The British consul, Richard Charlton, complained repeatedly of the effect of the monopoly. (Letter to George Channing, June 1825; also "Letter from the British Consulate to a senior officer on any of H.B.M.'s ships." Archives of Hawaii.)

discovered or a wood similar to it."[20] Captain John Kendrick of the *Lady Washington* left about the same time, as something of an afterthought, two men on Niihau to collect sandalwood to deliver to him on the next trip of the ship back from Boston.[21] But the wood collected in these earliest ventures was a false sandalwood, and when it was transported to Canton, the Chinese would give nothing for it.[22]

In consequence of the discouragement, it was not for over ten years that any significant trade was carried on in the true sandalwood also growing in the Islands. In 1804–1805 900 piculs[23] are recorded as imported at Canton. By 1809 sandalwood was a regular article of Hawaiian export. The peak of the trade was from 1810 to 1818, due to the conjuncture of relative abundance of supply, a good market in China, and knowledge of the opportunity.[24] In 1817–18 ships were arriving at the Islands at the rate of four a month; they were nearly all American, and nearly all engaged in the sandalwood trade.[25] Within the Islands the

[20] *Log of Captain Joseph Ingraham,* May 26, 1791. Copy in Archives of Hawaii. See *Paradise of the Pacific* for April 1935, for Bruce Cartwright's discussion of the origins of the trade.

[21] Vancouver's Journal, October 1791.

[22] Amasa Delano, *A Narrative of Voyages and Travels* (Boston: 1817), speaks of seeing 30 tons of such wood from one ship at Canton. His date for this is 1790. He must have been in error by a year or two, in view of the dates above.

[23] A Chinese measure of weight, equaling 133 1/3 lbs.

[24] Cantonese customs statistics give imports of

19,036	piculs in	1811–12
15,825		1817–18
9,800		1820–21

By the last named year wood was scarcer, and much more effort was needed to obtain it . . . From Hawaiian reports it is clear that these figures are not even close to being inclusive, although Canton was nearly the only port to which the wood was brought. Perhaps smuggling explains part of the discrepancy. There is reason to believe that some increase in trade took place during the later 1820's. Source: Gutzoff: *Sketches of Chinese History,* vol. II, appendix IV; reproduced in Bruce Cartwright, "The Sandalwood Trade," *Paradise of the Pacific,* April 1935.

[25] The most active group of traders was a company organized around Captains William Davis and Jonathan Winship of Boston. Some of the company stayed in Hawaii to collect wood, others transported it to China. These same captains had in 1812 made a monopoly agreement with Kamehameha to have for ten years the exclusive privilege of exporting sandalwood (and cotton!) from Hawaii. The War of 1812 ended the venture, since armed merchantmen of both England and the United States were in the Pacific, attacking enemy ships, and so increasing the risks of commerce. (*Solid Men of Boston in the Northwest,* manuscript in the Bancroft Library, University of California. Quoted in Ralph Kuykendall, *The Hawaiian Kingdom, 1778–1854* (Honolulu: 1938), p. 86.)

trade was monopolized by Kamehameha.[26] When wood was needed, he simply ordered his chiefs to see to its collection. They retained for themselves a share generally amounting to four parts by weight for every ten parts collected.

The price during the period from 1810 to 1818 varied between $8 and $10 a picul ($120–150 a ton) in money. But normally the value of the wood was given in barter terms. In a Spanish manuscript dating from 1811 to 1814, equivalents are given as follows:

a large, wide coat	12	piculs	
12 hammers	1	"	
14 4 pounder cannons	7	"	each
500 balls for these cannon	18	"	
10 piculs of ammunition	35	"	
80 swords	80	"	
600 lime trees	30	"	[27]

The sandalwood trade was, as we have before indicated, often combined with the fur trade. The Americans had worked out an economical routine, bringing out from the East Coast "British printed cottons, broadcloths, and hardware, which they sell to the natives at an extravagant price, taking sandalwood in return." While the wood was being collected by agents, the ships proceeded to the Northwest Coast for beaver and sea otter skins, coming again past the Islands on their way to China to pick up their wood.[28]

[26] This was apparently largely for a conservational and general welfare reason. See note, p. 66.

[27] Archives of Hawaii.

[28] Letter of the British Consul, Richard Charlton, to the Honorable George Channing, June 1825. Archives of Hawaii.

The inventory of goods received by Kamehameha in return for a shipload of sandalwood carried to China in Captain Winship's voyage of 1811–12 affords an illustration of what was being brought to the chiefs at this time:

3 paintings on paper
2 doz. ordinary cotton stockings
1 box of Chinese wood
2 crystal lamps
1 bundle of metal pipes
6 boxes
1 bundle of blue stones and white for a gaming table
12 Chinese chairs
1000 large beads
10 boxes silk handkerchiefs
6 shiny hats for soldiers

In 1821 the first United States "Agent for Commerce" noted with approval the consistent success which the American fur and sandalwood traders had met with in the preceding decade. During the year 1821 alone 30,000 piculs of wood had gone to China, commanding in that market at least $300,000.[29]

By the 1820's Island demand for goods had become more sophisticated. With the goods brought for King Kamehameha (see note 28) may be compared typical goods in 1821: blankets, "cambiricks," India cottons, silks, "common cloths," turpentine, hardware, muskets, powder, large guns, spirits, wine, rice, molasses, in addition to "all fancy articles." [30] In 1825 among British manufactures especially in demand are listed printed cottons, calicoes, broadcloth, earthenware, hardware, and clothing of all kinds.[31] Occasionally schooners, brigs, and other vessels were sold to Kamehameha for the price of their volume in sandalwood.[32]

Trade was carried on by barter into the twenties. Though the natives were aware of the value of dollars in 1809, they were less securely conscious of value in them than in consumption goods.[33]

12 black straw hats
50 silk hats
6 reels thread
50 Chinese cutlasses
3 pieces flowered flannel
6 fishing rods
100 Chinese mats
135 lbs. large glass beads
1 iron hearth
1 saddle
3 pieces flowered satin
3 boxes of sweets
1 large cloak

Source: Foreign Office Records, Archives of Hawaii.

[29] Dispatch of John C. Jones, Jr. to John Quincy Adams, Secretary of State, dated December 31, 1821. National Archives of the United States.

[30] *Ibid.*

[31] Richard Charlton to the Honorable George Channing, June 10, 1825. Archives of Hawaii.

[32] Often a hole of the same dimensions as the ship was dug in the ground and filled with sandalwood. Once the King is said to have been done in by a Yankee trader who persuaded him to permit a rectangular hole to be dug with vertical sides which took no account of the sloping sides and sharpened bow and stern. The King carried out his side of the trade, but learned to bargain more shrewdly thereafter. ("Reminiscences of G. D. Gilman," *Hawaiian Annual* for 1894, p. 85.)

[33] See pp. 103–105.

In the 1820's bonanzas of $300,000 a year and more were still being received into the Islands from export of the wood. King Liholiho, who succeeded Kamehameha at his death in 1819, was a weaker monarch, and soon gave up the royal monopoly of sandalwood, permitting his chiefs to sell it on their own account. The desire of the nobility for the exotic merchandise of the foreigner was great. Their avarice was excited the more by traders competing for increased business. The merchandise could be gotten in return for a mere scribble. Promissory notes were easily signed: the future when the notes were to be paid was distant and doubtful.

Warehouses of the chiefs came to be stacked high with ill-assorted goods, more than could possibly be used, and subject to rotting and rusting away:

> Chief Kuakina at Kailua possessed great quantities of foreign goods stored in his warehouses, while his people went naked. I have often heard my father tell of seeing one of Kuakini's large double canoes loaded deep with bales of broad cloth and Chinese silks and satins which had become damaged by long storage. They were carried out, and dumped in the ocean.[34]

The competing traders were of two minds about the debts: they wanted to collect them, but the greater the pressure they put on the chiefs to pay, the less goods could currently be sold. Such a result was not altogether to be desired, with more or less perishable goods coming in which had been ordered months before, and with other merchants about pressing to establish favorable contacts and sell their own merchandise.

The chiefs naturally preferred to receive goods in exchange for sandalwood, rather than canceled IOU's. In some cases they were unwilling to pay when they found that ships they had bought as sound turned out to be rotten, fit only for dismantling. This was painfully true of at least two ships bought by Kamehameha, and of a brig of Liholiho's,[35] and it must have been the case with others as well.

Protests by the traders to the United States government finally brought American warships to the Islands in 1826 and 1829 to investigate the matter. The chiefs acknowledged claims of about

[34] S. E. Bishop, *Reminiscences of Old Hawaii* (Honolulu: 1916), p. 26.

[35] Tyerman and Bennet, *Voyages and Travels* (London: 1840), 2nd edition, p. 121.

15,000 piculs of wood.[36] A general assessment was made on the population for the collecting of the debt: every man was to deliver at least one-half picul of sandalwood (half of any additional amount he cut to be his own), and every woman was to bring a mat, a piece of tapa, or a Spanish dollar.

The amount was not completely paid, however. Some debt was still outstanding in 1836; and the accounts were finally settled only in 1843 by payment of $14,000.

The end of the sandalwood traffic was already in sight in the twenties. Where wood had once been plentiful[37] (and in the nineties had probably been first identified in the midst of firewood casually cut in the lowlands), now it could be obtained in desired quantities only by prolonged expeditions into the uplands. Goaded by their avarice and the demands of the traders, the chiefs were compelled to send commoners in numbers of up to several thousands into the forests, to be gone for weeks at a time. In 1822:

> On one occasion we saw nearly 2000 persons laden with fagots of sandalwood, coming down from the mountains to deposit their burthens in the royal storehouses, and then depart to their homes, wearied with their unpaid labors, yet unmurmuring at their bondage.[38]

Ellis in 1823 speaks of villages nearly deserted, with all the inhabitants in the mountains cutting the wood; and of "three or four hundred people" returning from such an expedition.[39]

Sometimes the natives burned forest areas in the effort to detect sandalwood by its odor when burning.[40] By 1829 the scarcity of wood was acute enough to lead the Governor of Oahu, Boki, to set out on a badly planned expedition to the islands of Rotuma and

[36] See R. S. Kuykendall, *The Hawaiian Kingdom, 1778–1854* (Honolulu: 1938), Appendix D, pp. 434–436, for an excellent analysis of the amount of the debt, as resolved from conflicting testimony.

[37] In the earlier years of the trade, a severe famine extending from Hawaii to Kauai is attributed to the trade, so many were the chiefs and commoners devoted to cutting and transporting wood. "Kamehameha, observing this, thereupon charged the chiefs and people that they be not too absorbed in sandalwood gathering, and *kapued* it for the government." (Translation of account of the native historian, S. M. Kamakau, in *Hawaiian Annual* for 1906.)

[38] Tyerman and Bennet, *Voyages and Travels,* p. 109.

[39] William Ellis, *Journal,* pp. 227, 273, 295, 298. Cf. also Bingham, *A Residence of Twenty-one Years in the Sandwich Islands,* pp. 26, 50; J. M. Lydgate in *Hawaiian Annual* for 1916, p. 53; Ethel Damon, *Koamalu,* p. 53.

[40] Ellis, *op. cit.,* p. 45.

Erromanga in the New Hebrides, where wood was reported abundant—a venture which ended in death and disaster to most of the participants.

To these troubles were added those of a less stable market. During early 1831 sandalwood cargoes did not sell for enough to pay the freight on them, according to one report; and by fall there was still little sale for the wood.[41]

By the middle thirties income from the wood had dropped to a tenth and less of its maximum value, both from lower valuation ($7, rather than the previous $8–10 per picul) and from diminution in supply. Instead of over $300,000 a year, we have:

1836	approx.	3700 piculs at $7	$26,000
1837		1770	12,000
1838		860	6,000
1839		3000	21,000
1840 through 1843		none	—
1844		724	5,000[42]

The sandalwood epoch was over.[43] Where there had formerly been splendid groves, there were now only isolated and scraggly bushes at a few places; and part of those remained only because they had been protected by law.[44]

By 1842 the chiefs could still explicitly account for more than 100,000 piculs, or close to $1,000,000 of revenue. Even when discounted in its significance as real income because of high prices

[41] Richard Charlton, British Consul, to Captain Waldyman, September 22, 1831. Archives of Hawaii.

[42] Figures for 1836 through 1838, Appendix IX of Captain Charles Wilkes, *Narrative of the United States Exploring Expedition, 1838–1842* (Philadelphia: 1845). Data for 1839–1844, Report of William Patty, Collector of Customs, as quoted in *The Polynesian,* January 18, 1845.

[43] A century later a project was under way to cultivate sandalwood trees. On a hill above St. Louis heights, Oahu, was "a grove of over 1500 sandalwood trees raised from seed obtained from Mysore, India, and . . . planted in November 1932 and January 1933, as an experiment to determine whether it is feasible to re-establish the industry."

Sandalwood has in recent years been grown mainly in India, and shipped to New York for distillation. It was valued in the 1930's at up to $500 a ton. (See "Sandalwood" by C. S. Judd, Territorial Forester, in the *Paradise of the Pacific,* April 1935.)

[44] Wilkes in his visit noted only a few bushes on the slopes of Haleakala, on the Ewa-Waialua plains of Oahu, and at the base of the Waianae mountains on Oahu. Cf. Berthold Seeman, *Voyage of the H.M.S. Herald during 1845–51,* quoted in *Thrum's Annual,* 1905, p. 71.

paid for imports, this still represents a considerable influx of foreign goods.

Social Results of the Fur and Sandalwood Trade

The period of the early explorers, fur and sandalwood traders was "to the natives a time of wonder, delight, and incipient disease; to their chiefs an El Dorado of iron and destructive implements . . . The dawn of a new day had sent its grey streaks across the dark sky of Hawaiian night."[45] New consumption goods of European, American, or Chinese manufacturer soon were introduced, as mentioned above. There resulted an extraordinary mixture of haole and native goods. At first hardly more than the king and high chiefs had foreign goods. Gradually they came to be used also among the lower strata. Something of the consequence can be imagined from the description of the King's grass shack in 1818: it contained a large chest filled with arms, a mahogany bureau, two tables, one of which was covered with a blue cotton tablecloth, two or three chairs of European make, and a cheap mirror. There were ground glass dishes, a set of silver table ware, and some fine porcelain ware. The soldiers around the King's house had swords and muskets with bayonets. Some of them wore white shirts, some waistcoats, and some were naked.[46]

Typical among early importations of consumption goods were Guayaquil cocoa, flour, soap, "good Manila rice," hemp, Manila cordage, "Blue Nankings," English prints, American cottons, woolens, copper sheathing, nails, Russian canvas, English saddles, spirits of turpentine, French wines, crockery and glass, harness, iron pots and pans, writing and letter paper, quills, ink, and lard.

Under a different heading come plants and animals left by early navigators, which altered productive techniques just as the other goods changed consumption habits. Among the plant introductions were melons, pumpkins, and onions (by Captain Cook), greens (attributed to Captain Portlock), "an assortment of garden seeds," and over a hundred orange shoots (by Vancouver).[47] Captain Vancouver, who ought to be well remembered for his

[45] Fornander, *The Polynesian Race*, II, 322.

[46] Captain V. Golovnin (of the Russian Navy), *Tour Around the World of the Sloop of War Kamschatka, 1817–1819*. Translations from the 10th and 11th chapters by Joseph Barth, in *The Friend*, July 1894.

[47] Menzies, *Hawaii Nei 128 Years Ago*, pp. 19, 39; Cook, *Voyages*, II, 217.

kindness and generosity, is known also to have left in 1793 a quantity of animals: a bull, five cows, two ewes, and a ram.[48] The cattle were tabued by Kamehameha, and left to multiply in peace. In 1796 the grapevine was brought by Captain Broughton, and in 1803 four horses[49] by Cleveland. By 1809 sheep and goats were already an article of trade.[50] Irish potatoes were introduced about 1820; and by 1825 cabbages, Indian corn, limes, and pineapples exchanged at the regular market then functioning in Honolulu.[51] Captain Meek brought the mango (fruit) tree in 1824. By about this time turkeys, ducks, donkeys, mules, and European varieties of chickens, pigs, and dogs had been introduced.

Along with these importations of undoubted usefulness came another about which there is more doubt. Already in 1791–1794, 11 white men were reported to be in the service of the king.[52] By 1816 there are listed 45 permanent residents,[53] to which should be added something like 100 stranded seamen and other transients. The Islands were becoming a clearing center for sailors: sometimes they were dropped for insubordination; sometimes because the ship captains wanted to release themselves from the obligation of paying their men the wages or shares agreed on, and to sign on instead the cheaper native seamen.[54] Often the men were dis-

[48] Menzies, *op. cit.*, p. 69.

[49] "Men sit on his back and ride; he has no horns on his head." David Malo, *Hawaiian Antiquities* (Honolulu: 1903), p. 65.

[50] Campbell, *A Voyage round the World*, p. 121.

[51] *Diary of Andrew Bloxam*, p. 30.

[52] Captain V. Golovnin, "Golovnin's Visit to Hawaii in 1818," in *The Friend*, LII, July–August 1894.

[53] *Columbian Sentinel*, November 6, 1816.

[54] "A practise has for many years existed with the commanders of ships touching the Sandwich Islands either for supplies or trade, to turn on shore all seamen against whom they could allege any trivial misconduct, and employ in their lieu natives of the Islands, by this means lessening their passage bills, but depriving their country of valuable subjects. American vessels have been sold to the natives and their crews discharged, without any means of support, thus left to the protection and mercy of the rude savage.

"These abuses of the laws of the United States I have been able to remedy . . . I have been enabled to return to their country many of the distressed seamen, & obtained employment for others, who were found dependent on the hand of charity. The enormities and crimes committed by such seamen have been of the most serious nature to the American trade & reflected disgrace on the American character." Manuscript dispatch of John C. Jones, Jr., U. S. Agent for Commerce, to John Quincy Adams, Secretary of State, December 31, 1821. National Archives of the United States.

charged because they liked the Islands; or, they simply deserted.

Turnbull was pessimistic as to the chances of keeping a crew once the Islands were reached:

Such is the difficulty, nay almost impossibility of maintaining the necessary complement of men in these voyages that I could almost recommend that no one should make the attempt. Nothing . . . can withstand the seduction and artifices of the southern islander; women, and a life of indolence, are too powerful for the sense of duty in the minds of our seamen. Had we relaxed our efforts for a single moment, our ship would have been deserted! [55]

It had become fashionable for a chief to have one or more white men in his employ to act as interpreters, gunners, technical experts in several trades, and as intermediaries in commercial projects. The King was reported in 1810 to have "a considerable number" of carpenters, joiners, blacksmiths, and bricklayers in his service.[56] Such men, if they behaved themselves, ranked as chiefs, with all privileges of the order. Often they bought or were given an area of land, with natives to work on the land as their servants.[57]

Such men, directing native helpers, built for Kamehameha over 30 sloops and schooners. By 1821 the King and chiefs had accumulated a small fleet of vessels, including 10 large brigs, part of them built in this fashion, and part bought from traders—often at exorbitant prices by home standards. They were kept busy coasting between the islands, transporting provisions, and gathering sandalwood.[58]

[55] *Voyage round the World,* p. 203.

[56] Campbell, *A Voyage round the World,* pp. 166–167. These men trained natives in skilled trades, though often they conveyed their knowledge grudgingly, or refused it. But soon a number of natives were skilled workmen: native blacksmiths are spoken of as early as 1803, carrying on the trade with ingenuity and persistence.

"Such is the astonishing assiduity of these people, and such their eagerness to improve their condition by imitating the callings of the Europeans that it is not unusual to see some of them exercising the trade of a country blacksmith, having for an anvil a pig of iron kentlage, obtained from some ship; a pair of goat-skin bellows, made by himself or some of his countrymen; and his charcoal wood fire; making articles suited to the wants of his countrymen, or repairing and mending such as stand in need of it, with an ingenuity surpassing what might be expected under such circumstances." (Turnbull, *Voyage round the World,* p. 232.)

[57] Samuel Patterson, *Narrative of the Adventures and Sufferings of Samuel Patterson* (1825), p. 70; Campbell, *A Voyage round the World,* p. 145.

[58] Kamehameha's first ship constructed after foreign technique had been built for him long before, in 1794, by ship's carpenters of the generous explorer George

But though some of the haoles were industrious, most of them were dissolute and idle: "It is no uncommon sight to see a party of them broach a small cask of spirits and sit drinking for days until they see it out . . . I do not recall any who knew more than the letters of the alphabet." [59]

By 1823 there was a total of a little under 200 foreigners in Hawaii. Of these a fluctuating proportion of close to three-quarters were drifters, and stranded or runaway sailors.[60] There were "15 or 20" permanent residents on all the islands. A few were well-to-do, with herds of cattle, goats, and many plantations: their ties were to the chiefs who had given them place and land. The remainder, save for the missionaries,[61] were the clerks and managers of four American mercantile houses in Honolulu. These houses had been established as a consequence of the fur and sandalwood trade,[62] two with head offices in Boston, one in New York, and one in Bristol, Rhode Island. Each generally had one ship cruising between the Islands to collect wood, and others that touched for repairs and provisions and with supplies of new goods, on their voyages between the Mexican, South American, and Northwest coasts; and China. Imported merchandise was paid for by sandalwood and specie. The total trade of the four was about $100,000 a year.[63]

The consequence of these foreign intrusions on native health, habits of life, and economic adjustments was slow catastrophe, no less destructive because spread out over decades.

The coming of the foreigners was a disaster to native health. Venereal disease introduced by the Cook expedition spread rapidly through the group, and was devastating in its effect. Likewise common diseases of foreigners, such as measles, influenza, and common colds, to which the Hawaiian race had not been inured by prolonged contact, were often fatal. The dissolute

---

Vancouver, as a friendly gesture. (Manuscript letter, signed by Vancouver, dated at the "Sloop Discovery," Toeyah Bay, Owhyhee, March 2, 1794. Copy at the Archives of Hawaii.)

[59] Campbell, *A Voyage round the World,* pp. 166–167.

[60] C. S. Stewart, *Private Journal of a Voyage to the Pacific Ocean and Residence at the Sandwich Islands,* 3rd edition (London: 1830), p. 156.

[61] Ch. VI.

[62] The whaling trade had not existed long enough up to this time to be a factor. (Chapter V).

[63] C. S. Stewart, *op. cit.,* pp. 154–156.

habits of the majority of the foreigners who drifted to the Islands were imitated. Ellis repeatedly speaks of drunkenness among the people through whose districts he passed on his tour: "At Kealakomo, to our great regret, two-thirds appeared to be in a state of intoxication, a circumstance we frequently had cause to lament in the villages through which we passed." [64] Another enfeebling influence came from the sandalwood expeditions into the rugged upland regions, where for weeks at a time, hundreds or thousands underwent wet and cold weather and arduous work, with inadequate food, and next to no clothing or shelter. Their resistance to exposure was the less because they were used to the congenial temperature and moderate work of the coast.[65]

These physically detrimental influences were combined with disruption of the social order. The process can be best traced in the decline and eclipse of the tabus, the keystone of the old social fabric. Almost every time the haole came ashore he offended against the tabus—either intentionally in order to lead the native away from idolatry and superstition, or unconsciously, in ignorance and drunkenness. And the shocked Hawaiian found no vengeance from heaven falling on the culprit. The prestige of the white accentuated the confusion he was causing through his disregard of sex and eating taboos, those relating to occupations, and those sanctioning political and social values generally.[66] In 1810 women were breaking the taboos restricting them when it could be done secretly;[67] and though Kamehameha upheld the tabus strictly during his lifetime, their prestige had been so weakened at the time of his death in 1819 as to allow of their formal abolition by the new king, Liholiho.[68]

[64] *Journal*, p. 196. Their drinks were made of fermented sugar cane juice, sweet potatoes, or ti root. By 1822 at least two distilleries had been set up. (Tyerman and Bennet, *Voyages and Travels*, pp. 111–112.)

[65] See Sir George Simpson, *Round the World 1841–2* (London: 1847), from which relevant passages are given in the *Hawaiian Annual* for 1905, p. 70.

[66] See Andrew W. Lind, in E. B. Reater (editor), *Race and Culture Contacts* (New York: 1934).

[67] Campbell, *A Voyage Round the World*, p. 188.

[68] This was not done without a civil war. Liholiho's motives seem to have been two, a desire to improve the condition of his wives, who like other women were handicapped by the operation of the tabus, and a wish to diminish the power of the priests and avoid the necessity of expending labor and property upon them. The advice of foreigners and of a few of the chiefs, and a report of what Pomare in the Society Islands had done toward the destruction of their tabus were significant influences. (Ellis, *Journal*, pp. 6, 37, 95.)

With the passing of the tabus, the priesthood was debased; and the chieftain class lost a main prop for their exclusiveness and unchallengeable authority.

The disruptive physical and social effects sketched are not to be clearly separated from the equally devastating consequence of a shift from a subsistence economy to one organized on an alien model for trade and gain. A revolution in values took place. Foreign consumption goods were spreading constantly, especially among the chieftain class; and foreign productive goods and techniques were expanding among all classes, their advance furthered both by their superior effectiveness and by the prestige of the haole.

Before the haole conspicuous consumption had held only a minor place in the native economy: most goods spoiled rapidly, and the chiefs generally demanded no more than they could use. Now a long list of foreign goods, useful only for war or ostentatious display, was desired by the chiefs to an extent which jeopardized food and shelter to their retainers. Silks, crepes, broadcloths, tobacco, alcohol, dollars, guns and ammunition accumulated among the chiefs' possessions so long as the sandalwood held out, while the welfare of the commoners declined as they were driven farther up the rugged heights in search of the elusive wood.

But even as the native economy was orientating itself painfully to the sandalwood and fur trade, and had already evolved considerably from its state in Cook's day, the chief driving force vanished with exhaustion of the wood supply. There had been a sudden economic tie, and now nearly as sudden a break. The plight of the economy would have been thereafter much worse than it was, had there not been rising to fill the gap a new source of demand, the whaling trade.

CHAPTER V

WHALING

AMERICAN WHALERS achieved early in the nineteenth century an unchallenged dominance in the Pacific. On the New England coast the pursuit goes back to days preceding the coming of the white man, when Indians followed whales in their canoes, using long wooden harpoons attached by line to a wooden float. When the colonists arrived, they appropriated drift whales—those cast up on shore through accident or disease—and fished close to shore Indian fashion, using a harpoon with a log attached to it. But very early, in standard nineteenth-century practice, they were running their line from a small boat to the harpooned whale. Such shore fishing appears to have become a regular business by 1638.

During the eighteenth century the price of whale oil irregularly increased.[1] But costs were increasing too. As whales grew scarcer along the coast, deep-water fishing was necessary. By 1730 Nantucket had 25 vessels of from 30 to 50 tons employed in "deep" whaling, cruises being of something like six weeks' duration.[2] The blubber was processed into oil on shore. Vessels rapidly increased in size, and voyages became longer. Whalemen are reported active off the Gulf of Saint Lawrence by 1761, the coast of Guinea in 1763, the Western Islands in 1765, and along the coast of Brazil in 1774.

The Revolutionary War was a crushing disaster to the American

[1] Average price per ton (8 barrels)

1730—£ 7	1753—£21
1742— 18 13*s*	1762— 17 15*s*
1744— 10	1772— 44 to 45

(The figures are taken from E. P. Hohman, *The American Whaleman* (New York: 1928), p. 31.)

[2] W. S. Tower, *History of the American Whale Fishery* (Philadelphia: 1907), pp. 26–27. Cf. Obed Macy, *History of Nantucket* (Boston: 1835), pp. 42, 44, 46.

whalemen, and an advantage to their British and French competitors. Both competitors were already subsidized by their governments, the British having the heavier bounty.[3]

After the War, the principal market (the British) for sperm oil, then the main product of the industry, was virtually closed by an alien duty of £15 per ton.[4] A slow recovery of the American trade was broken by the Embargo of 1807, and the War of 1812, with advantage again accruing to whalers of other nations.

In 1815 began a 45-year period of unexampled expansion and prosperity for whaling. Where in 1815 there were 1230 tons of whaling vessels listed afloat out of United States ports, already by 1818 all previous records were surpassed with 16,750 tons. The previous maximum of 1803, 12,390 tons, was surpassed about one-third. By 1820, 36,445 tons are listed, a figure which increased irregularly to 57,284 in 1829, and 136,927 in 1840,[5] close to the end of the period we are at present considering.

The first whaling in the Pacific Ocean was the venture of Sam Enderby into the South Seas in 1789, the beginning of a series of visits important in the founding of the Dominions of Australia and New Zealand. Already before 1790 New England whalers had been active in the South Atlantic off Brazil, the coast of Africa, and the coast of Patagonia. Auspicious reports from merchant vessels led them farther afield. In 1791 six Nantucket ships and one from New Bedford rounded the Horn, finding sperm whales abundant off Chile. At first whaling was restricted to an area fairly close to the coast. As increasing numbers of ships came,

[3] Of 150 Nantucket ships at the beginning of the War, 134 were captured or sunk by the British, and 15 were shipwrecked. Two or three old hulks remained in 1785.

Before the War Britain had less than 80 whalers; there were 314 after the War. The American change was the reverse, from 360 before to 80 afterward.

Thomas Jefferson in 1791, when he was Secretary of State, analyzed the advantages and disadvantages of the American whaling industry. He concluded that advantage of location would place our fisheries on a somewhat sounder basis than those of other nations, "such as to relieve our treasury from the necessity of supporting them, but not to permit it to draw support from them, nor to dispense the government from the obligation of effectuating free markets for them." *Report of the Secretary of State on the Subject of the Cod and Whaling Fisheries* (Washington: 1791), pp. 8–10.

[4] Tower, *op. cit.*, p. 41.

[5] Tower, *op. cit.*, p. 121. Nantucket and New Bedford immediately outstripped all other ports, and gained an unchallenged lead. Far behind them Fairhaven, New London, Sag Harbor, and Westport competed with varying success for third place.

fishing extended farther and farther north until the equator was passed; and in 1818 Captain Gardiner of Nantucket found a fruitful "Offshore Ground," beginning some 1400 miles west of Peru, stretching about 5° to 10° south latitude, and 105° to 125° west longitude. By 1820, 50 ships were cruising there.[6]

Years before this, whalers are occasionally mentioned as touching Hawaii. South Sea ships had come north for trading reasons or for "refreshments" on their way to or from the grounds. Such was the *Duke of Bedford,* mentioned in Honolulu harbor in 1810 on her way to England. The first American whalers at Hawaii were the *Balaena* and *Equator* of New Bedford, making their landfall at Kealakekua in September 1819.

The real flood of whalers did not descend on the Islands until the news spread of the discovery about 1820 of rich sperm whale grounds off the coast of Japan,[7] 40 days' sail distant from Hawaii. Only two years later there were 11 American whalers in Kealakekua Bay at one time, and 23 ships in Honolulu harbor.[8]

The convenience of the port of Honolulu is indicated by its central position among the Pacific grounds. The Gulf of California was distant 15 days' sail under the trade wind. It came to be frequented in the early thirties and remained a cruising ground into the 1850's. By 1838, with diminishing returns from the Japan and Yellow Seas, the rich Kodiak or Northwest Coast ground off the Russian possessions had been discovered, 30 days' sail from Hawaii. Continuously "the line," or equatorial grounds, attracted whalers, especially during the winter months which brought stormy weather in northern waters; and for this area there could be no more advantageous place for repairs and provisions than the Islands. North a month's sail were the Bering and Okhotsk Seas, and the Arctic Ocean north of Bering Strait. The region was opened in 1848 by a whaler from Sag Harbor with a completely successful expedition; and grew rapidly in importance until it was the leading whaling region of the world. The diminishing numbers of whales had fled from the harpoons of their hunters to a last refuge amidst the ice.

[6] A. Starbuck, *History of American Whale Fishery to 1876,* p. 96.

[7] See Dispatch of John C. Jones, United States Commercial Agent, to John Quincy Adams, Secretary of State, December 31, 1821. United States Archives.

[8] Tyerman and Bennet, *Voyages and Travels,* pp. 372, 396.

In 1830 the British Consul in Honolulu described the routes followed generally by the whalers of that time:

> The vessels engaged in whaling . . . generally arrive here in the months of March or April, and Sail toward the coast of Japan in May, where they cruise until the beginning of September (often in sight of the coast), when they leave and return to these islands, where they arrive early in October and remain until the latter end of November . . . Those not full proceed toward the Equator and cruise between the parallels of 5° N and 10° S until February, when they proceed towards these Islands to refit previous to their proceeding to the coast of Japan.[9]

Shortly before the year 1830 a New England ship with a capacity of 2000 barrels cruising in the Pacific Ocean could return home with a cargo of sperm oil from the Japan and Yellow Seas in two years.[10]—This in contrast with the six weeks' voyage sufficient when deep sea whaling was first practiced. After 1830 the time required for a full ship gradually increased. Already by 1844 declining returns were evident to the Hawaiian Minister of Foreign Affairs.[11] He compared typical catches of sperm oil for two periods:

(in barrels)	1824	–25	–26	–27	1838	–40	–42	–43
Out 9 months	800	250	450	1300	235	300	200	100
Out 18 months	1600	1200	1300	1400	600	1050	850	700

The average-per-month comparison is 76 in 1824–1827, 34 in 1838–1843. The return to be anticipated had dropped more than half.

But, despite the ominous decline in returns, visits of whaling ships at Hawaii continued and increased, because of still worse prospects at the cruising grounds in other oceans.

Arrivals of whaling ships in the two chief whaling ports, Honolulu and Lahaina, are recorded for 1824–1844 as follows:[12]

[9] Richard Charlton to Captain Waldyman, dated August 8, 1830. Archives of Hawaii.

[10] Starbuck, *History of American Whale Industry*, p. 113.

[11] R. C. Wyllie, in a report to Seaman's Chaplain S. C. Damon, in *The Friend*, May 1844.

[12] Data from R. S. Kuykendall, *The Hawaiian Kingdom* (Honolulu: 1938), p. 307. Basic sources are records of William Richards and E. Spaulding, in *Sailor's Magazine and Naval Journal* (New York), August 1834; and records of S. Reynolds, a merchant of Honolulu who kept a journal of visits to that town 1823–1843, as reproduced by R. C. Wyllie in *The Friend*, May 1844.

	Whalers
1824	104
25	78
26	138
27	98
28	157
29	173
1830	157
31	159
32	198
33	189
34	111*
35	76*
36	73*
37	129
38	148
39	116
1840	86
41	133
42	172
43	383
44	490

* Honolulu only.

There is a considerable contrast between the fluctuations in the numbers of whaling visits and the relative stability in visits of trading ships (Appendix II, pages 225–226, column 2). There are several elements in the explanation.

The drop from 104 whalers in 1824 to 78 in 1825 is partly explained by "high price of provisions and high port charges at Woahu [Oahu], the only harbor in the Islands where vessels can lie in safety during the winter season." [13] One contributing cause of the high cost of provisions was the portion of each sale which the chiefs were accustomed to exact as taxes. At the regular market at Honolulu, by this time evolved primarily to supply

Of the above whalers probably over four-fifths were American, less than one-fifth were British. Only a few came from other countries. The preponderance of the American ships is the more noteworthy in that they received no legislative protection, unlike the British from 1813 to 1824, or the French from 1824 to 1850.

In order to obtain figures for numbers of individual ships which made landfalls at Hawaii, a subtraction of about one-third should be made from the above "arrivals" for whalers who touched more than once; for many of them visited the Islands twice a year, in the spring and fall.

[13] Dispatch, Richard Charlton to the Honorable George Channing, June 10, 1825.

visiting ships, prices were regulated by the chiefs, and two-thirds of whatever the natives sold went to them.[14] The harbor dues had originated in an unprofitable venture in 1817 by Kamehameha into the sandalwood trade, when he sent a shipload of wood to Canton. One excuse of the Captain for the net deficit was that he had been charged heavy dues for pilotage and anchorage. The King concluded he could do the same. By 1823 the fee for anchorage in the outer harbor at Honolulu was $60, having been

CHART 1

ARRIVALS OF WHALING, MERCHANT, AND NATIONAL VESSELS AT HAWAII, 1824–1880

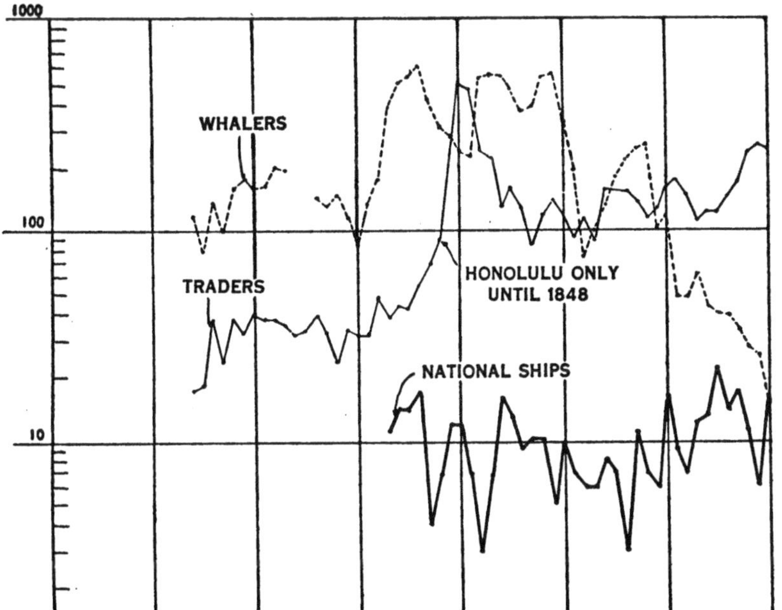

For sources of data of this and following charts, see Appendix II

raised from $40 several years before; and in the inner harbor or basin it was $80, having been previously $60. Pilotage was charged at the rate of $1.00 per foot of draught of the vessel.

[14] Ellis, *Journal*, p. 311.

The decline in visits in 1825 led the chiefs to sharply reduce the official charges and the cost of provisions. The number of visits rose abruptly.

The fundamental factor influencing the level at which the industry generally was carried on was the price of sperm and whale oil, as compared with the luck experienced during the previous season or seasons. In few industries are returns so capricious as in whaling, bonanza catches alternating with wretched luck. Average spring and fall catches from 1835 to 1838—and the averaging already implies a significant loss of variations from ship to ship—varied from a high of 91 barrels a month to a low of 54 barrels.[15] Price fluctuations were likewise great, and increased by the exigencies of wars. Whale oil prices per gallon varied from $140 in 1814 (due to the Embargo and War of 1812 in the United States, and the Napoleonic Wars in Europe, which cut off supply and increased demand), to 26 cents in 1828 (as the whale fleets multiplied in response to high prices), to 39 cents in 1830, to 23 cents in 1832, 42 cents in 1836, and 30 cents in 1840. Sperm oil showed a smaller range of fluctuation, from $1.25 a gallon in 1814, to 45 cents in 1824, to $1.00 in 1840.

The stability, by contrast, in numbers of trading visits is a reflection of diversification of routes and of types of trade. The sandalwood and fur trades were only two of the types of commerce included under "traders"; and their dwindling through the 1830's was compensated for by the others. Other traders were mainly engaged in the general transpacific commerce which had opportunity to get under way in the 1820's with the rise to independence of South American states and the end of the Spanish monopoly of their trade.

An attempt at an absolute and relative estimate of the volume of the early whaling trade meets with the difficulty of lack of data. But some crude figures can be obtained. The total value of a whaling hulk and gear was in 1844 thought by the Minister of Foreign Affairs to be about $40,000, of which $22,000 was for the hulk, and $18,000 for the outfit. These vessels spent annually in the Islands from $800 to $1500 per visit for provisions, equipment, and repairs. Of this amount, about $200 went for

[15] They were both takes of American ships. Six months' passage was allowed for each ship, and hence subtracted from the total time at sea, in arriving at these figures. (*The Friend,* May 1844.)

vegetables, meat, and other local produce; and \$600–\$1300 for (imported) articles taken from the stores.[16]

During a typical year in the twenties, according to our figures, there was a (gross) money income at Honolulu from whalers of \$71,000 to \$134,000; in the thirties of \$69,200 to \$129,750. (The figures for ship arrivals at Lahaina suggest that at least as much more ought to be added for whalers getting provisions at other Island ports, to get a figure applicable to all the Islands.) As the fur and sandalwood trade waned, the chief stimulus to mercantile activity was coming to be the whaling trade.

The relative importance of the whaling trade to the Islands is indicated crudely by a comparison of the above with gross exports (including reëxports) from Honolulu. The latter added up to \$65,850 in 1838, and to \$94,400 in 1839.[17] The whaling trade was as important, measured in these money terms, as all other exports put together. And much of the other exports were of a complementary character, not able to exist independently had the whale trade vanished.

Point is given to Wyllie's lugubrious prediction: "The prosperity of these islands depends mainly on the whale ships that annually flock to their ports . . . Were the whale fishery to fall off, the Islands would relapse into their primitive insignificance." [18]

Social Effects Attributable to the Whaling Trade

The whalers furnished a seasonal and unstable stimulus to commerce and agriculture. A considerable number of skilled workmen, chiefly blacksmiths and carpenters, were kept busy during the spring (March and April) and fall (September and October) seasons. Fresh vegetables were demanded in quantity, with corresponding simulus to cultivation.

The demand for meat furnished a comparatively great incentive for the production of cattle and salt. By this time the cattle left by Vancouver on Hawaii had multiplied into great herds in the mountains and inland plains. The King, chiefs, and later the government, sold or leased to haoles the right to shoot them; and the meat was salted and used for provisioning native and foreign

[16] *The Friend,* March 25, 1844, and July 1, 1844. English ships, which had formerly come in larger numbers, averaged more—from £250 to £350.

[17] Pierce and Brewer estimates. *Polynesian,* September 1840, p. 54.

[18] *The Friend,* July 1, 1844.

vessels.[19] About 1830 John Parker, from Massachusetts, evolved such a right into the beginning of the now huge Parker ranch.[20] On other islands too both tame cattle and wild cattle were running loose; and by the end of the thirties beef was being provided to the whalers on an increasingly continuous and rational basis.

The growth of whaling furnished the first large-scale incentive to the utilization of bills of exchange. They came into use in the twenties, and soon were the common method of transmitting funds to the United States and Europe.[21]

As had happened before with the sandalwood commerce, the active presence of the whale trade in local waters suggested to people resident in Hawaii that they might themselves undertake such ventures. The first whaler owned in Honolulu is reported to have been the enterprise of Henry A. Pierce and Captain G. W. Cole, who commanded her. Her first trip, in 1832, was successful, netting 1000 barrels of sperm oil. A brig, the *Waverly*, was fitted out in 1835 as a trader and whaler, but met disaster on her first voyage.[22] Another, the bark *Honolulu*, carried on some whaling in the forties. It was not until the 1850's that more than one whaling ship was listed as owned in Hawaii.

But many native Hawaiians were taken off the Islands as seamen.[23] Groups of them are in fact reported to have penetrated to Canton and the Northwest Coast before 1820. The number serving on board ship came to be so large as to be wrongly considered one of the causes of the declining Island population. They obtained a reputation as excellent seamen. The traveled *Kanakas*, when they returned to the Islands, were readily distinguished from their brethren by their "superior cleanliness, dress, and assimilation to foreigners."

One most significant social influence from the whaling trade lay in the large numbers of men who flooded the port villages when the fleets were in, wild for pleasure after months of work and

[19] Ellis, *Journal*, p. 303. *Pacific Commercial Advertiser*, August 11, 1859.

[20] Louis A. Henke, *A Survey of Livestock in Hawaii*, "University of Hawaii Research Publication No. 5" (Honolulu: 1929), p. 37.

[21] See pp. 101–102.

[22] See the *Hawaiian Annual* for 1913, pp. 47–49, 64–65. The *Waverly* was cut off and burned by natives on Strong's Island, and all hands were murdered.

[23] William Patty, Collector of Customs, reported 275 on board ship during the year and a half period from January 1843 to June 1844.

isolation and danger at sea[24]—pleasure which generally meant to them alcohol and women. The saying was, "No God west of the Horn." Debauchery was conventional, and sanctioned by custom and time. The seamen bitterly resented efforts to deny them their normal diversions.[25]

In addition to the visiting seamen there were the more nearly permanent derelict seamen, who had been discharged for either a real or alleged cause,[26] or had deserted at the Islands; these, having no means of support, lived in squalor, often with natives.

[24] The American consul wrote in 1827 that there were not less than 600 men on shore at the fall and spring gatherings (25 to 30 ships, with about 25 men to the ship)—"all unruly." There is continual report through this period of the dissatisfaction and mutinous tendency of the crews. "Owing to the want of discipline, the length, and arduous duties of a voyage, these people generally become dissatisfied, and are willing at any moment to join a rebellion or desert the first opportunity that may offer. This has been fully exemplified in the whale ships that have visited these islands. Constant desertions have taken place, and many serious mutinies, both contributing to protract and frequently to ruin a voyage." (Dispatch of John C. Jones, "U. S. Agent for Commerce and Seamen," to Henry Clay, Secretary of State, dated July 1, 1827. National Archives.)

The British consul thought no differently: "The crews of the Whale ships are often very troublesome and it is not unusual for them when dissatisfied to refuse to lower the boats to catch Whales, to the great loss of the Owners. They also desert at the different Islands . . . They meet with great encouragement from the Chiefs to desert, and there is scarcely a season that they do not carry off a boat from the Ships. It is true that the Seamen forfeit their wages for deserting or refusing to obey the lawful commands of the Commander, but as they are on shares in the Whale ships, if the ship should be unsuccessful during the early part of the voyage they become dissatisfied and having nothing due (but often in debt), they take the first opportunity to desert, often leaving the ship in great distress." (Richard Charlton to Captain Waldyman, dated August 8, 1830. Archives of Hawaii.)

Both consuls recommended to their governments that a man-of-war cruise about and visit occasionally to improve discipline and general order.

[25] In 1825 the crew of the British whaler *Dolphin* threatened a Maui missionary whom they considered guilty of persuading the chiefs to promulgate a law tabooing the ships against visits of Island women. In 1826 Lieutenant Percival of the United States naval ship *Dolphin* "tried to have four base women released from jail."

In late January of that year a company of sailors armed with clubs and knives invaded a religious meeting and demanded a repeal of the laws against fornication. When Captain Clark of the British Whaler *John Palmer* "enticed four base women aboard," the governor of Maui, Hoapili, detained the captain on shore, insisting the women be given up. The captain sent orders to fire if he should not be released within an hour; and the crew fired four balls, intelligently aiming them in the direction of the mission house. The captain was allowed to return to his ship, but sailed without releasing the women, as he had promised. (For more detail, Sheldon Dibble, *History of the Sandwich Islands* (Honolulu: 1909), pp. 190–196.)

[26] P. 69.

In general, their moral fiber succumbed before the mildest temptation.

The influence of these men was without alleviation destructive of the native social order. The prestige of the haole made even his worst example imitated, and, had there been no more reputable class of foreigners about, the future prospect for the impressionable native—such of them as survived the diseases that had been imported [27]—would have been somber indeed.

A few generalized conclusions may be presented as to the effect of the whaling trade upon Hawaiian culture. The existence of a feudal system implied the organization of the whole group around the central hierarchy of the nobility. The nobles (chiefs) justified themselves originally by the protection they gave from other nobles, and by the stability they furthered within their particular lands. But after Kamehameha's victories and the uniting of the Islands under one head, stability and protection were provided by the central government. That government was strong, and under an able administrator minimized local autonomy for several reasons—among them, for the sake of a uniform policy toward traders and whalers.

At a time when the functional justification of the chiefs had thus been lost, orientation of the society around them, which would otherwise have persisted for a prolonged period through inertia, was being broken up by intrusion of the foreigner. It was replaced by orientation toward the whaling ports, and toward the chance for pecuniary gain there present.

We can define four more specific ways in which the whaling trade served to break down the native culture: (1) It diverted

[27] Social opinions of the reputable foreigners and chiefs, formed in large part out of social need, are illustrated in the schedule of "Fines for Malconduct of Seamen":

"Hanging, as a murderer, for maliciously and knowingly violating those laws whereby a contagious disease is communicated ashore. $60 fine for any Captain who leaves on shore any men without written leave from the government. $10 for coming ashore with a knife, swordcane, or any other dangerous weapon. $2 for every seaman seized ashore after 9:30 p.m. at firing of second gun from the fort. $1 to $5 for halloing or making a loud noise in the streets at night. $6 for striking another in a quarrel. $5 for racing or swift riding in the streets or unfrequented roads. $6 for desecrating the Sabbath the first time, $2 the second time; fine doubled on each offense thereafter. $6 for catching a deserter near harbor; $12 if ten miles off. $6 for drunkenness. $10 for lewd, seductive, lascivious conduct. $5 for fornication. $30 far adultery. $50 for rape." (*The Friend,* September 1844.)

increasing quantities of labor and agricultural resources into producing commodities for sale to visiting whalers (a more continuous influence than that of the sandalwood trade), thereby withdrawing them from production for internal consumption. But originally, in Cook's time, the full effort of the population had been necessary for the provision of their own subsistence. (2) It helped to develop further the tastes of the chiefs toward foreign goods, beyond the point to which the sandalwood trade had carried them. By providing new ways to consume conspicuously, it gave incentive to heavier taxes at a time when both the social situation and the productive routine could less well support even the old taxes. (3) It attracted an appreciable quantity of young men to sea on the whalers, and to the waterfront in port towns to work as laborers. By their voyages to strange places and by their contact with whites they acquired alien viewpoints and habits of life. Both their sentiments and their earnings inclined them to treat obligations to the chiefs lightly; and their residence on ship or at the seaports helped them to do so with impunity. (4) Common association with derelict white seamen, from whom much of evil and few virtues were to be learned, and with whaler crews bent on pleasure, led toward lax social habits, debauchery in morals, and shiftless economic ways.

CHAPTER VI

THE MISSIONARIES

THE MISSIONARIES furnished a third major influence on the economic development of the Islands during this period. Their influence powerfully shaped the social and economic evolution of Hawaii.

The time of their arrival could not have been more propitiously chosen. When the first band landed at Kailua in 1820 they were promptly met with the cheering news that "Liholiho is king—the tabu system is no more—the gods are destroyed—the temples demolished—the islands are at peace." The bulk of the work of discrediting and disintegrating the old religious system had already been done during the four decades of visits by explorers and traders before them: the Islands were a religious vacuum. The missionaries saw divine favor in this. The fields were made ready for the harvesting, they thought, and awaited only the diligent workman.

There were 7 ministers, teachers, and other workers in the 1820 company, 8 more in 1823, 9 in 1828. By 1844, 53 more had arrived, or 77 in all.[1] They were spread throughout the four main islands, Oahu, Maui, Hawaii, and Kaui; and later on Molokai. There was a decided concentration at Honolulu, already the largest city.

Converts were abundant. Their theology was sometimes confused,[2] but their enthusiasm was all that could be desired.[3]

[1] The total sent to the Islands by the directing Board in Boston, before the missionaries were put on their own, was 92, all arriving by 1857.

[2] A creed worshiping Jehovah, Jesus Christ, and Hapu, a former prophetess, developed on Hawaii. (Jarves, *History of the Hawaiian or Sandwich Islands,* p. 262.)

[3] Mark Twain later reported on the phenomenon: "They all belong to church and are fonder of theology than they are of pie; they will sweat out a sermon as long as the Declaration of Independence; the duller it is, the more it infatuates them; they would sit there and stew in a trance of enjoyment till they floated away in their own grease if the missionaries would stand watch-and-watch and see them through. Sunday schools are a favorite dissipation with them, and they never get enough. If there was a physical as well as mental intoxication in this limb of the

The kind of religion that came down from Tremont Street in Boston and from New Bedford and New Haven to the Islands where it was always summer had not changed greatly from that of the seventeenth-century Puritans. It was still "a religion of fear, of prohibitions, of rigorous observation of solemn formalities such as the recitation of Scriptural texts, and a doleful keeping of the Sabbath."[4] There was small tolerance in them for rich and varied human belief and action, out of accord with their northern and New England background.

The intent of the missionaries was to work through the existing class of nobility, to focus first efforts upon them, and, when they were converted, to use their influence to convert more readily the remainder of the people.[5] The policy was most successful, conjoining with the susceptible psychological position of the natives to favor rapid proselyting. Already, by the beginning of 1823, 24 high chiefs, men and women, were attending a school established for them in Honolulu. As early as 1824 a proclamation of Queen Kaahumanu indicates missionary influence. Not only murder and theft were enjoined, but also boxing or fighting, and work or play on the Sabbath. And in 1827 the King published six laws, forbidding murder, theft, fornication, selling of rum, prostitution, and gambling.[6]

---

service, they would never draw a sober breath. The Hawaiian reads a whole world of moral tales, built on the good old Sunday school book pattern exaggerated —heroes who walk around the world with their mouths full of butter, and are simply impossibly chuckle-headed and pious. And he knows all the hymns you ever heard in your life, and he sings them in a soft pious voice, to native words that make 'On Jordan's stormy banks I stand' sound as grotesquely and sweetly foreign to you as if it were a dictionary grinding wrong end first through a sugar mill." (In Wright and Fry, *Puritans in the South Seas* (New York: Henry Holt & Co., 1936), p. 320.)

[4] Wright and Fry, *op. cit.*, p. 303.

[5] In items 1 and 2, of the *Missionary Minutes of 1838*, rulers are admonished to be just and honorable in dealings with their people. Item 3 reads: "Rulers in power are so by the province of God, and in an important sense by the will or consent of the people, and ought not to shrink or resign from the cares and responsibilities of their offices: therefore, teachers of religion ought to guard the subjects against contempt for the authority of their rulers, or any evasion or resistance of government orders, unless they plainly set at defiance laws of God." (Printed in *Report of U. S. Senate Committee on Foreign Relations* (Washington: 1894), pp. 142–143.)

This stand implies a whole theory about the manner in which it is desirable that social change shall take place. Subsequent events do not evidence its invalidity for Hawaii.

[6] W. F. Frear, "Hawaiian Statute Law," in *Hawaiian Historical Society Papers* (1906), p. 27.

All liquor shops but two were suppressed on Oahu by the end of 1838: "Lahaina,

Ship captains who failed to observe the Sabbath or were in other ways unacceptable found their ungodliness an inconvenience when they tried to carry on trade or recruit sailors in Hawaii; so also did merchants who had similar habits.[7]

It is not surprising that a bitter antagonism soon split the white community. Two aspects of western civilization were competing for the attention of the natives and all newcomers had to take their stand with one group or the other. On the one side were the missionaries with their prolonged religious training, somber theology, and devoted intent to reform the morals of the Hawaiians and to elevate them into civilization. On the other were most of the business community of the haoles, concerned with secular, commercial problems, not well educated formally—though often they had traveled much—and certainly not aiming toward reform. Each party had its adherents. Calumnies flew thick and fast between the two camps, and visitors to the Islands reflected in their one-sided bias the views of the group with whom they were thrown.

The missionaries were accused of causing the people to starve by taking them away from their crops to learn to read and spell, and to build churches; of causing to be enacted unpleasant Sunday "Blue" laws; of prohibiting innocent sports such as swimming, fishing, surf-board riding, and horseback riding.[8]

Maui, March 13, 1838. I give notice beforehand to you foreigners who keep grog shops on Oahu that at the end of the licensing for the last six months you will not again receive license for selling liquors, for I intend to suppress most of the grog shops on the Island of Oahu this year. But two houses only will be left where grog may be sold. By me, Kamehameha III."

[7] Cf. Wright and Fry, *Puritans in the South Seas,* p. 306.

[8] Among the opposition, the most vehement whom I have come upon is T. H. James: "In short, civilization as it is unfortunately going on at present under the management of the American missionaries is only another word for extinction . . ." (Letter to "a Noble Lord," 1832, in *Hawaiian Historical Society Papers* for 1915.)

Shaw, a gold seeker from California, represents a segment of the prevailing spirit among traders: "Many of the missionaries have made themselves notorious by neglecting their spiritual duties for temporal affairs; persuading the king to issue unpopular edicts, such as driving the natives to religious worship, compelling them to build churches, and undertake other work unremunerated, to the neglect of their household duties and respective callings . . . To preserve their declining power they assiduously and artfully labored to exclude commerce from the Islands, forbidding the cultivation of cotton, sugar, and coffee, destroying several plantations, and declaring cultivation impious, where so many indigenous plants existed." (*Golden Dreams and Waking Realities, Adventures of a Gold Seeker in California and the Pacific Islands* (London: 1851), pp. 253–254.)

The failure of the Titcomb experiment in silk production at Koloa, Kauai was unjustly laid to the ecclesiastics, who were said to oppose the necessary feeding of

On their side the missionaries claimed that they were grossly calumniated: "When a strange ship arrives, and the officers complain of the extravagance of the harbor fees—this impost is immediately declared to be enacted by advice of the missionaries: the high price of refreshments is assigned to the same cause." [9] They claimed that they were being opposed in their efforts to introduce Christianity by the traders, "who are generally devoid of all religious principles and practise the greatest fraud on the natives in their dealing with them; which tends to corrupt their morals." [10]

The feud between the missionary and trading classes lasted with diminishing force into the fifties. The details of the respective accusations and calumnies are not important: what is interesting is that the antagonism and mutual sabotage existed. Both the traders, with their commerce, and the missionaries, with their proselyting and educational activities, were in some degree obstructed by the presence of the other.

More significant were the direct efforts of the missionaries to extend education and improve techniques. It is true that the prime intent was to win souls to Christianity; but in addition there was the will to "civilize in the broadest sense." The spirit and purpose of the American Board of Commissioners for Foreign Mis-

---

the worms on Sundays, "on penalty of excommunication, and the pains of an endless shower of hell fire beyond the grave." (G. W. Bates, *Sandwich Island Notes,* New York: 1854.)

The British Consul reported without approval in 1831 that the government was under the control of American missionaries, but it is unclear whether his lack of enthusiasm was due to their being missionaries, or Americans. (Richard Charlton to Captain Waldyman, letter dated September 22, 1831, Archives of Hawaii.)

The Sandwich Island Gazette, a newspaper begun in 1836, maintained a specifically anticlerical policy, excoriating "meddling fanatics," and writing enthusiastically of new inventions and commercial developments.

[9] "though we ourselves . . . scarce ever taste a banana or melon, because we do not feel at liberty . . . to purchase fresh provisions at the price demanded by the chiefs." (C. S. Stewart: *Private Journal of a . . . Residence in the Sandwich Islands,* New York: 1928, pp. 159–160.)

[10] J. N. Reynolds, *Voyage of the Potomac, 1831–34* (New York: 1835), p. 422. The Reverend Jonathan S. Green had perhaps the most pessimistic views as to the true nature of trade and traders: "As to her influence [commerce] at the Sandwich Islands, I am confidant she is digging the grave of this people . . . The merchants probably intend the chiefs shall become indebted to them, till they can grasp their lands, and become too deeply rooted to be removed." (Letters of the 22nd and 24th of November 1836, quoted in the *Sandwich Islands Gazette,* March 17, 1838.)

sions[11] in Boston, which was in charge of the effort, is given in its "Instructions to Missionaries in Hawaii":

> Your views are not to be limited to a low and narrow scale; but you are to open your hearts wide and set your mark high. You are to aim at nothing short of covering these Islands with fruitful farms and pleasant dwellings and schools and churches, and raising the whole people to an elevated state of Christian civilization. You are to obtain an adequate knowledge of the language of the people; to make them acquainted with letters; to give them the Bible with the skill to read it; to turn them from their barbarous courses and habits; to introduce and get into extended operation and influence among them the arts and institutions and usages of civilized life and society . . . and to inculcate the duties of justice, moderation, forbearance, truth and universal kindness. Do all in your power to make men of every class good, wise, and happy . . . To effect all this must be the work of an invincible and indefectible spirit of benevolence.[12]

The proportion of every effort which was to go to medical aid and secular education is given a rough quantitative measure in the numbers of persons of secular occupations among the individuals sent over by the American Board. There were in all twelve companies, and a few independent arrivals, which can be grouped as shown in the table on page 91.

The substantial proportion of men and women who were not missionaries—25 teachers, 8 doctors, 5 printers, 1 bookbinder, 1 farmer, as compared with 51 ministers—gives an impression to some extent illusory of the extent of secular activity. For "printers" were printers chiefly of religious publications. Books of the Bible, a hymn book, primers, and scriptural tracts were among the early products of the press at Honolulu,[13] in addition to a small number of proclamations and commercial pamphlets. Teachers were concerned at first with training to read, chiefly so that the Bible might then be read. The missionary group was in fact sometimes criticized for giving too much time to "preaching the Gospel" only, not enough to general educational work.[14]

[11] An interdenominational Board with strong Congregational and Presbyterian representation.

[12] *Instructions of the Prudential Committee of the American Board of Commissioners for Foreign Missions to the Sandwich Island Mission* (Lahainaluna: 1838), pp. 19–20.

[13] In 1834 a second press was set up at Lahainaluna.

[14] Thus the U. S. Commissioner wrote to the Secretary of State: "One great mistake has, I am afraid, been made by the missionaries; they have employed more of their time in *preaching* than in teaching. Civilization and Christianity ought to

OCCUPATIONS OF MEMBERS OF THE MISSION

Company	Date	Men						Women
		(all save one were married)						(single, mostly in teaching)
		Total	Ministers	Printers	Doctors	Teachers	Others	
1st	1820	7	2	1	1	2	1 farmer	
2nd	1823	7	5		1	1		1
3rd	1828	6	4	1	1			3
4th	1831	4	3 (one of these also a doctor)			1		
5th	1832	10	8	1	1			
6th	1833	4	3 (one a teacher also)	1				
7th	1835	3	1	1			1 book-binder	2
8th	1837	15	3		2	9	1	2
9th	1841	4	3 (two also teachers)			1		
10th	1842–3	4	4					
11th	1844	4	4					1
12th	1848–54	7	5		2 (one also a D.D.)			
"Independent Arrivals	1855–57	8	6			2		
Totals		83	51	5	8	16	3	9*

* Note: This chart excludes Hawaiian helpers returning from training in New England, and in the Islands. From the convenient records in Jean Hobbs, *Hawaii: A Pageant of the Soil* (Stanford: 1935), pp. 143–156.

Nevertheless the obvious need for instruction in "the mechanical arts" led to increasing emphasis there. The need was the greater

go hand in hand." (Letter of January 16, 1844. National Archives of the United States.)

And one of the missionaries, the Reverend Sereno E. Bishop, speaks of a tendency on the part of the Board of Foreign Missions to feel that the true work of the missionary was to spread the Gospel, and not to inculcate information beyond that needed to understand the Bible—save to natives who should themselves later be teachers, and who would hence need such information. (*Reminiscences of Old Hawaii* (Honolulu: 1916), p. 41.)

since often the traders and other resident whites had tended illiberally to keep the natives in ignorance, and so maintain their own superiority and prestige.[15]

By 1838 such training in techniques had become a matter of explicit policy:

We deem it proper for members of this mission to devote a portion of their time to instructing the natives into the best method of cultivating their lands, and of raising flocks and herds, and of turning the various products of the country to the best advantage . . . The missionary should endeavor to call forth ingenuity, enterprise, and patient industry, and give scope for enlarged plans for profitable exertion, which . . . would clothe the population in beautiful cottons, fine linen and silk, and their arable fields with rich and various productions . . . [and] would adorn the land with numerous comfortable habitations.[16]

Individual missionaries were constantly confronted with problems relating to the use of resources; and as they solved them were constantly expanding the natives' technical knowledge. In turn the missionary became carpenter, blacksmith, road-supervisor, land surveyor, surgeon, and blacksmith.[17] The Reverend John S. Emerson at Waialua on Oahu was kept occupied with such matters:

His work of reform necessarily included an attempt to stir the natives to industry—to help them become good householders. "I cannot go on preaching to a lot of people sitting on their haunches with no purpose in life," he wrote to his brother. Stone walls were laid to keep out roaming cattle, horses, and pigs from cultivated lots; and the native laborers whom he employed learned from him the right way of handling the crowbar and sledge hammer,[18] how to yoke oxen, and the use of the drag. After some choice

[15] As an example from 1809, Campbell reports that when he undertook to construct a loom for making sails, he incurred "the displeasure of many of his countrymen . . . When a brother of the Queen's wished me to teach him to read, Davis would not permit me, observing, 'They will soon know more than ourselves.'" (*A Voyage round the World* (fourth American edition, Roxbury, Mass.: 1825), p. 141.)

[16] *Minutes of the General Meeting for 1838* (Lahainaluna: 1838).

[17] G. W. Bates, *Sandwich Island Notes* (New York: 1854), p. 352.

[18] "The laying of a stone wall was an object lesson closely watched. I have seen great husky men straining and tugging with crowbars, vainly trying to lift some big rock out of its bed and get it into its place in a wall; when taught the method of leverage the task became easy. I have seen them with sledge hammers striking heavy blows on some unwieldy stone they could not fit into its place. My father would come along, examine the stone as to its natural cleavage, and with a stroke or two of the hammer split off a piece with the greatest ease, and so make it fit

piece of land had been enclosed, he taught them how to break up the soil with the plough and harrow, and to plant and cultivate in such a way as to produce a rich crop . . . He also encouraged fertilizing.[19]

As a means of getting funds to support schools, churches, and the mission movement generally, the missionaries encouraged cotton growing and experimented in its manufacture. Several efforts in cane growing and sugar production were carried on under missionary auspices.[20]

The work bore fruit in increasing numbers of natives who were skilled in trades. At Wailuku, Maui, by 1844:

There are three or four mechanics in this place, and others who have left, who have acquired their information under the direction of the missionaries . . . The owners of fourteen carts . . . and more than thirty oxen . . . were first instructed in the use of carts and oxen by missionaries.[21]

To be added to the informal instruction of the missionaries in trades and manual activities is the formal instruction given in their schools. By about 1824, when the missionaries had learned the Hawaiian language sufficiently well to print a few primers and pamphlets, and had obtained the sanction and help of the chiefs, the schools were expanding rapidly. Kuykendall reports the number of students at 2000 by the end of 1824, 27,000 by 1828, and 52,000, or something like two-fifths of the population (in 1100 schools) by the fall of 1831.[22] Adults were more numerous than children in these early schools. The fad passed, and interest in education dwindled down to a lower but more solidly based level during the 1830's.[23]

The early schools taught only reading and spelling. A little

as it should. 'His blows are mighty,' he would say, whereas the simple fact was they were wisely given." (O. P. Emerson, *Pioneer Days in Hawaii*, New York: 1928, p. 128.)

[19] *Ibid.*, pp. 126–127. The taro was fertilized before, according to native custom, by burying weeds in the mud around the plant; but other plants which were less demanding on the fertility of the soil were not so intelligently treated.

[20] P. 174.

[21] Reverend E. W. Clark, in *Answers to Questions Proposed by R. C. Wyllie* (Honolulu: 1848), pp. 9–12.

[22] *Op. cit.*, p. 106.

[23] Partial returns from a survey in 1841 gave 357 schools, with 505 teachers and 18,034 students. (*The Friend*, December 18, 1844.)

Almost all these teachers were natives; but most of them had been trained by missionaries. It was estimated that by 1830 over half the people could read; and that by 1846 80 per cent could read and write.

later on some arithmetic was added. In the thirties the mission schools had matured to a more elaborate curriculum, though of the severely impractical pattern common on the mainland: the Hanalei school taught reading, writing, composition, elements of natural philosophy, geography, arithmetic, geometry, sacred geography, Church history, moral sciences, and natural theology.

But natives who were to be teachers required technical training if they were to fulfill the obvious need; and it was always fit that girls should be trained in household duties. So we find "industrial training" given at Lahainaluna by 1831, a time when such instruction was almost unheard of in the United States. "Manual labor" was being taught at Hanalei and Waioli on Kauai, and at Waialua on Oahu in the late thirties. At Kaluaaha Mr. Dwight taught his school girls to sew effectively. A school inaugurated in 1835 at Wailuku, Maui, gave instruction in spinning, knitting, and weaving; and afterward braiding, washing, ironing, sewing, and feeding silk worms[24] were taught. By 1844 at least seven people there were making butter for the market, as a direct or indirect result of mission training.

What evaluation shall be made of missionary activities? It is clear that the net effect is to the good—in contrast with mixed impressions when we look to the influence of other white residents.

This conclusion is not upset by the embarrassing circumstance that the missionaries who arrived to save the souls of the natives came to possess, in the persons of their relatives and descendants, title to much of the Islands' worldly goods.[25] The missionaries,

[24] Andrew W. Lind, *An Island Community* (Chicago: 1938), pp. 170–171; also p. 97 below.

[25] One or two of the missionaries can be questioned as devoting a doubtfully large proportion of their interest to land speculation. One bought, or bought and sold, 47 parcels of land in his lifetime; another, 30. The ten who transacted the most business averaged 22 parcels, though many of these were quite small. Of all 83 in the mission, 38 made no purchases at all; and of the transactions listed, some were made after separation from the mission. (Jean Hobbs, *Hawaii: A Pageant of the Soil,* Stanford: 1935, Appendix B.) The record seems on the whole a good one.

Missionary pay was normally $450 a year, not a high rate even in days of low prices. In 1850 the Hawaiian Government sought to compensate the missionaries for faithful and low-paid service in the Islands by permitting each missionary who had served eight years to buy up to 560 acres of land at a reduction of 50 cents an acre below the market price. (Privy Council Resolution of August 19, 1850. Cf. *Polynesian,* May 7, 1852.)

Toward the middle of the nineteenth century and after, relatively lucrative government jobs were sometimes available to missionaries.

and more especially their children and other relatives, had the considerable advantage of being early comers. They were energetic, trained to anticipate the future, and acutely conscious of the sharp upward trend in land values in the middle and late nineteenth century. As they preached thrift to the natives, so they practiced it themselves, adding good example to good doctrine. They improved their lands, experimented in and furthered agriculture, and showed the native the way to get ahead. This seemed to them worthy work: the Puritan code gave credit to the honest and shrewd businessman.

A few doubtful cases—and a dour theology—should not blind us to the general "invincible spirit of benevolence" which suffused the actions of the missionaries. The morale of the native had already been effectively disrupted: his decadence in the face of the intrusion of an alien civilization was rather checked than accelerated by the presence of a new body of doctrine around which he might orientate himself. With respect more narrowly to economic factors, the discipline inculcated by the New Englander was of as much service as the techniques which he directly and indirectly taught. We are inclined to be rather more generous than Robert Louis Stevenson, who thought that "with all their deficiency of candour, humour, and common sense, the missionaries are the best and most useful whites in the Pacific."

CHAPTER VII

OTHER DEVELOPMENTS

PIONEER INDUSTRIES

THE EPOCH 1776–1844 was an experimental time, when the course of development of foreign markets (and especially the most important of them, the west coast of the North American continent), and the types of production for which the Islands were best suited, were unclear. Although Hawaii was becoming orientated toward transpacific trade relationships and the foreign population was increasing, still the chief connections which existed (fur, sandalwood, whaling) did not seem to be secure or lasting. Hawaii had not learned where its chief advantage in production lay; and many experiments were to be made before failure and success gradually outlined the future.

Salt continued to be produced, in part as a secondary result of the fur and whaling trades, in part for its own market in the Russian settlements. A cargo of salt was carried to Kamchatka in 1819,[1] in return for "Russian cordage and canvass, Hardware, and dried fish." It was no longer produced for small scale trade in tidal pools according to old native custom, but was dug from the bottom of Moanalua Lake near Honolulu. For drying, it was piled up in conical heaps, within circles of stones of five feet or less in diameter. Grass was spread underneath, and stones and grass on top, to keep it clean and protected against rain until it was barreled and taken away to market. Since the evaporated salt contained the impurities of sea water, it came to be considered not pure enough for the purpose of curing provisions, and by 1857 salt was being imported for that use.[2] Salt was then being produced for commerce at the Puuloa Salt Works, twelve miles west of Honolulu, on the south shore of the Pearl River. Sea water was pumped by a windmill into a flat reservoir, and allowed to evaporate. The resultant salt was ground between mill wheels

[1] "U. S. Agent for Commerce and Seamen" John C. Jones, to the Secretary of State, December 31, 1821.

[2] *Pacific Commercial Advertiser,* November 5, 1857.

powered by a windmill.[3] The mill had an annual capacity of 2000 tons of coarse salt. About half this amount was being exported at the time.

Exports of salt varied in annual value from $1400 to $4400 in the years 1836–1839. The peak of the industry was reached in 1847;[4] and dwindling export quantities are listed as late as 1881.

Silk production was encouraged by missionaries on Maui, in 1835 and after, through their instruction in ways of caring for silk worms. A serious effort toward silk production was carried on in Kauai from 1836 to 1844. Sherman Peck and Charles Titcomb leased about 3000 acres of land from Ladd and Company at Koloa. The native or black mulberry was set out, and in 1838 Peck brought back from the United States the *morus multicaulis,* which grew thriftily. Chinese and American worms were imported, though much trouble was experienced with hatching the latter until it was found they needed to pass through a winter season. They were crossed with the Chinese worms, with much success. In 1840, 100,000 trees were growing, with whose leaves 500,000 worms could be fed at once.[5] Prospects were hopeful: another company was set up at Koloa, and Titcomb started a second plantation at Hanalei.

Then a series of disasters descended on the ventures. An unexampled drought in the summer of 1840 withered the trees; a species of aphides, or wood louse, sucked the sap; a spider "the size of a chestnut" attached itself by millions to the trees; strong trade winds in the fall and kona winds in the winter stripped the leaves, and covered the ground with them.[6] The Koloa plantations turned to sugar growing; and though Titcomb carried on longer at Hanalei, he also turned toward coffee growing in 1844.[7]

Certain other minor industries, such as cotton, coffee, and livestock, which became more important after 1844, are discussed below.[8] Sugar is discussed in Chapter 12. Small quantities of tobacco, arrowroot, and kukui nut oil were also being shipped

[3] The old mill and planned improvements are described in the *Pacific Commercial Advertiser,* April 18, 1861.

[4] *Polynesian,* January 8, 1848. There was a brief but large volume of export in 1869 and 1870 also.

[5] *Polynesian,* August 1840.

[6] *Polynesian,* July 10, 1841; *Hawaiian Annual,* 1911, pp. 67–71.

[7] U. S. Commissioner George Brown to Secretary of State, July 1, 1844, National Archives.

[8] Pp. 154–172.

out by 1844. No one of these had a value of more than $500 annually.[9]

All such products put together are of small importance compared with the supplies furnished to whaling and trading ships. "Provisions" to ships increased irregularly in comparative significance until by 1841 they were a little over twice the value of "exports."[10]

General obstacles to developing Island resources during this early time were the land tenure situation, lack of markets, and, especially, inertia on the part of the foreigners toward local opportunities. In the early years dominated by trading relationships, the active foreign population looked on the Islands as a temporary residence where they could heap together enough spoils from the whaling fleet to enable them to spend their later years back in their northern homes. Hence their interests were short run: the permanent resources of the soil which demanded time and patience to develop seemed of minor importance compared to golden streams of income from the seasonal fleets of whalers.

Growth of Commercial Businesses

During the 1820's and 1830's Hawaii was already on the way to becoming a center for commerce. The attainment of independence by Spanish colonies in the Americas in the twenties, and the consequent freeing of trade to other than Spanish vessels, was one important stimulus to transpacific commerce. Trade to California, the nearest part of the Continent, was also expanding rapidly at this time. Vessels sailing between the South American coast, Chile or Peru, from Mexico, or from California; and bound for China, Manila, or the East Indies, stopped at the Islands for fresh provisions or repairs, and to obtain cargo or to discharge what cargo they might have remaining from their other traffic. There were also vessels centering their trade more specifically on the Islands—those owned by American residents there, or by New England mercantile houses with branches in the Islands. These ships voyaged primarily between the Northwest, California, and Mexico; and China (Canton almost exclusively) and Manila in the Far East.[11]

[9] Accounts of Messrs. Pierce & Brewer, "respectable merchants of Honolulu," the *Polynesian*, September 12, 1840, and September 4, 1841.

[10] R. C. Wyllie's accounts in *The Friend*, June 1844.

[11] Japan was tightly closed to commerce. Hence whalers in the adjacent Japan and Yellow Seas were based on Hawaii.

Reynolds' diary[12] lists 17 ports as those from which Traders came, in contrast with Whalers, nearly all of whom came from a few compactly situated New England ports, or from England. Pierce and Brewer's account of imports from January 1, 1836 to August 17, 1840 [13] lists ten areas from which significant quantities of imports came: (1) From the United States: cotton cloths, prints, chintz, hardware, copper, cordage, canvas, naval stores, iron, paints, furniture, flour, bread, wines and spirits, soap. (2) From the "Coast of California and Islands adjacent": sea otters' skins, land furs, bullock hides, soap, horses, etc., "but principally otter skins and bullock hides." (3) From Chile: the same products as those from the United States. (4) From Mexico: principally specie and bullion. (5) From China: blue nankins, blue cottons, teas, silks, and some English goods. (6) From Islands of Ascension, Tahiti, and Southern Islands: turtle shell, pearls, pearl shell, and sugar. (7) From Norfolk Sound, the Columbia River, and Northwest Coast: lumber, spars, salmon. (8) From England: long cloths, chintz and prints, hardware, spirits, etc. (9) From Prussia: cotton goods, broadcloths, gin, etc. (10) From Manila: the manufactures of China, England, and the United States, and cigars, rope, hats, etc.

Corresponding to this general Pacific trade, as well as to the fur, sandalwood, and whaling trades, was the growth of stable businesses in Honolulu. The first was that of James Hunnewell, established on a permanent basis in 1826, and later to evolve into the present-day C. Brewer & Company. The trade was chiefly that of collecting sandalwood in exchange for merchandise. Hunnewell claimed conventionally that business was not profitable: "I now have more business than I can attend to with advantage, not very profitable, but pleasing to be trusted." [14] His books show assets in 1830, after four years of activity, of $67,000, as compared with original capital and stock of $5000, an expansion rate of 310 per cent a year.

The prospects of profit attracted a branch of the Hudson's Bay Company to Honolulu in 1834.[15] Its house, managed by Pelly and Allen, came to take a foremost rank, one whose fluctuations

[12] P. 77, footnote.

[13] (Not a completely accurate account.) *Polynesian,* September 12, 1840, p. 54.

[14] Quoted in C. G. Tilton, *The History of Banking in Hawaii* (Honolulu: 1927), p. 14.

[15] There are reports of occasional shipments of goods to Richard Charlton, British Consul, before this time.

of shipments and of fortune closely influenced all the other merchants. By 1840 a shipping routine had been worked out by the Company, an annual ship of merchandise arriving from England at Vancouver in the spring, taking lumber from there to Oahu during the summer, bringing back to Vancouver salt and other goods, "but generally not enough for ballast," and in the fall sailing for England with pelts obtained during the preceding year.[16] By 1840 £10,000 of goods were imported by the Company in one year. The effective competition of the Hudson's Bay Company distressed American merchants, and led to accusations that the Company was intending to monopolize Hawaiian trade.[17]

By this time there was a respectable aggregation of merchants. For 1844 we have a list of six general or commission merchants:

American:	C. Brewer and Company
	E. and H. Grimes
	Ladd and Co.
	Paty and Co.
English:	Pelly and Allen (Agents for Hudson's Bay Co.)
	Henry Skinner and Co.

There were in addition 11 storekeepers, who maintained 15 shops:

American:	Stephen Reynolds	2 shops
	Cummins and Co.	2
	Eli Jones	2
	E. C. Webster	2
	G. M. Moore	1
	Robert Davis	1
	. . . The U. S. Naval Storekeeper Bensen had liberty to trade.	1
British:	J. Montgomery	1
Chinese:	Samping and Co.	1
	Ahung and Co.	1
	Tuhune	1 [18]

[16] Reverend Samuel Parker, *Journal of an Exploring Tour*, 3rd edition (Ithaca: 1842), pp. 312, 347–348.

[17] See J. J. Jarves, *History of the Hawaiian or Sandwich Islands* (Boston: 1843), pp. 366–367. The Company withdrew from the Islands in 1860 when discovery of gold and settlement of Canada gave employment for the Company's capital nearer home. (*Polynesian*, August 1860.)

[18] From the list given by R. C. Wyllie in *The Friend*, August 1844.

The United States Commissioner to Hawaii at that time, George Brown, estimated the property of the "general merchants" to be worth from $15,000 to $100,000 apiece.[19]

Advertisements were informative, rather than "competitive," being simply announcements of facilities and services, as:

Pierce and Brewer
Comm. Merchants
Honolulu, Island of Oahu

Having constantly on hand and for sale on liberal terms Merchandise imported from the United States, England, Chile, and China, and adapted to the trade of the North Pacific. They offer to purchase the productions of the Sandwich Islands, and of California; and Bills of exchange on England, France, Russia, and the United States.[20]

The bills of exchange merit some comment. The transferring of purchasing power between Hawaii and other parts of the world was a constant problem. If cargoes were sent, the judgment of the ship's captain and his bargaining skill had to be trusted, unless an agent of the exporter was at the port of destination. Often bullion or coin was sent by way of the captain's strong box. Frequently a sum was entrusted to the captain with instructions to buy a cargo at one port, sell it in a good market, and bring back the profit. But there was danger of robbery, or of mutiny; even some risk still of piracy—the men who traveled the seas were not all honest folk. And there was chance of fire or shipwreck in which goods or metal would be lost without hope of recovery; whereas if they had been stolen there might be a chance of getting them back.

Sometimes the money was entrusted to a traveler, even a stranger of repute, who was going in the right direction. Here too entered the danger of human frailty; and if the traveler's route was indirect, or if there had to be relays, an undue amount of time was taken.

[19] Dispatch to the Secretary of State, January 16, 1844. National Archives of the United States.

[20] *Polynesian,* June 6, 1840. Pierce's list of the commodities most salable in Honolulu (1835) suggests the requirements of a pioneer community: "Cider, lemon syrup, raisins, boots and shoes, cotton shirts, flannels, brushes, crockery, hardware, window glass, nails, wire, iron, safes, combs, umbrellas, hosiery, table-covers, calico, gingham, cotton handkerchiefs, brown cottons, thread, paints and oils." (In Josephine Sullivan, *History of C. Brewer and Company,* Boston: 1926, p. 49.)

Hence there was much incentive to diminish risk by using bills of exchange.[21] They were, Kuykendall reports,[22] in use as early as 1823; and with the growth of the whaling trade they came to be the ordinary method of making remittances to the United States and Europe. The discounts varied greatly, from a small premium to a substantial deduction of 25 per cent or more, depending on the need for foreign balances and the assurance of payment.[23] Toward the end of the whaling season, when there were few bills being offered and much need for funds in the eastern United States to take care of debts for merchandise, bills were often at par, and sometimes commanded a small premium.[24] A freely competitive situation would have resulted in a discount equaled to the interest rate (usually about 1 per cent a month or approximately 3 per cent on the usual bill) plus an addition for risk. The discount generally paid seems to be explainable in part as the result of tacit or explicit monopolistic pricing by the merchants: knowing the whalers had to have money, they profited by their necessities.[25] The isolation of the Islands, and the high degree of spacial differentiation of product to which it gives rise[26] have often given opportunity for monopolistic pricing.[27]

Advertisements of Honolulu mercantile firms during the thirties and forties usually specified that "approved paper" was acceptable for merchandise, as did that of Pierce and Brewer above.

These merchants owned a small trading fleet by 1841. American traders held four brigs of from 100 to 260 tons and two schooners; British merchants had one bark and one brig. Native

[21] Cf. Cecil G. Tilton, *History of Banking in Hawaii* (Honolulu: 1927), pp. 14–16.

[22] *Op. cit.*, p. 95.

[23] The highest rate of discount I have come upon (though after this period), is 43 per cent, when to an 1863 consular draft on the Treasury of $98.01 was added $73.50 difference in exchange. Evidently this is to be explained chiefly by risk, the United States being in the middle of the Civil War. By June 1865 there was a 13-cent gain on a draft of face amount $99.87. (Dispatches of U. S. Consul Alfred Caldwell to the Secretary of State, dated December 31, 1863, and June 30, 1865.)

[24] This variation over a brief season seems explainable only in terms of lack of foresight.

[25] See dispatch of Thomas Miller, U. S. Consul at Hilo, to W. S. Marcy, Secretary of State, dated January 12, 1857. National Archives of the United States.

[26] That is, the absence of competition from conveniently located substitute products.

[27] Cf. p. 107, footnote.

chiefs still owned a few other vessels.[28] By 1844 two wharves had been constructed in Honolulu for receiving goods.[29]

Techniques

All foreign influences combined had not sufficed to change productive techniques greatly by the end of this period, save in specialized spheres where foreign supervision and capital entered directly. The ax and knife were used generally by the natives; but not heavier tools or specialized forms of tools. Bishop reports that in his youth in Kona he never saw "a plow, sythe, sickle, or, he thought, a spade or shovel." [30] But bone fishhooks had disappeared by the thirties; and metal hooks were much traded in. Fishermen often preferred a peculiar form of hook, filed from large needles, without barb, the point being bent to one side and curved inward.[31]

No beasts of burden were yet in use in outlying districts in the twenties and early thirties, though there were a few in Honolulu. Burdens were carried on the native shoulder yoke, of a form like that used by the Chinese. There were no wheeled vehicles in the native areas. In the late thirties some carts and oxen were being made use of in Honolulu, and even in less backward communities away from Honolulu (as in Wailuku, Maui), and horses were slowly coming into use. Honolulu was uniformly in advance of other areas.

Spread of the Use of Money

From the days of the earliest voyagers, occasional coins passed into circulation in the Islands; but money was not exchanged against goods to advantage. Men-of-war, which had no goods to

[28] *Polynesian,* September 1841. Bishop describes these ships: "Nearly all coasting vessels were small, varying from 30 to 50 tons, schooners or brigs. They were mostly owned by the King or chiefs, and commanded by white or native skippers and mates. They were usually in a very filthy condition, swarming with cockroaches and reeking of bilge water. We white passengers generally occupied the decks, on which our mattresses were spread, but had to dispute our scant space with a swarming crowd of natives, with their calabashes and dogs . . . Many of these people were constantly smoking the coarse tobacco of their own raising . . . The native skippers would be indifferent to making progress, and the helmsman would fall asleep at his tiller, so that the morning would find us further from our destination than the night before." (*Reminiscences,* pp. 31–32.)

[29] *The Friend,* September 1844.

[30] *Op. cit.,* pp. 28–29.

[31] *Ibid.,* p. 29.

exchange for provisions, were soon complaining of the high prices which they had to pay. The natives became conscious of the high estimation which the white man, with his peculiar ideas, placed on these round bits of metal; but preferred to have "goods" with their clear and immediate utility. Before coins could come to have for the native a similar significance as for the foreigner, Island trade would have to be divorced from its internal, subsistence orientation, and become focused to a consciously large extent on exchange with foreigners. There was the further disadvantage for the commoner that if his chief learned of his possessing a coin, it would eventually be extracted from him; whereas a consumption good, soon worn out or eaten, must be taken away immediately, or not at all.[32] Later, sandalwood effectively served as the "standard commodity." It also had real merit for the purpose: it did not easily deteriorate, it was classed into fairly clear grades,[33] it was divisible, and its market was then relatively steady.

By 1810, the natives (primarily the chiefs) were hoarding such foreign currency as came to them: the knowledge of a safe market in the now frequent visits of trading ships caused it to be valued. But throughout this period and into the forties the amount of cash that got into the hands of the commoners was negligible. A little came into possession of the chiefs, mostly in payment for furnishing provisions. For sandalwood, goods were generally received in payment.[34] Money in the possession of

[32] "Our guide said that . . . he had offered a native a dollar to fetch him a draught of water from the stream below. The man refused, saying 'What good would a dollar do me, for it would soon become known that I had it, and then I must give it up to the chief?' "—This was in 1822. (Tyerman and Bennet, *Voyages and Travels*, 2nd edition (London: 1840), p. 119).

Trade became so standardized around nails and pieces of iron in the nineties that we might look on iron as the medium of exchange of that time. (Pp. 59–60.) In 1894 Menzies, surgeon with Vancouver, reported: "When the fishing boats came into the bay at Honomalino we had an opportunity of observing their manner of traffic with one another, as the whole village and people from other villages flocked around them, and a brisk market was kept up until they disposed of all their fish for small nails and bits of iron. Sometimes we observed they drove very hard bargains. Of these nails the fishermen make their fishhooks, and no doubt are obliged in their turn to purchase potatoes, yams, cloth, etc., from the planters." (Archibald Menzies, "Hawaii Nei 128 Years Ago," in *Hawaiian Annual* for 1908, p. 77.)

[33] Captain V. Golovnin, *Tour Around the World in 1817–19,* translation by Joseph Barth in *The Friend,* July 1894.

[34] Ellis, *Journal,* p. 311.

chiefs was quickly dissipated again into the hands of the traders. The chieftain group went into debt steadily during the twenties, and was still in debt in the thirties.

Prices, usually stated in terms of sandalwood during the 1810's, around 1820 came to be often stated in terms of money. The clearest conception of the value of money was maintained around the ports. Inland, as Andrew Bloxam found in 1825, the matter was hazy:

> They ask a dollar for the most trifling thing, having no idea of the value of it. This I found several times in my excursions around the island, a small shell or coconut would be offered me for a dollar, and they would not relinquish it for anything else.[35]

In the thirties natives in the outlying districts were still not familiar with the appearance of money. It could not be said to be generally the medium of exchange. Missionaries paid for provisions or native services with a few yards of cotton cloth, with fishhooks or horn combs, and, more often, with school books and slates.[36] In the experimental plantations, such as Titcomb's silk plantation at Koloa, Kauai,[37] and the Ladd sugar plantation,[38] the laborers were paid by orders on the store for goods, with a reduction in real wages because of high prices of up to half. However, labor services were priced in terms of money.

The coins predominantly in circulation were Spanish or Spanish-American dollars, half-dollars, quarter-dollars, rials, and half-rials. Hardly any British or United States coins were present in the early years, and nearly all coins in circulation were silver.[39]

[35] Diary of Andrew Bloxam, MS. in Archives of Hawaii, p. 33.

[36] Bishop, *Reminiscences*, p. 29.

[37] P. 97.

[38] Pp. 175–176.

[39] By 1844 certain other coins were common enough for formal exchange values to be announced for them:

Gold		Silver	
Doubloon	$16.00	Shilling	.25
Eagle	10.00	Franc	.20
Guinea	4.50	Rix dollars of Hamburg	$1.00
Sovereign	4.50	Ruble	.75
Napoleon	4.00	Rupee	.50
Ruble	2.00	Rix dollars of Denmark	$1.00
Ducat of Holland	2.00	Rix dollars of Holland	$1.00

(*The Friend,* May 1844.)

We have a few estimates of the amounts of money circulating in different areas in 1844. Major Low in his visit to Puna and Hilo on Hawaii speaks of "a few hundred dollars" in circulation, partly by means of which a trade of $12,000 a year was carried on, though most of this was barter. At Kealakekua on Hawaii the monetary circulation was thought to be $1,000; on the whole Island of Kauai, $5,000.[40] At least $50,000 was thought to be lying in idle deposits in Honolulu, and as much more in circulation. To this "money" ought to be added bills of exchange from whalers and ships of war, aggregating during the two seasons $137,000 to $200,000.[41] But all these estimates are subject to a wide margin of error.[42]

Prices

The sharp rise in barter prices toward the beginning of the century has been mentioned.[43] The natives became conscious of the fact that the seamen had no adequate substitute for fresh provisions (especially when there was scurvy aboard) and for repairs. We might speak in later terminology of a very inelastic demand curve, with an opportunity for the discreet seller to exact a monopoly price. But a good thing could be run into the ground. Demand was more inelastic in the short run, that is, after ships had arrived, than in the longer run when news had gotten around as to the prices in the Islands, and shipmasters had had time to decide whether to get part of their supplies on the Coast or elsewhere. This limitation on their monopoly power had come sharply to the attention of the chiefs in 1825.[44] A feature of monopolistic pricing is present explicitly in differentially high prices charged to ships, as compared to local residents.[45]

The demand of visiting ships on Island resources was in any case of sufficient intensity to result in a strikingly high level of

[40] Major Low of the British Indian Army, reported in *The Friend,* for December 2, 1844.

[41] R. C. Wyllie, Minister of Foreign Affairs, *The Friend,* May 1844.

[42] In 1847 there was established a Hawaiian currency coördinate in value with the currency of the United States, with denominations of a dollar, half-dollar, quarter, eighth, and sixteenth. No coins were actually struck. (Session Laws of 1847, p. 185.)

[43] Pp. 59–61.

[44] P. 78.

[45] See records of prices of foodstuffs in current issues of the *Polynesian,* and *The Friend.* One example is given in note 47 following.

prices compared to those of earlier years,[46] and higher prices in Honolulu than in districts less frequently visited.[47] For example, in 1844 sweet potatoes were $1.25 per barrel in Honolulu, but only $1.00 in Kealekekua.[48]

Wages for unskilled labor varied from 12½ cents to 50 cents a day, or from $2.00 to $6.00 a month,[49] being highest near the port towns. On Kauai, wages were commonly 12½cents a day, plus provisions. They were paid in the form of goods. On Maui common wages were 12½ cents also; in Lahaina, the whaling port, they were 25 cents, and, if the laborer worked aboard ship, 50 cents. Servants in the thirties were generally paid their keep, and were envied by their less fortunate brethren who lacked adequate food and clothing. Skilled workmen received much more: in the Kealekekua district of Hawaii carpenters were being paid $1.25 to $1.50 a day and blacksmiths $2.00.[50]

A native type of house could be built for about $5.00 new, as late as 1840; but the 113 stone, wood, or adobe houses in Honolulu by 1844 were valued on the average at about $2400 apiece. A simple stone shop for the blacksmith trade cost $700 in 1839.[51] Despite these great differences in cost, foreign types of buildings

[46] Pp. 108–112.

[47] A few sample prices for provisions (Honolulu: 1844) follow:

Potatoes, $2.50 to $3 per bbl.
Sweet potatoes, $1.25 per bbl.
String beans, $1 per bushel
Corn (maize), $4 per bushel
Tomatoes, 75 cents per bushel
Pineapples, 50–75 cents per dozen
Oranges, 25–50 cents per dozen
Watermelons, 37½–50 cents per dozen
Cabbages, 12½ cents per dozen
Pumpkins and squashes, $1 per dozen
Beef (to families), 6 cents lb.
(to ships), 6¼ cents lb.
Fowls, 25 cents each
Eggs, $1.25 to $2 a 100
Pigs, according to size, 50 cents to $2 each.

(Prices obtained from F. W. Thomson, late high sheriff, and published in *The Friend,* September 1844.)

[48] Major Low in *The Friend,* December 1844. It is noted that prices were as late as this time being quoted on Maui in terms of "yards of coarse cotton cloth."

[49] U. S. Commissioner George Brown to the Secretary of State, January 16, 1844. National Archives.

[50] Major Low, *op. cit.*

[51] "Journal" of John N. Colcord, Hawaiian Historical Society Library, p. 76.

were increasing rapidly in numbers. Rents in them were at substantial levels: the three hotels in town were taking in boarders at $1.00 a day.[52]

A dual standard of living is clearly present, one for the mass of natives, another for the foreigners and high chiefs.

Public Revenue

Up to the year 1817 taxes (feudal dues) to the King and chiefs were little changed in type from what they had been in prediscovery days, but there was a change in the psychological background of taxation. Kamehameha adopted the policy of requiring strong chiefs to live near him so that he might keep an eye on them, and avoid revolts. With this new policy the feudal lords came to be divorced from the soil, from direct contact with and concern for their retainers.[53] There was a clear tendency for taxes to increase from this reason; and also from the other reason which we have mentioned, that of the introduction to the chiefs of new luxuries and new wants.

By 1817 taxes were showing some signs of becoming more regularized, especially for foreign holders of land, some of whom paid an amount, stated in money terms, in proportion to the number of laborers employed on the land.[54] In that year a new tax was introduced: harbor dues were established for vessels anchoring in the outer or inner harbor of Honolulu, and also a charge for pilotage, part of which went to the government.[55]

There was also the revenue from the sandalwood trade, which might be considered a kind of tax.[56]

By 1831 the revenue of the central body of chiefs (government)

[52] William Miller to H. U. Addington, Letter of February 27, 1844, Foreign Office File 58/25. Archives of Hawaii.

[53] "Formerly the chiefs lived on the land, personally attended to their cultivation, and took a strong interest in the prosperity of their vassals, on whom they had to depend in time of war. But when the centralizing policy of the Conqueror and the attractions of the capital had drawn them away from their lands, they were succeeded by rapacious agents or konohikis, and the old feudal ties gradually lost their power. (W. D. Alexander, *Appendix to the Surveyor General's Report* (Honolulu: 1882), pp. 8–9.

[54] On land where 10 to 20 men were employed, $40 was in one case paid annually. Golovnin, *Tour Around the World, 1817–19,* translation by Joseph Barth in *The Friend,* July 1894.

[55] P. 79; also Tyerman and Bennet, *Voyages and Travels* (London: 1831), p. 396.

[56] Pp. 63, 66.

was derived chiefly from the half of the collected sandalwood which was reserved to the crown, from shipping dues, now levied on a tonnage basis, and a levy of 50 per cent—sometimes more—on provisions sold in the market at Honolulu.[57] There was little expenditure by the "government" as such, the few people who were employed by the government being supported by allotment of land, from which came to them a large share, perhaps half, of the produce grown by the commoners. Public works—such as roads or irrigation trenches—were performed by unpaid labor of the commoners.

During the thirties imposts were also laid on the more profitable kinds of labor. Housebuilders, and also persons who washed clothes, paid a heavy annual tax for the privilege of carrying on their trade.[58]

In the later 1830's (up to the tax law of 1840), the government tax of a farm was specified in terms of a swine, a dog, fish line, fish net, and kapas and paus, all in specified sizes and quantities in accord with the extent of the farm.[59] In addition to this there were imposts made by the lower and higher landlords (chiefs) and governors. Where the number of children was large, additional claims might be levied against the family, on the justification of its increased productive power. Unpaid labor was required for the king and landlord on, generally, Tuesday and Friday of each week, adding up to something over eight days a month, of which half went to the king, half to the landlord.[60]

Protection against arbitrary taxation was promised by Kamehameha III's Declaration of Rights of 1839, a statement of the general intent of the government.[61]

Taxes on the general population were lowered in 1839 (the law was revised in 1840), and a regular poll tax imposed. Briefly, the taxes in 1840 consisted of:

1. Poll tax: man $1, woman 50 cents, boy 25 cents, girl 12½ cents.

[57] Letter of Richard Charlton, British Consul, to Captain Waldyman, September 22, 1831, Archives of Hawaii. Also Francis Warriner, *Cruise of the United States Frigate Potomac* (New York: 1835), p. 237.

[58] William Richards, *Letter to Commander Wilkes,* pp. 22–23. Archives of Hawaii.

[59] Pp. 23–26.

[60] This was specified in the Laws of 1842, pp. 133–135.

[61] *Fundamental Law of Hawaii* (1842), pp. 3, 10, 33.

2. Land tax: "There shall be no state, county, town, and district tax," only the following: a large farm—a swine one fathom long (or $10); a smaller one—a swine three cubits long (or $7.50); a swine one yard long (or $5).[62]

3. Labor tax: "Hereafter a tax in labor shall not be required on every week of the month. The first week in the month people shall work two days for the King and one for the landlords; the second week in the month they shall work one day for his Majesty the King and two days for the landlords; and the next two weeks the people shall have for themselves. But if there is important work to be done which is for the benefit of the people at large, then there shall be twelve working days . . ."[63]

The exemption from labor on payment of money effectively freed people of some income, especially foreigners, from the labor requirement. It may be noted that the tax system as a whole bore relatively far more heavily on the poorest section of the community, the commoners, than on the rest. Even so the exact specification, and hence limitation, of the taxes was a great advance on the past.

Several interesting items of social policy are implied in the tax law. One was a measure against chiefs who sought to maintain their old unchecked rights of levying such claims on their tenants as they pleased: tenants were to be freed for six months from

[62] Other alternatives are given: two yard-long swine equal one fathom swine, or four one-cubit swine.

The Laws say hopefully, "Money is the standard by which all taxes and assessments are to be estimated, and it would be very well if all men would pay their taxes in money"; but the following were acceptable: kukui nuts, at $1.50 per barrel; arrowroot, at 3 cents a pound; tumerick, at 3 cents a pound; fish, "valued as is right"; cotton, 6 cents a pound; also nets, or any other article which the tax officer can certify. (*Laws of 1842,* pp. 55–56.)

Money taxes had sometimes been levied before 1840 in an irregular fashion, "sometimes on lands, but usually on polls." (*William Richards to Commander Wilkes,* p. 23.)

An amendment approved in 1846 allowed the working out of land taxes by labor on the public roads. (*Session Laws of 1845,* "Act Organizing the Executive Departments," Sec. 1, Art. 1, Chap. 3.)

[63] These specifications of taxes are from *Fundamental Law of Hawaii* (1842), pp. 12–17.

The labor tax could also be commuted in money. Absence with notice could be compensated for by payment of 25 cents a day; without notice, 50 cents. An annual payment of $9, of which half went to the King, half to the landlord, relieved one of any obligation to labor. There were fines also for lateness. (*Fundamental Law of Hawaii* (1842), p. 16.)

working for landlords who had caused them to work when they should not have done so. The abrupt decline of the Hawaiian population[64] was a concern of the writers of the measure—hence a provision favoring families with many children. All fathers with three children were relieved of the labor tax, and successive exemptions corresponded to increased quantities of children, until, with six or more, they were freed of all tax. Lastly, to give incentive for the cultivation of fertile lands held out of use, and to diminish idleness there were penalty taxes.[65]

This tax law was amended significantly several times; but it remained the basis of the tax system of the rest of the century.

A small portion only of the taxes indicated were actually collected; according to Richards, about a sixth:

> Estimating families at two adults and two children to a family, the present rate of the whole taxation . . . would be to a family about eleven dollars and thirty cents, nine dollars of which may be paid in labor, one dollar in produce, and one dollar thirty cents in money . . . But the revenues of the government must not be estimated by this calculation. For according to this, the revenue would be more than three hundred thousand dollars, whereas it is probable that not more than the value of fifty thousand is really collected and realized . . . This includes all that is paid for rent and in every way to all the lower ranks of chiefs. What the King actually receives in money is about fourteen thousand dollars annually.[66]

The first tariff laws date from this time. A measure effective on January 1, 1839 imposed a duty of $1 a gallon on imported wine. The trading class was not pleased. The *Sandwich Islands Gazette,* representing their view as opposed to that of the missionaries, urged that temperance would not be furthered by the law, and that it might lead to general tariffs which would obstruct trade and hinder the development of the country.[67] The trading interest was dominant: there was no group of local manufacturers to urge a different argument.

[64] Pp. 114–116.

[65] See also pp. 118–119.

[66] *William Richards to Commander Wilkes* (1841), pp. 27–28. Before 1840 a total of as much as $25,000 had occasionally been collected, but usually not half that sum. (*Op. cit.,* p. 23.)

[67] See Kuykendall, *The Hawaiian Kingdom, 1778–1854,* p. 163, where reference is made to the *Gazette's* articles of September 8, and November 24, 1838, and May 11, 1839: *Report of Minister of Finance* (1851), p. 13.

The wine duty was in effect repealed by pressure brought by the Captain of a French ship-of-war six months later.

The first general tariff act of the Kingdom was approved in May of 1842, and became effective at the beginning of 1843. Section 7 provided that "There shall be an ad valorem duty of 3% laid on all goods, wares, and merchandise, and on every article of trade imported into these Hawaiian Islands from foreign nations. None of the above articles shall be landed on these shores until the duty or bonds for payment be given." [68]

The net revenue of the Kingdom was in 1842 about $41,000, in 1843, $50,000. The first true public debt had been floated by 1843, to an amount of $39,000, at interest "not over 12%." [69]

Living Conditions

The change in living conditions during this period was less than one might have thought likely. One principal reason was that the ability of the chiefs to demand anything they wanted made possession of any desirable foreign article a doubtful blessing. The chiefs were of course bringing in foreign textiles and ill-assorted household equipment; but little change took place in the clothing, housing, utensils, or furniture of the commoners until the 1840's.

By 1823 the influence of foreigners who built houses with windows and doors had led the natives to enlarge the doors to their grass shacks. Formerly the doors had been so small that one had to crawl through. Some had begun to think windows convenient.

In the early 1830's Honolulu was yet a village of, by appearance, hay mounds.[70] The royal palace and churches, built also in the native fashion, were large and airy. The houses of the chiefs, too, were neatly kept, often with a foreign type of bed, but with few other articles of furniture, and no tables or chairs. But houses of the commoners were small and filthy.[71] They were irregularly scattered in enclosures of rotten adobe walls.

Foreign residents in Honolulu had dwellings of stone or frame-

[68] *Laws of 1842,* p. 123.

[69] R. C. Wyllie in *The Friend,* May 1844.

[70] Or, as William Miller, the later British Consul, called it with some imagination, a "Village of Wigwams." (Letter to H. U. Addington, February 27, 1844, F. O. 58–25. Archives of Hawaii.)

[71] J. N. Reynolds, *Voyage of the United States Frigate Potomac* (New York: 1835), pp. 402–403.

work, though in other parts of the Islands they usually had to be content with grass houses.

There was as much variation in dress as in housekeeping. A visitor estimated that one person in fifty dressed completely in European clothing, while one-seventh were partly so clothed.[72] The men were perhaps a little better off in this respect than the women, though in response to advice of missionaries the younger women even away from Honolulu generally wore some clothing in addition to the pau. At meetings men often wore the little *kihei,* or shoulder cape; or, sometimes, simply a cotton shirt.[73] But in general, away from Honolulu, clothing was made of tapa only.

The mixture of the native and the foreign presented a strange picture in the Honolulu of the mid-thirties, with all degrees of assimilation to European habits represented in close conjunction. The visitor saw through half-opened blinds of spacious town houses "elegant scarfs and fair countenances" of fine ladies, while he passed through a crowd of islanders with "disheveled hair and naked limbs." [74] There were at that time about 300 houses in the town, the great majority of grass only.[75]

In the mid-forties Honolulu had the aspect of a rising city. William Miller, the British Consul, described it in 1844:

> Its streets are well laid out, and although not paved, from the porous nature of the substratum are clean and dry. Most of the houses are still of dried grass, & stand at a considerable distance from each other. Amongst them are thirty or forty good dwellings made of Stone, or Adobe (sun burnt brick) occupied by Foreigners and native Chiefs . . . There may be thirty married couples among the Foreigners.[76]

[72] Francis Warriner, *Cruise of the United States Frigate Potomac* (New York: 1835), p. 240.

[73] J. N. Reynolds *Voyage of the United States Frigate Potomac,* pp. 402–403; S. E. Bishop, *Reminiscences of Old Hawaii* (Honolulu: 1916), pp. 14–15. Bishop writes of Kona in the early thirties:

"One day when my father was about to sail to Honolulu his six new shirts hung out on the line together. A great amazement pervaded the minds of the villagers at the incredible opulence of their spiritual father, and the premises were surrounded with crowds to gaze at the miracle." (P. 15.)

[74] Translated from the French of Adolphe Barrot, who visited the Islands in the French sloop-of-war *Bonite,* in 1836. *The Friend,* April 1, 1850.

[75] J. K. Townsend, *Narrative of a Journey Across the Rocky Mountains,* etc. (Boston: 1839), p. 193.

[76] Letter to H. U. Addington, February 27, 1844, F. O. 58–25. Archives of Hawaii. Miller reports that all but four families of the foreigners were Americans.

Among the natives around the port there had already developed a group who, attached to no land, gained their living by their skilled and unskilled labor, earning from $50 to $200 a year or more. They were the "best clothed, most civilized, and best paid" class of natives. Here is the first appearance of a permanent working group, earning money incomes. Since they held no lands they were excused from the land and labor taxes, being subjected only to the poll tax of $1 a year. In addition to these, there were natives living without regular labor, the rabble of the town.

In several other parts of the Islands the habit of regular work in return for a regular money (or goods) return was making headway about the centers of the early plantations; but foreign living habits and commodities were spreading there less rapidly.

Population Decline

Following the appearance of the Cook expedition in 1778, the native population declined with extraordinary rapidity, losing nearly 57 per cent of its numbers by 1823, 45 years later; and 73 per cent by 1850, when the first complete census was taken.

	Hawaiian		Non-Hawaiian	
1778	300,000	(estimate)		
1823	134,750	(" plus correction)	175	(estimate)
1832	124,049	(census " ")	400	"
1836	107,354	" " "	600	"
1850	82,035	(census)	1,532	" [77]

What is the explanation of the decline? Many of the explanations offered by missionaries and others of the time have the fault of referring to causes which would have been as operative before Cook, when the population was relatively large, as to later times.

[77] These figures are all from Romanzo Adams, *Interracial Marriage in Hawaii* (New York: 1937), pp. 3, 4, 8. The figure for 1778 has been commented on before (pp. 6–7). That for 1823 is based on an estimate by missionaries, scaled down by Adams on the basis of information on Island resources which the missionaries did not themselves have. The figures for 1832 and 1836 are derived from results of a census by missionaries and school teachers. There were, however, only estimates for three small islands, which Adams corrected as before on the basis of more adequate present knowledge of the local resources, and hence of what population the area might reasonably have supported.

For example, infanticide, abortion, oppressive governance, and damp and dirty grass houses are suggested.[78]

A more logical explanation of the decline can be grouped under four headings. First, were the wars which continued for nineteen years after Cook's first visit, and often were most bloody, as well as disruptive of agriculture and fishing.

Second, was the continuing foreign interference with the native economy and its flow of productive effort. There was an important, widespread, diversion of labor from producing food for home use to producing it for consumption by visiting ships, and to collecting sandalwood. In each case the returns to the Islands were largely in the form of importations valued by the chiefs as items of conspicuous consumption, with a negligible import of goods increasing the material welfare of the people at large. Also there was the exposure and hardship of expeditions into the cold wet uplands for the purpose of collecting sandalwood, doubly hard on people used to the ideal climate of the seashore, and without adequate food, clothing, or shelter for the higher regions.

Third, and of primary importance, was a decline in morale, consequent both on the introduction of a specific vicious foreign habit, the intemperate use of alcohol; and upon the wasting away before the superior prestige of the foreigner of native institutions and mores. We have spoken before of the use of alcohol, in quoting reports of a traveler who found whole districts helplessly drunk. The decline of native institutions and mores was a dominant influence following the abolition of the tabus in 1819, and it was perhaps the fundamental cause over the whole period. The waning away and vanishing of their habits of thought and way of life, of the whole fabric of the ancient native culture, led to a deep-seated pessimism, a lack of heart for living, and to a collapse of physical resistance associated with the psychological trouble. There is testimony from many contemporary comments, of which a sample is, "The Hawaiians can lie down and die the easiest of any people with whom I am acquainted." [79]

[78] U. S. Commissioner George Brown to Secretary of State, January 16, 1844, National Archives of the United States; G. W. Bates, *Sandwich Island Notes* (New York: 1854), p. 346; Ellis, *Journal*, p. 32; and the opinions of missionaries listed in *Answers to Questions Proposed by R. C. Wyllie* (Honolulu: 1848).

[79] Quoted in Andrew W. Lind, *An Island Community* (Chicago: 1938), pp. 96–97, where there is an interesting series of such comments.

Last among the causes is disease. Of all the diseases introduced by the white man, syphilis, dating back to Cook's visit, was the most deadly, and especially so in the earlier years. But several other diseases were mortal to a race which had not become inured to them by prolonged contact. A disease called the *mai okuu,* the cholera or perhaps bubonic plague, reportedly took over half the population about 1804: "People dismissed freely their souls and died." Influenza and mumps took their thousands of victims during this period in two epidemics (1826 and 1839), and, later, in the forties and fifties, measles, whooping cough, diarrhea, and smallpox successively decimated the population.

The problem of native survival was much in the minds of missionaries in the thirties and forties; and anyone who had a new social proposal to advocate urged that its effect would be to ameliorate the population problem. Missionaries argued for greater morality and religion.[80] Anti-missionaries lectured on the "unnatural habits of life" inculcated by the missionaries.[81] Others spoke of the damp and dirty grass houses;[82] and at least one writer developed a theory that lack of adequate thatching for the houses was to blame, since cattle had eaten the preferred *pili* grass.[83] Representatives of the government and those whose minds turned toward business saw secure tenure of land and property, differentially low taxation on large families,[84] and the development of new industries and of commerce as effective anodynes.[85]

No remedy was effective. Despite what was done, or left undone, the population decline continued, though more slowly, during the rest of the century.[86]

[80] See, for example, in *Answers to Questions Proposed by R. C. Wyllie,* a questionnaire on Island conditions and problems sent out by the Minister of Foreign Affairs to the missionaries, who were scattered through native areas, and presumably had detailed knowledge. Also Ellis, *Journal,* p. 32.

[81] For example, their advocacy of clothing, which the natives used imprudently for its prestige value, wearing it in hot weather out in company, taking it off during rains and at night. G. W. Bates, *Sandwich Island Notes,* p. 346.

[82] Dispatch of George Brown, U. S. Commissioner, to the Secretary of State, dated January 16, 1844. National Archives of the United States.

[83] W. A. Kinney, *Hawaii's Capacity for Self-Government All but Destroyed* (Salt Lake City: c. 1927), p. 39.

[84] P. 111. The British Consul, William Miller, had advocated this.

[85] For example, R. C. Wyllie, "Communication to the Reverend Samuel C. Damon, Seamen's Chaplain," in *The Friend,* May 1844.

[86] The increasing slowness of the rate of decline caused a projection of the trend up to 1850 to fly wide of the truth. The *Polynesian* then predicted that there

The disaster to the Hawaiian race attendant on the appearance of the foreigner is the more impressive in that there could not have been a more peaceful or congenial invasion of new people.

Collapse of Native Morale

The decay of native morale needs a more detailed statement. In the days of the first visitors, say from 1778 to 1810, report is unanimous as to the energy and productive aptness of the native.[87] By the twenties and early thirties there is complaint of Hawaiian laziness and lack of desire for improvement. They would not, for example, dig wells where wells were needed: "In the first place, they have no funds, and if they had, are too indolent to use them for fear they should never see the dollar again . . . They have no taste for improvement." [88]

In 1832 the impression was that the Islands were growing constantly poorer, and that, even so, "considering the amount of labor employed," it was surprising how much was produced. "Want must be felt unless more attention is given to agricultural pursuits." [89]

By the 1840's the report is unanimous that the native is shiftless, indifferent, just won't work at all. Wyllie wrote without sympathy:

> In the whole Islands you nowhere see natives at hard labor or regular labor, except for short intervals for the Kings & Landlords and at their own caprice. The carrying of burdens from place to place is the hardest labor to which they subject themselves . . . They might ease themselves of that almost entirely, were they not too slothful to take the trouble of raising Asses, Mules, Horses, or Oxen . . . It may safely be reported that the whole labor of the entire able-bodied population does not amount to four hours per day during the year, even including the labor days for the King and Landlords.[90]

The problem of social morale (like that of population, from which it cannot really be separated) was much in the minds of

---

would probably be fewer than 100 Hawaiians living in 1930. (Issue of January 26, 1850.) Actually there were nearly 61,000 pure and part Hawaiians.

[87] Pp. 49–50.

[88] "Colcord's Journal," pp. 129–130. MS. in Hawaiian Historical Society Library, Honolulu.

[89] J. N. Reynolds, *Voyage of the Potomac* (New York: 1835), p. 414.

[90] *Answers to Questions put by Mr. Dudoit, Consul of France,* April 22, 1846, MS. in Archives of Hawaii.

socially minded people of the time. What could be done with respect to immediate causes?

About one matter, the transformation of economic values resulting from foreign contacts, clearly nothing could be done. The King himself was financially embarrassed, though he would have been wealthy by old standards of values:

> The King pointed out the improvements in his house he had in contemplation, but complained he had not money enough to carry them out. Although his income is very considerable in tapas and native produce, and would have constituted great wealth in former times, yet from the depreciation of these articles, it is now of little value.[91]

One might of course pass laws against laziness; and one did. Chiefs were to be penalized for maintaining a retinue of sluggards:

> As for the idler, let the industrious put him to shame, and sound his name from one end of the country to the other. And even if they should withhold food on account of his idleness, there shall be no condemnation for those who thus treat idlers . . . If a landlord or a chief, should give entertainment to such a sluggard, he would thereby bring shame on the industrious. For three months the tenants of him who thus entertains the sluggard shall be freed of labor to their landlord. Such is the punishment of him who befriends the sluggard. Let him obtain his food by labor.[92]

Another law of 1842 remonstrates with the people for complaining of burdens, when those have been regularized and much lightened compared to the past. "The people are not oppressed, but are idle." And outstanding idlers among the people are to be punished:

> 1. If a farm is seen to be grown over with weeds and little food upon it, and yet a good farm for cultivation, in such a case the tenant shall be dispossessed, though he shall not be dispossessed without a trial.
>
> 2. . . . Forbearance shall be exercised for one year more, and then if the idleness of the people continues, it shall be the duty of the tax officer whenever he sees a man sitting idle, or doing nothing on the free days of the people, to take that man and set him to work for the Government, and he shall work till night. The Landlords also may do the same with tenants of their lands when they are idle. This law is passed on account of the idleness

[91] Captain Charles Wilkes, *Narrative of the United States Exploring Expedition* (Philadelphia: 1845), IV, 238.

[92] *Fundamental Law of Hawaii* (1842), p. 18.

of the people on their own free days. While they are at work for themselves, they shall not be set to work for others.[93]

From lack of subsequent reference to this law, one would conclude it was not enforced.

The nobles and the king sought to encourage industry by a homestead ordinance, that:

> Those men who have no land, not even a garden, nor any place to cultivate, and yet wish to labor for the purpose of obtaining the object of their desires, may apply to the land agent or the governor, or the King, for any piece of land which is not already cultivated by another person, and such piece shall be given to him.[94]

But there was specific complaint by missionaries and haole residents as to the detrimental effect of other government policies and laws. At least three missionaries objected to the labor tax, arguing it trained the natives in habits of shirking labor, since they had no reward for their toil. One missionary thought the poll tax encouraged prostitution.[95] The willfulness of the chief's laws was a continued source of confusion, especially in the thirties and earlier forties, since they retained much local authority, and were unwilling to fall in always with pronouncements from Lahaina and Honolulu.[96]

On one proposal missionaries and commercial people were in substantial agreement, the desirability of giving the native an incentive to work by offering him security of possession of personal

[93] *Fundamental Law of Hawaii* (1842). Sanctioned by the Nobles and Representative Body, and signed by the King on May 16, 1842.

[94] Passed in 1839. In Statute Laws of 1845–1847, II, p. 86.

[95] *Answers to Questions Proposed by R. C. Wyllie*, pp. 77–78. A traveler of 1846 quotes a human view by "an Indian" (i.e., native) of Oahu: "Ah sir! this civilization is the ruin of us. All want money, sir; money they must have: our daughters and our wives are not our own; they must have money and there is but one way to gain it. It is a sad curse, civilization; formerly each was willing to give, so none was needed; now he who has keeps, and he who has not, wants . . . And they say it is all for our good." Frederick Walpole, *Four Years in the Pacific* (Paris: 1850), p. 290.

[96] An example: In 1836 the King published an announcement that the right to fish in the sea should no longer be restricted according to ancient custom to chiefs and tenants along the shore line of their lands. One of the chiefs six weeks later published a contrary ruling, forbidding anyone to fish off the shore of his estate, under penalty of loss of the fish. "So the people know not what to depend on. There is no security." (John S. Emerson: *Journal*, entry for May 3, 1836. Archives of Hawaii.)

property and land; and of opening land to foreign enterprise by providing secure tenure. These views will be considered at the beginning of the next section, for they were part of the pressure leading up to the Land Reform of the forties. This Reform, or "Mahele," was a decisive break between the feudal past and the capitalist future in Hawaiian economic development.

In conclusion, Hawaii at the end of the third decade and beginning of the fourth decade of the nineteenth century had reached ebb tide in native morale. Although the disintegration had been peaceful, it was no less complete. The Hawaiian was dying out as a race; he was stricken as well in his psychological and social health. The superior prestige of the foreign invader had destroyed the social ties around which clung individual and group self-respect: the old religion was gone, the tabus were gone, the austere inviolability of the chiefs was obsolete, the functional basis of the feudal order was undermined; and new strange codes of behavior and social values were being pressed by the assured stranger. That the new techniques of the foreigner were superior to the old ways did not compensate for the disappearance of the old and familiar; nor for the upsetting of the old organization of production, which, after all, had served; nor for the turning upside down of economic values as foreign demand grew for special Island products, and as foreign commodities of greater effectiveness and high prestige value came on the market.

We can understand the despair felt when a higher civilization has penetrated a society, and the old has dwindled and disappeared. In Hawaii the prophecy of a native priest was often repeated: "The hibiscus shall grow, the coral shall spread and stretch forth its branches, but man shall cease." [97]

[97] From H. T. Cheever, *The Island World of the Pacific* (New York: 1851), p. 26; quoted in Lind, *An Island Community*, p. 97.

SECTION III

LAND REFORM TO RECIPROCITY, 1845–1876

CHAPTER VIII

LAND REFORM

We have carried our story of the disintegration of the native feudal economy to its low ebb of decay and lost morale.

The theme shifts in this section to the building of a new structure. Its central motive is the growth of a plantation economy, replacing previous temporary and casual relationships with the outer world by a permanent attachment to the trade network that commercial enterprise was throwing across the Pacific. On the horizon at the end of the period is a political bond to the Republic at the east which was already dominating Hawaiian commerce. Chief augury of the future is the uneven expansion of the sugar industry. The whaling trade continues preëminent during most of the period, but declines abruptly at the end. The settlement of California was more than a transient promise of diversified agricultural development: it also forecast closer future ties. And there were minor industries on which hopes were lavished.

Socially, there was the continued growth of the port towns, especially Honolulu. Increasing numbers of foreigners spread their secular and spiritual gospels in Island valleys and settlements; and eventually the expansion of the plantations led to the importation of contract labor. The native population declined more slowly, and was acclimatizing itself to the new culture. And there was the prerequisite to expansion of the plantations and of commerce: a conscious, rapid, and in its way astonishingly successful transition from the feudal system of land holding to a system of fee simple tenure.

Pressure toward Land Reform

We have mentioned the frequent advocacy of alodial tenure as a specific for economic stagnation. Essentially the campaign has been continuous ever since the haole first visited the Islands, but it reached a culmination in the forties. The haoles were subject to the same uncertainties of tenure and taxes as were the natives, and were the more dissatisfied because they were conscious of the security of owners in the countries from which they had come. They did not in general "own" land at all, but possessed only a right of use. Some had also the right to transfer land to others.[1] Such transfer was difficult enough, for the land was unsurveyed, and might be specified by name only.[2]

The Minister for Foreign Affairs, R. C. Wyllie, carried on perhaps the most persistent campaign, and as a person of consequence his words carried weight. He spoke of the low wages for native labor, and the truck system already established, urging laws to allow foreigners to hold land and employ native labor: "For the demand for native labor would be increased, and wages would rise in proportion . . . Demand for labor would stimulate the natives to take care of their offspring as a source of profit." [3]

It was repeatedly argued that foreigners could not be expected to bring in much-needed capital to develop the land until their ownership rights were secure; and that natives must know surely that what they produced would not and could not be taken from them.[4] The United States Commissioner agreed that, despite the natural indolence of the natives, they would work and work well if an "adequate object to industry" were put before them.[5] The eight missionaries who answered Wyllie's question on the subject were unanimous in listing security of land as one means—and

[1] Josephine Sullivan, *History of C. Brewer & Co.* (Boston: 1926), p. 18; G. F. Mathison, *A Visit to Brazil, Chile, Peru, and the Sandwich Islands* (London: 1825), p. 385.

[2] As John Young, before his death in 1835, left to his wife "one land" situated in the district of Puna, called Kamomoa. He left four other "lands" specified no more exactly. ("John Young, Companion of Kamehameha," in *Hawaiian Annual* for 1911, p. 103.)

[3] *The Friend,* July 18, 1844. Wyllie argued elsewhere: "Thus even the poorest of Your Majesty's subjects would stand on a footing of independent right—he would know that the land he cultivated was his own, and could not be taken from him; and he would have the powerful stimulus of self interest to improve it, and to put a good dwelling on it; every child would be of value to him as he grew up, to help him in cultivating the ground; laborers would be induced to marry, in order to have children to help them; those children would be better taken care of, and would become more moral by being removed from the haunts of vice in the seaports." (*Reports of the Minister of Foreign Affairs, 1852–62,* Report dated December 1, 1847, p. 67.)

[4] *Ibid.*, p. 66; "Colcord's Journal," p. 129 (MS. in Hawaiian Historical Society Library, Honolulu; Bishop, *Reminiscences*, p. 29; *The Friend,* July 1844.

[5] George Brown to the Secretary of State, Dispatch dated January 16, 1844, National Archives of the United States.

sometimes the only means mentioned—of overcoming indolence.[6]

The minister and doctor Thomas Lafon, who came in 1837, was an enthusiastic antislavery man. His zeal may have hastened somewhat the land reform, and the release of the makaainanas from their inferior status.[7]

The haoles were not loathe to advocate their own interest. When the United States Commissioner visited Hawaii in 1844 he found the Americans on the island without complaint "except that they couldn't get land for cultivation, of which there are thousands of acres now useless." [8] The *Polynesian* urged that the interest of the Islands demanded decidedly that no hindrances be put in the way of agricultural enterprise, but instead that bounties should be offered, and land even given away on the condition that it be cultivated.[9] Other pressure came from the advertised examples of commercial advance in New South Wales 1836–1840, in the Canary Islands, and in the Philippines after alodial land tenure was introduced. Lord Byron on his visit in 1825 had urged the king to continue the first Kamehameha's general habit of accepting hereditary succession to landholdings; and subsequent visiting naval commanders had urged secure individual tenure.[10]

Native Resistance

The operations of Ladd & Co. at Koloa after 1835 [11] gave substance to the promises of agricultural development if secure tenure were granted; but there was a contrary influence in the fear to which its lease of 1841 also gave example, that foreigners might take over the country, or at least embroil the government in bickering, if they were granted such a right.[12] Fear of the increasing

[6] *Answers to Questions Proposed by R. C. Wyllie* (Honolulu: 1848), pp. 7–13.

[7] Bishop, *op. cit.*, p. 53.

[8] "This will be remedied in time, I think, as at present these people are in the unenviable position of the dog in the manger; they will neither work themselves, nor allow others the wherewithal to work upon." (George Brown to the Secretary of State, Dispatch of September 6, 1844. National Archives.)

[9] July 1841, p. 10.

[10] Sanford B. Dole, "Evolution of Land Tenure in Hawaii," *Hawaiian Historical Society Papers,* December 5, 1892; printed in Report of Senate Foreign Relations Committee (1894), p. 98.

[11] Pp. 175, 178.

[12] The Ladd & Co. agreement had given to the company right to lease any unoccupied lands for 100 years at a low rental. The franchise was transferred to a Belgian company in which Ladd & Co. had interest, and there was trouble for the government over the matter for several years.

power of foreigners reached in 1845 the point of petitions to the government seeking to have the king dismiss foreign advisers and deny further land holdings to haoles.

The government yielded only gradually to continuing pressure. The great chiefs were certainly in favor of secure tenure for themselves—and their own economic interest made them less able to resist the similar aspirations of others; but they opposed so far as they could the extension of the principle. They were unable to conceive of any other way in which discipline and the hierarchy of rank could be maintained. An old chief said to Richards, "If we cannot take away their lands, what will they care for us? They will be as rich as we." [13] With respect to foreigners there was fear not only of loss of sovereignty over individual lands but also of a rapid increase in their numbers and wealth until the native should be an impoverished outcast in his own country. Such a view had led by 1841 to an exclusive policy, of short leases at relatively high prices, with longer leases paying still higher fees per annum. The editor of the *Polynesian* thought the system "admirably calculated to answer its purpose, by discouraging foreign enterprise and permanent investment of capital." [14]

The fears of the natives were not decreased by partial loss of sovereignty to Captain Laplace of the French Navy in 1839, or the temporary complete loss of sovereignty in 1843 to Captain Paulet of the British Navy. In effect, the recognition of independence by Britain, France, and the United States in 1842–43 was granted only at the cost of relinquishing considerable native control.[15]

Native resistance to abrogation of feudal tenure took the form essentially of delay: discussion, compromise, and partial pronouncements and laws inched the way toward fee simple tenure—in contrast with resistance by force and bloodshed in other parts of the Pacific and the world. Looking at the successive steps, we see the self-interest of the king and chiefs—their gain in security

The temporary cession of the Islands to Great Britain in 1843 was in part a consequence of land claims of Richard Charlton, the British Consul. (Sanford B. Dole, *op. cit.*, p. 100.)

[13] *Letter of William Richards to Commander Wilkes*, p. 13.

[14] Issue of June 17, 1841.

[15] Cf. Ralph S. Kuykendall, *The Hawaiian Kingdom* (Honolulu: 1938), pp. 191–205; Andrew W. Lind, in *Race and Culture Contacts* (New York: 1934), pp. 239–240.

(the chiefs) and hoped-for gain in income (the king and chiefs) —easing the pain of relinquishing feudal rights.

When Kamehameha III had come to the throne in 1833 he asserted his full and unqualified feudal right over all persons and property: "Life and death, to disapprove and to approve, all pleasures, all the laws and everything in the nation are all mine." [16] But only six years later influence on the king and chiefs had been adequate to lead to a "Declaration of Rights," a statement of the benevolent intent of the government. Its ideas and phrasing indicate the religious sentiments of the missionaries and suggest the influence of our own national documents:

> God has made of one blood all nations of men to dwell on the earth in unity and blessedness. God hath also bestowed certain rights on all men and all chiefs and all people of all lands. These are some of the rights which he hath given alike to every man and every chief of correct deportment: life, limb, liberty, freedom from oppression, the earnings of his hands and the productions of his mind—not, however, to those who act in violation of the laws . . . In making laws . . . it is by no means proper to make laws for the protection of the rulers only, without also providing protection for their subjects; neither is it proper to enact laws to enrich the chiefs only, without regard to enriching their subjects also.[17]

Specific defense against arbitrary exactions was assured the commoners: "Protection is hereby assured to the persons of all the people; together with their building lots, and all their property." [18] The landlord was not to "causelessly dispossess his tenant." [19]

The tax laws of 1839 and 1840 carried out the implications of the Declaration by specifying the maximum amounts and kinds of taxes[20] which might be collected.

In the Constitution of 1840 is a postulate as to inherent right in the land on which was founded the later land distribution. It is therefore a basis of present landownership:

> Kamehameha I was the founder of the kingdom, and to him belonged all the land from one end of the Island to the other, though it was not his own private property. It belonged to the chiefs and people in common, of whom

[16] Quoted in Lind, *An Island Community*, p. 45.
[17] *Constitution and Laws of Kamehameha III* (1842), p. 9.
[18] *Ibid.*, p. 10.
[19] *Ibid.*, p. 33.
[20] Above, pp. 109–111.

Kamehameha I was the head and had the management of the landed property.[21]

This was the first official pronouncement as to any rights of the commoners in the land. We may well doubt whether the old Conqueror or succeeding rulers had ever conceived of themselves as holding property (and authority) in trust, rather than by absolute right: but the theory here expressed was a basis on which land distribution could be carried out as a measure of justice and due, rather than of charity and expediency. The moral pressure for such distribution was greater if such a theory were accepted and maintained.

What had so far been done? There had been a "reform," that is, a movement toward an alodial, relatively unconditioned land tenure, only in two respects: (1) in the tax law of 1840 had appeared a partial division of feudal dues into tax to the government, and rent to the landlord;[22] (2) the claims of the nobility on the commoners had been made definite and explicit. These are small reasons for considering the developments so far a homogeneous part of the Land Reform, despite use later made of the measures. More fundamentally the development so far had been conservative, an effort to maintain the old feudal system against the pressure of change by improving it: (1) by giving the commoners and individual chiefs an assured interest in the enterprise; (2) by making less onerous and more regular its exactions.[23] In the best Macaulay tradition, it was an effort to preserve by reforming.

The government was several times compelled to emphasize that the regularization of feudal obligations did not mean their abrogation. The king announced in 1841: "The subjection of the people to the chiefs from former ages down is a subject well understood; so also are some of the ancient laws. That subjection and those laws are not now discontinued as a matter of course, but there are many new laws."[24] In 1842 the basic claim of the king

[21] *Constitution and Laws of Kamehameha III*, pp. 11–12.

[22] The law is abstracted on pp. 109–110.

[23] As evidence of the backward orientation, one measure of the Constitution of 1840 took away a personal right the commoner held even during pre-discovery days. In view of the crisis in production and the population decline, commoners were forbidden to desert their cultivated lands without cause.

[24] *Polynesian*, March 6, 1841.

to the soil was reaffirmed, to warn against sales of land and fixed property which assumed they were being held in fee simple.[25]

The laws for regularization of feudal dues were less effective than they might have been through persistence of old habits, not only among the chiefs, but also among even the officers of the new system, who feared to carry through any ruling which, contrary to prolonged and honorable custom, was against the wish or interests of the chiefs.[26] Arbitrary taxation and offenses against the persons of the commoners continued for some time, especially in the outlying districts.[27]

In 1841 the government attempted to assert itself against foreigners, who variously held good, doubtful, and squatter claims. Those who had written titles or leases were not to be disturbed; all others were to negotiate leases with governors for a fixed term of years, with a maximum length of fifty years, and at higher rentals as the lease was longer.[28] But the government was not strong enough to press the issue against the objections of American and French consuls and the foreigners generally; and the matter was dropped.

[25] "It is hereby clearly proclaimed that lands and fixed property upon them can never be sold at auction, neither can they be permanently transferred. They cannot even be leased for years without consent of King and Premier. This kind of property . . . can never be seized for debt, for the Government has never relinquished its right in the soil." (Proclamation of Kamehameha III, Lahaina, May 1842. *Laws of 1842*, p. 121.)

The above is qualified to this extent, that a person who holds no personal property may have land and real property sold for debt, but only to a "native born citizen."

The provision against leasing without consent of the government was an effort to keep check on the entry of new agricultural enterprises. Naturally it was an irritating obstacle to plantation men; and point is given to the complaints in the *Polynesian* and *Friend* against antagonistic government policy.

[26] *Letter of William Richards to Commander Wilkes*, p. 18.

[27] The Government addressed proclamations to governors and chiefs from time to time: "All the Governors are hereby forbidden to lay new burdens of their own invention on the lands. When you condemn anyone unjustly, do not lay the blame on the laws of the kingdom, and when you lay grievous burdens on the people do not cast the blame on his Majesty the King, nor on the law; do not behave thus, lest even the country people rise up before you, and expound the meaning of this book." (*Constitution and Laws of Kamehameha III*, 1842, p. 27.)

A later proclamation advised: "Ye chiefs of the nation, reflect well on these fundamental laws of the kingdom. From this time on change your procedure. A change in accord with this law will be both more just and be really better for yourselves . . ." (*Op. cit.*, p. 31.)

[28] Announcement in the *Polynesian*, June 1841.

Steps to Land Reform

The principles of the Mahele (meaning literally "to divide"; and, in this connection, the Land Division of 1846) were foreshadowed concretely in the distribution of fishing grounds in 1842. Irregular and complicated rights in fishing were to be divided into three groups: "His Majesty the King hereby takes the fishing grounds from those who now possess them, from Hawaii to Kauai, and gives one portion of them to the common people, another portion to the landlords, and a portion he reserves to himself." [29]

Agitation for alodial titles continued for several years without outward results; but in late 1844 the harassed government had already concluded to appoint a commission to inquire into the whole disturbed land question, and to decide on all claims and matters of title. Such a group, appropriately called the "Board of Commissioners to Quiet Land Titles," was set up as part of an act organizing the executive divisions of the government, passed in December of 1845. The climate of opinion, dominated by the foreign business interest, missionaries, and haole ministers in the government, ensured that the organization of policies governing land tenure implied in the duties of the Commission would not be undertaken according to feudal principles, but according to the private property principles of western societies.

From this time on the transition was continuous and rapid.

The state of mind to which the king and chiefs had themselves come by this time is indicated by a provision in the same act that the Minister of the Interior, subject to further approval, could sell lands to natives under fee simple title (but not to foreigners unless they had previously gained such a claim); and by a project undertaken in 1846 under their decision to sell small plots of land in fee simple to natives in Makawao, Maui, and Manoa Valley, Oahu. About a thousand acres were finally sold in this experiment.

The Land Commission was composed of five members, two Hawaiians, two whites, and one half-white. Its powers specified that it was "to be a board of investigation and final ascertainment or rejection of all claims of private individuals, whether native or foreigners, to any landed property acquired anterior to the pas-

[29] *Constitution and Laws of Kamehameha III*, p. 21.

sage of this act." [30] The awards of the Board were to be binding on the government, and on the claimant unless appeal were made to the supreme court. But since, according to later decision, the government retained usually a part interest in lands so awarded, the claimant had to pay a commutation to the government before he received a royal patent in fee simple to his land.[31]

The Commission did not have power to change the system of land tenure, nor to divide the lands out of the undefined community of interest in which most of them remained. They could only pass on the validity and dimensions of specific grants made in the past by the king or by chiefs. For the great majority of lands, further decision was needed by the government before any alodial titles could be extracted out of the mass of common right.

But the Board did, after consideration of the ancient land system, draw up "Principles adopted by the Board . . . in . . . adjudication of claims presented to them" which were influential (but not determinant) on later decisions, and on the Mahele proper, or division between king and chiefs. The Constitution of 1840 with its tripartite interest was accepted as a fundamental guide; and the Board suggested hesitantly that the king would be generous in comparison with his former feudal rights if he allowed a third of the lands to the commoners, a third to the chiefs, and himself retained a third. On this basis they suggested that the share of the government when any patent was given might be reckoned at one-third of the unimproved value, a decision which later held, with some exceptions.[32]

After formulating its "Principles," the Land Commission worked only on house lots in and near Honolulu up to December of 1847, in view of the difficulty of making division between the king (and government), and chiefs on other property, where the interest was normally undivided. On December 18, in conclusion to many fearful and hopeful discussions in the Privy Council,

[30] Statute Laws, 1845–1847, I, p. 107.

[31] Since payment of commutation was not compulsory, the government interest remained in some land for many years, until a 1909 law enforced payment. (Laws of 1909, pp. 118–121.)

[32] In 1847 the proportion was reduced to one-fourth for house and building lots of Hawaiian subjects. And in 1849 a further resolution exempted native tenants completely from payment of commutation for their cultivated lands and house lots. (Privy Council Resolutions of June 8, 1847 and December 21, 1849, the latter enacted August 6, 1850.)

agreement was reached there that: (1) The king should retain his private lands as his own property; (2) One-third of the remaining lands should be set aside as the property of the government; (3) One-third should go to the chiefs and konohikis[33] "in proportion to their possessions"; (4) The last third should go to the commoners. Lands previously granted in fee simple were not to be affected.[34]

This also, like the "Principles" of the Commission, was a statement of intent, not actually to be carried out with any exactness. Separate agreement was made for each area of land, with final division varying more or less from this intent.

Accordingly, chiefs and konohikis came before a committee of the Privy Council, and in forty days, January 27 to March 7, 1848, arrived at acceptable divisions between themselves, and the crown and government. They either gave up a part of the lands over which they held authority, and received in return a claim to the remainder; or paid instead the specified commutation of one-third of the unimproved value. Their claim was to be taken to the Land Commission, and exchanged for an alodial right.

On March 8, the day after this division ended, the king further divided the crown and government lands into two parts, setting aside for the government the larger share, and withholding for himself what he considered "a reasonable amount of land" as his own estate.[35]

Lands so distributed were still subject to claims of the commoners. But though the commonors were able to buy land in accord with the provisions of the 1846 act setting up the Land Commission, there was no procedure by which they could obtain an award of their rightful share of the lands of the kingdom, to which the Principles of the Commission had asserted their claim. There was some doubt as to the desirability of the change: the commoners would apparently lose as well as gain, losing their common right on the land of their landlord to fishing, hunting, and gathering of forest products (and now of pasturage of their ani-

[33] Land agents of the chiefs.

[34] Privy Council Record, IV, 280–288.

[35] W. D. Alexander, *Appendix to the Surveyor General's Report*, pp. 16, 25, 26. The Crown Lands were in 1865, after they had been encumbered with mortgages and in part sold, declared inalienable, to be inherited by successors to the Kingship.

mals),[36] in exchange for ownership, and remission of the labor tax to landlords.

But one of the main arguments (altruistic in part but not wholly so) for land reform had been the stimulus to energetic work which secure ownership would provide. The uncertain political status of the kingdom gave additional reason for securing to the natives what might otherwise through a change in government be permanently lost to them. This last main step in Land Reform was taken in late 1849, with a resolution of the Privy Council providing that alodial titles should be given to all commoners for lands which they occupied and cultivated. No commutation was required, save for the most valuable of such lands, house lots in Honolulu, Lahaina, and Hilo.[37] In addition certain government lands were to be set aside for sale to commoners who had not otherwise secured adequate lands.

These claims of the native tenants made up the bulk of the work of the Commission. It continued its investigations and awards, the duration of its activity being extended several times. Before it was finally disbanded in 1855,[38] 11,309 claims had been filed before it.[39] In each case an application for the land had to

[36] A Special act of June 20, 1851 continued such rights to people who had been granted alodial title. They were to have right of way; and might obtain water, thatch, house timber, ti leaves, and the like, provided they did not sell such supplies. (Confirmed in *The Civil Code of 1859,* p. 356.)

[37] Resolution of December 21.

[38] Still later, in 1860, another time allowance was granted for claims to be brought forward. Tenants were often diffident about making claims, did not wish to make claims in opposition to konohikis and alii, sometimes were suspicious of the worth of their titles once they had them.

Even when, after 1850, titles were given free to all native tenants for their cultivated lands and house lots (Act of August 6, 1850), they must have often been discouraged by the $6 to $12 surveying and general costs fee made for each kuleana title. Alexander, in charge of surveying at a later date, argues this was a small amount. (Appendix to *Surveyor General's Report,* p. 10.) But in view of the wage levels of the time and the current value of land, his argument is not convincing. Wages in the forties and fifties were normally between 12½ cents and 33 cents a day for unskilled labor, plus certain perquisites. (See below, p. 193.) This means, at Alexander's lowest figure, 18 to 48 days; at his highest figure, 36 to 96 days' labor, for a title many thought of little value.

As to the value of land, it is likely that the $6 to $12 fee often exceeded the value of the kuleana, even granting the superior fertility of kuleana land. Land was exchanging in the late forties and fifties for from 25 cents to $1.50 an acre, with $1 about the median.

It is clear that many commoners were presented with a doubtful bargain.

[39] W. D. Alexander, *Appendix to the Surveyor General's Report,* p. 10.

be made, testimony as to the merit of the claim listened to, the boundaries surveyed, and final awards made.

Inaccuracies of surveying constituted a persistent course of confusion into the future: there was no uniform procedure as to how much land ought to be included in a kuleana; the pieces surveyed were of all shapes and sizes; and the surveyors of all degrees of conscientiousness and skill. The procedures of three surveyors sent to Hawaii illustrate the lack of uniformity: The first was a stranger to the country. Following directions to include what the claimant had cultivated and improved, and finding in the upland that the people were cultivating only two or three acres of taro, he did not take into account that it was necessary to let the land lie fallow two or three years, and consequently surveyed only the amount actually being cultivated. In many cases the people abandoned their new lands as insufficient for their needs. The second surveyor, a native Hawaiian, thought the people had the main right to the land on general principles. He sent in surveys of from 15 to 40 acres—which were also awarded. The third multiplied the amount of land under cultivation by the number of seasons it would have to lie fallow, and came out with from 6 to 12 acres for the ordinary run of upland kuleanas. He was having hard going in the taro patches, with an ever-watchful konohiki to contest his progress; and when reports of what was going on the neighboring districts came to him, he waited awhile, rather puzzled, to see what would turn up. But when he found his reports too were approved by the Commission, he continued on his own principles.[40]

To confound the confusion an act of 1852, designed to speed up

[40] For a fuller account, see C. J. Lyons, "Land Matters in Hawaii," *The Islander*, August 6, 1875, p. 143.

Alexander corroborates this report, saying that the surveyors were practically irresponsible. Only a few were competent: many were not only incompetent, but also careless and unscrupulous. "Some used fifty foot chains, and others the four pole chain divided into links; some attempted to survey by the true meridian, others by the average magnetic meridian, while most made no allowance for local variations of the compass . . . Some surveys . . . were made with a ship's compass, or even a pocket compass. Few of them took much pains to mark boundaries, or to note the topographic features of the country. Rarely was one section or district assigned to one man. It is said that over a dozen were employed in surveying Waikiki, not one of whom knew what the others were doing, or tried to make his surveys agree with theirs where they adjoined . . ." (*Appendix to the Surveyor General's Report*, p. 28.)

awards,[41] empowered the Land Commission to make grants of whole ahupuaas or ilis by their proper names, without survey.[42] Some areas sold cut across half a dozen ahupuaas. Though there was explicit exemption of kuleanas within such districts, the former were not surveyed until specifically applied for. This existence of titles within titles was another leading cause of the unmitigated confusion as to boundaries that existed in the sixties.

When by 1860 something like nine-tenths of the available land had been taken up, the government was completely in the dark as to what remained.[43] Most of its lands were by then mere remnants, irregular and worthless pieces remaining after the valued land had been sold. The government could not with any certainty dispose of them to new applicants. To clear up the confusion, a general government survey was undertaken in 1871.[44]

The question of landownership by unnaturalized foreigners, of under what terms they might retain lands they already held or/and gain new lands, continued to be agitated through the forties. The unsuccessful effort of the government to put on a lease basis all foreigners save those who held fee simple grants has been mentioned. Wyllie phrased the continued government viewpoint:

> Their policy not to grant lands in fee simple to Foreigners is founded upon this—that if lands were put up for sale, since the natives have little money, Foreigners would in every case become the purchasers, so that from their superior wealth and industry, the natives would soon become excluded from their own soil, reduced to a hopeless servitude and finally wholly extinguished.[45]

But the shift to a more liberal land policy became explicit soon afterward. In 1847 the Legislature was induced to enact[46] that foreigners might keep lands of which they were then possessed on payment of the regular commutation—putting them thus on the same basis as native Hawaiians. But they could not sell such

[41] Passed June 19, 1852.

[42] A Commission of Boundaries was established in 1862 to legally settle the dimensions of these ahupuaas and ilis. The work progressed slowly. Many owners were indifferent, and surveys were expensive. (Alexander, *op. cit.*, p. 20.)

[43] C. J. Lyons, "Land Matters in Hawaii," *The Islander*, August 20, 1875.

[44] Alexander, *op. cit.*, p. 30.

[45] "Answers to Questions put by Mr. Dudoit, Consul of France," April 22, 1846; Archives of Hawaii. (MS. in Wyllie's own handwriting, and nearly illegible.)

[46] Act of June 28. *Statute Laws, 1846,* II, 78–79.

land save to native subjects. Foreigners were not satisfied. Discussion continued; and a law permitting them to hold and convey land in fee simple, rejected in 1848, was passed in 1850.[47]

The victory of alodial tenure was as complete as law could make it.[48]

Aftermath

Approximate figures for the gross land distribution by 1855 are as follows:

Government lands	1,495,000 acres
Crown lands	984,000
Chief's lands	1,619,000
Kuleanas	28,600
Total	4,126,000[49]

The astonishingly low figures for the tenants' share are compensated for to some extent by consideration that these were the most productive lands of the Islands when they were watered in accord with their rights, while the other lands were often rough, or had dry upland sections or vast lava stretches.

What did the commoners think of the new days of alodial tenure and freedom from arbitrary exaction? In the early days after Reform their confidence in the laws was often shaken because of violations by local chiefs.[50] As the changes continued,

[47] Act of June 10, 1850.

[48] With the coming of a later administration, when the best land had been sold, and the limit of land resources was evident, there was a return in some measure to a close land policy. In 1874 an act provided that no property of more than $5000 value should be sold unless there were consent of the King and a majority of the Privy Council. (W. D. Alexander, *op. cit.*, p. 23.) Owners of land were often unwilling to sell. H. M. Whitney wrote in his *The Hawaiian Guide Book* (Honolulu: 1875): "While it is comparatively easy to lease land, it is difficult to purchase . . . The policy of the large land holders is not to sell but to lease." (Pp. 112–13.)

[49] *Senate Committee Report on Pacific Islands* (Washington: 1903), I, 86.

[50] "I am sorry to say that the people of this region have little confidence in what their rulers say about the security of lands . . . In the face of the Constitution, some twenty families in the single valley of Hanalei are stripped of the fruit their own hands had planted; and . . . are now, some of them, being literally driven from the spot where they have always lived and were born. They are told that the white man has paid their king dollars, and therefore they must be content with their lot." (E. Johnson, teacher of the mission, speaking of Hanalei, Kauai, in *Answers to Questions Proposed by R. C. Wyllie*, p. 13. His reply was dated April, 1847.)

rumors spread of shifting future events: that the whole thing would be overthrown, that certain lands would have no kuleanas taken from them, and the like. It was like a dream to people whose only tradition was that of hopeless inferiority.[51] Some thought it a ruse only, to tempt them to fence their fields, improve the land, and build better houses; that eventually all their efforts would go to enrich the chiefs, as had always been the case in the past.[52]

Fewer kuleanas were applied for than had been hoped. There are three reasons: the charges for surveying and transfer of title[53] often made ownership a doubtful or bad bargain; some of the kuleanas, surveyed by men not cognizant with the production routines or intimidated by the chief's man, were too small to sustain a family; and the commoner often feared to oppose the interest of his chiefs, or was doubtful of the validity of his prospective title.

Once obtained, the kuleanas passed rapidly into the hands of the rising sugar and rice plantation operators, or to land speculators.[54] The loss of the land by the natives was due not so much to "lack of foresight," compared with the haole, as to his alienation from the concepts of private property. More specific reasons can be listed: (1) The kuleanas were too small for support of a family, as we have mentioned, or were composed of several fragments awkwardly placed. Often such kuleanas were simply abandoned. (2) The attractions of port towns. (3) Nearly consistently booming land prices, giving a dazzlingly large return for a lease or sale. And often, after a lease to a plantation, landmarks which had defined the limits of the kuleana were cleared away; and the returning kanaka was unable to identify his land. (4) When there were no heirs, reversion to the government, or absorption in surrounding lands.

The *Hui* was a type of cotenancy which arose as a result

[51] C. J. Lyons, "Land Matters in Hawaii," *The Islander*, July 30, 1875, p. 135.

[52] Titus Coan, *Life in Hawaii* (New York: 1882), p. 124.

[53] Some of the missionaries helped to survey land, so reducing charges to the natives.

[54] Samples of price rises are conveniently collected in Appendix B of Jean Hobbs, *Hawaii: A Pageant of the Soil*, pp. 157–178. Appreciation was rapid and constant after Land Reform, with tracts selling for 2 to 13 times their original exchange price after a one- to ten-year interval. Speculation was at times feverish. See the interesting letter to Wyllie quoted in A. W. Lind, *An Island Community* (Chicago: 1938), p. 53.

of earlier communal use of land. Altogether, several hundred grants were made at the time of the Mahele to groups of individuals; and a few were sold later to such groups. Usually the number of interested persons was two to twenty; later sometimes as many as 200.[55] The extent was from several acres to over 2800 (the Mailepai Hui on Maui). The customary rules of the Hui suggest its affinity to the earlier land system: there was an allotment system by which each member could select a house lot and garden of five to ten acres for each "share"; there were pasturage rules specifying the number of cattle which could be run on the common range per share, with penalty rates for a larger number; and regulations as to cutting wood, fishing, fencing, and the like. A few of the huis persisted into the 1930's; but most disappeared. There were many difficulties: (1) The children of the original founders were often not interested in continuing the hui, having become accustomed to alodial tenure, or wanting to live in the cities. (2) As shares passed to children, or were sold to groups, the undivided share came to be very small, as little as 1-30th of 1-71st (in the Wainiha Hui of Kauai), altogether surpassing the mathematical abilities of the owners to deal with, and too small for the inheritor to bother with. (3) An increasingly serious bane was a wealth of unrecorded facts about divisions and rights. But the hui filled a useful purpose in the late nineteenth century as a transitional device on the road to alodial tenure.[56]

The alii were not more successful than the commoners in retaining the 1.6 million acres which were issued to them. Lack of ability to foresee the future value of land, debt, and poor management in general took their toll.[57] With royal lands also coming into private hands,[58] the proportion of land owned by haoles progressively increased. In 1856 only 209 land claims of the 15,514

[55] L. J. Watson (Land Superintendent of Alexander and Baldwin), in the *Honolulu Star Bulletin,* December 13, 1932.

[56] An interesting account of the prosperous Wainiha Hui is given in John M. Lydgate, "The Affairs of Wainiha Hui," in *The Hawaiian Annual* for 1913, pp. 125–237; also in L. J. Watson, *Honolulu Star Bulletin,* December 16, 1932.

[57] "Money is lent to chiefs and others on mortgages of their lands for 2 and sometimes 2½ per cent per month. Their extensive domains will soon go out of their hands at that rate. The king too is in debt." (Dispatch of Luther Severance, U. S. Commissioner to Department of State, 1851, in *Hawaiian Diplomatic Correspondence,* published by the Historical Commission of the Territory of Hawaii, vol. 1, no. 3, p. 17.)

[58] *Ibid.,* and p. 132, note.

registered with the government belonged to foreigners or their descendants. But of the land sold from government holdings prior to 1886, 64 per cent went to haoles; and, by 1896, 57 per cent of the land area paying taxes belonged to them.[59]

The Land Reform is a testimony to the possibility of carrying out far-reaching social adjustments by a conscious program, where there is compelling leadership, and problems are recognized.

One may conjecture that the disappearance of feudal tenure would have been achieved at far greater social cost, and perhaps not sooner, if the missionaries and other whites had opposed with violence and antagonism the feudal lords and the feudal tradition, instead of inculcating a code of ethics to which feudal tenure was incompatible, and allowing economic evolution to continue to the point where feudal tenure was no longer practicable.

The Reform was most significant to the commoners as a removal of the social burden of debased status and absence of any acknowledged rights. The *direct* economic advantage was not great. The chiefs and foreigners desiring secure tenure doubtless gained much more. The tenants' share was extraordinarily small; what they did obtain was secured only at the cost of high fees; and not being used to ownership, they soon lost much of their holdings through sale or foreclosure.

But the Reform must be viewed against its background. As social events go, in terms of concrete situation, relative solutions, and the possibilities of error, it was a success. It remains a major landmark in Hawaiian history, and a tribute to the men who conceived the possibility of carrying it through. The Land Reform and the social reform which accompanied it were the indispensables of economic advance. Capital could be invested with security: the road was clear for the rise of the sugar industry which has chiefly dominated the course of the Hawaiian economy since.

[59] Report of the Minister of the Interior, 1856; A. W. Lind, *An Island Community*, p. 57.

Though pure-blooded Hawaiians made up 63 per cent of landowners by 1896, they owned only 14 per cent of taxable land.

CHAPTER IX

THE PEAK OF THE WHALING TRADE, AND COLLAPSE

THE YEARS 1843–1860 were the golden age of Hawaiian whaling. During the spring and fall seasons sometimes over a hundred ships at a time lay at anchor at Lahaina Roadsteads or in the harbor of Honolulu. Agriculture was stimulated to diversified production of ship provisions; repairs were needed in quantity; merchants were busy disposing of imported supplies; and unruly seamen filled the streets.

The bulk of the American fleet during this time resorted to the Pacific, far more than to any other one area. Few ships of any other nation, in fact, touched at the Islands.[1]

The peak of whaling visits to Hawaii corresponds well with the peak of the whole American whale trade;[2] but the percentage variations between 1845 and 1859 are decidedly more violent when we look at visits to Hawaii than when we look at the total American industry. The reason evidently lay in the marginal nature of a venture to the distant north Pacific. Discouraging Pacific voyages diverted subsequent efforts toward shorter voyages in closer seas; but when luck had been good, there was a rush to Pacific waters. A chart of Hawaiian visits comes to be a sensitive index of all the trade.

During the whole boom period of the industry, prices of sperm oil, whale oil, and bone were (account being taken of a six- to eight-year cyclical variation) irregularly increasing. The price of bone, in fact, continued rising past 1900; but whale oil began a long decline about 1864, and sperm oil in 1866, under pressure

[1] *The Whaleman's Shipping List* of New Bedford (November 21, 1843) listed 593 whalers at sea, of which 324 were in the Pacific, 114 in the Indian Ocean, and only 88 in all other areas.

Visits during 1844 were itemized by the *Polynesian* according to country of origin. Out of 497 ships in all, 410 were American. French (26) and Bremen (19) ships came next to the Americans; and far behind English ships (5), New Brunswick (4), Danish (2), and Norwegian (10). Of the seamen, 13,000 were American, out of a total of 14,905. (January 4, 1845.)

[2] See Chart 2 below; also W. S. Tower, *History of the American Whale Fishery* (Philadelphia: 1907), p. 121.

of competition from petroleum. Up to those dates there was continuous stimulation from the side of price.

CHART 2

VISITS TO HAWAIIAN PORTS OF WHALERS, COMPARED WITH UNITED STATES WHALING TONNAGE

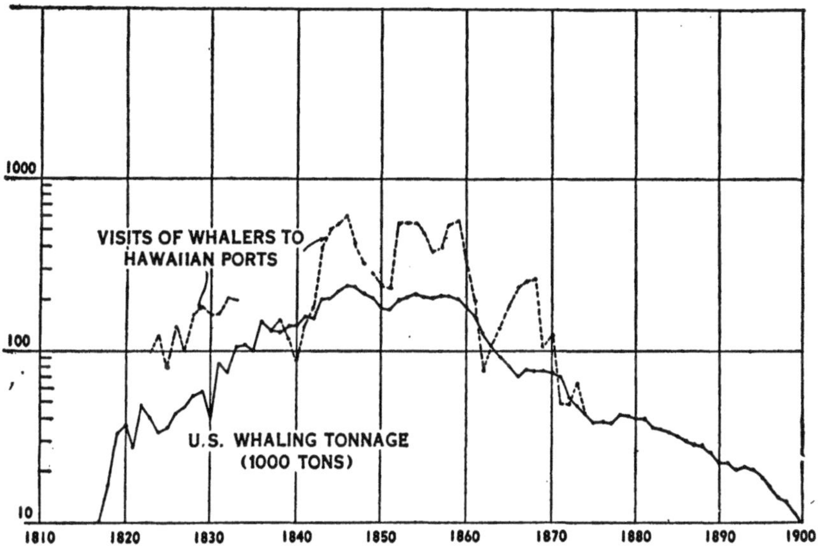

Data: Appendix II, column (1); and W. S. Tower, *History of the American Whale Fishery* (Philadelphia: 1907), p. 121.

The major rises in visits reflect, however, not price changes, but exploitation of successive new fishing grounds. By 1838 the Kodiak or Northwest grounds off the Russian possessions had been discovered. The great rise 1840–1846 indicates its exploitation. Similarly, the grounds in the Arctic Ocean north of Bering Strait were discovered in 1848, and by 1852 the spreading news of its existence is portrayed in a multiplication of visits.

As for declines in visits, no satisfactory correlation can be made of them with major or minor fluctuations in prices; and again other causes must be looked to. The drop from 1846 to 1852 seems attributable to three causes. One was the California gold rush. It had a depressing effect from 1848 through the 1850's. Men shipped from the East Coast only for the sake of reaching California, since vessels often put in here for supplies. It became necessary to offer heavy advance wages; and often "bounty jumpers" would desert anyway after receiving their wages. Even the officers sometimes left the ship stranded in Frisco Bay and lit out for fortunes in the hills. A second cause was the exhaustion of sperm fisheries off Japan, noticeable in 1838, and by 1844 forcing a diversion of nearly all whalers toward the northwest coast, and later to the Bering and Okhotsk Seas.[3] Corresponding to this shift was, perforce, a transition from sperm whale exports out of the Pacific to whale oil.[4] The third and most important cause was temporary poor luck in the newer, right whale grounds. In consequence there were often disgusted and mutinous crews to deal with. In 1845–1846 especially:

> With few exceptions the crews were restless and discontented, many had been on board for two years or more and instead of diminishing the debts which stood against them; i.e., for outfits at the time of sailing, they had been compelled to add to them in order to supply themselves with necessary clothing . . . They were disgusted with the occupation and determined at all hazards to leave their vessels.[5]

In 1848, when the luck was better and ships stayed overlong from port to take advantage of it, scurvy, always a menace, reached disastrous proportions. Some seamen died before reaching port, and many were invalided in the Honolulu marine hospital. Neither kind of experience conduced toward numerous ventures.

The smaller decline 1853–1856 seems to have been due in part to the possibility of using Japanese ports, which opened in 1854, but mainly to the comparatively high price of sperm oil, leading to voyages directed toward sperm oil only. Since the sperm oil grounds of the North Pacific (Japan and Yellow Seas) were exhausted, resort was made to other waters.[6]

BACKGROUND OF THE FINAL DECLINE

An inquiry into the causes of the secular decline of whaling beginning in 1859 denies the opinion that (1) competition of petro-

[3] Dispatch of U. S. Commissioner George Brown to the Secretary of State, dated May 4, 1844. National Archives.

[4] Consular reports for the thirties show sperm oil being carried by full whalers almost exclusively. Jones's semiannual report for the second half of 1835, for example, lists 48 sperm oil whalers at Honolulu, and none carrying whale oil. But by the middle fifties, whale oil was being carried nearly exclusively.

[5] Dispatch of U. S. Consul J. Turrill to the Secretary of State, January 25, 1848.

[6] *Pacific Commercial Advertiser,* March 25, 1857.

leum was the definite factor, as often argued. For the only direct effect of petroleum was upon price; and price continued its upward trend until the end of the Civil War. The price levels of 1870–1880, when whaling was a shadow of its former self, were on the average much higher than they had been in the boom decade of 1840–50; and the prices of 1880–1890 were not notice-

CHART 3

Prices of Whale Products, 1804–1880

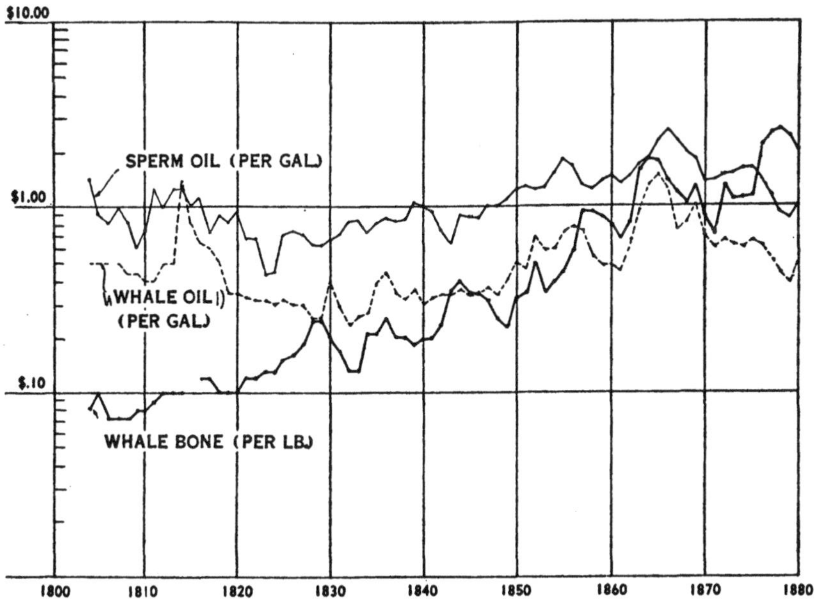

ably lower. The price of bone, free from the depressing effect of petroleum competition, soared to unheard-of heights—$4 and $5 a pound—by the end of the century. Still we may grant a temporary depressing effect from petroleum competition in 1860–1862 when that new industry was ruining its market through "overproduction"; and some pressure on prices after 1865.

(2) The Civil War proved to be a sharp, although temporary, depressant on whaling. A 60 per cent drop in numbers of whale ships afloat occurred between 1860 and 1866. Privateering, mainly of the *Alabama* and *Shenandoah,* resulted in the loss of 50 ships, out of a total of 514 in the industry in 1861. Another 40

were bought by the government and sunk at Charleston Harbor as part of the stone fleet, in the effort to blockade the port. At the end of the War 263 ships were left.

(3) To a real extent the "opportunity cost" of engaging in whaling was increasing for both owners and men. New England, the home of whaling, was becoming industrialized. There was the chance for the ship owners to grow up with growing industry. The opportunity was accepted.

As home industry developed, the disadvantages of whaling—especially its uncertainty—became more impressive by contrast. In few occupations are the returns so capricious: "In 1866 two New Bedford ships each made a profit of $125,000 on a capital of $25,000. On the other hand, of 68 vessels due to arrive in New Bedford and Fairhaven in 1858, 44 made losing voyages, the total loss being $1,000,000." [7] Average catches each season of ships of the North Pacific fleet reported by the *Polynesian*[8] 1852–1858 vary from 1244 to 607 barrels. Consular records of value of cargoes show throughout the whaling period wide and unpredictable fluctuations.[9] Riskiness, as a characteristic of the industry, is correlated with growing scarcity of whales in that the latter led to the taking of more and more risks. The danger of pursuit of the whales close to the permanent Arctic barrier was evidenced in 1871, when 33 ships, the bulk of the fleet, were lost in the ice through staying too late in the fall. The loss of the vessels was felt as a crushing blow in Honolulu, though whaling visits had already declined below the level of the thirties. In 1876 there was further disaster, when 13 more ships were abandoned in the ice.

Returns from the alternative occupation, manufacturing, were far steadier, being removed from the uncontrolled vagaries of wind, weather, and the luck of the hunt. In 1846, the peak of the whaling age, cotton manufacture was begun in New Bedford. Shipping capital flowed into textiles: whaling ships were transformed into cotton mills.

For the men, too, the alternative opportunity was no longer that of continuing on the farm: they too found surer hopes in the expanding industry and commerce of the growing seaboard cities.

[7] J. T. Jenkins, *A History of the Whale Fisheries* (London: 1921), pp. 241–242.

[8] January 1, 1859.

[9] For example, Jones's semiannual report for July 1–December 31, 1835 shows variation of worth of cargo from $10,000 to $67,000.

We have spoken of the paying of advance wages necessary during the fifties. By the middle sixties whalers were forced into the habit of sailing short-handed from the East Coast, picking up additional men from Portuguese Islands in the Atlantic. These "kanakas" were reported less effective whalemen than the older type of crew.[10]

(4) Preëminent among other causes of decline were conditions of increasing cost, due primarily to growing scarcity and shyness of whales. This factor had existed in the industry ever since the early colonists were impelled from utilizing "drift whales" to shore fishing, and from shore fishing to "deep" fishing. It was a basic limitation on the scale of the industry from the beginning.

We have mentioned the increasing length of voyages as one hunting ground after another was exploited. Now, finally, no new ground remained to be found in the world, and in consequence the time required to secure a full cargo increased out of all measure. "Prior to the year 1830 a ship with a capacity of 2000 barrels would cruise in the Pacific Ocean and return in two years with a cargo of sperm oil. The same ship might go to Delago Bay, or Woolwich Bay, and fill with whale oil in about 15 months, or to the coast of Brazil and return in nine months." [11] But the time required for voyages came to be four years for whale oil; and later up to six years were necessary, and still a full cargo was not achieved.[12]

Consequently the outlays for fitting and provisioning were greatly increased: "In 1790 a ship carrying 1900 barrels of oil would be outfitted for a two years' sperm voyage in the Pacific for $12,000; while in 1858, with a doubled capacity, the length of the average voyage had more than doubled, and the cost of outfitting had increased to about $65,000." [13]

The drop in oil prices due to petroleum was merely a *coup de grâce* to an industry which declining returns were already condemning to decay.[14]

[10] *The Friend,* December 1, 1886.

[11] Starbuck, *History of American Whale Fishery* (Waltham, Mass.: 1878), p. 113.

[12] The greatly increased prices for whalebone in the late nineteenth century led to hunting for that alone, oil being reclaimed only wastefully. But the demand for bone was not sufficient to sustain the industry.

[13] Starbuck, *op. cit.,* p. 110.

[14] The New York *Times* commented foreseeingly in 1855: "The time cannot be far distant when the business will have to be abandoned altogether, and some sub-

A special reason for the final decline of the whale trade in *Hawaii* lay in the growing port of San Francisco to the east, no less convenient for the grounds then being hunted, and after the completion of the first transcontinental railway in 1869, the natural shipping point of whale oil to the eastern market.[15]

Honolulu Whalers

The presence of foreign whalers continued [16] to suggest to Honolulu merchants the possibility of themselves carrying on the business. The bark *Honolulu* had made several voyages in the early forties. In 1845 there was effort to start a joint stock whaling company, and the cost of fitting and repairing a whaler that had gone ashore on a reef was investigated. But by 1852 four ships were listed whaling out of Honolulu. No more than one ship was engaged at any one time in the forties. In the 1850's Honolulu whaling came into its own, with up to 19 vessels out during one year (1858). The number of ships out varied irregularly, but not more irregularly than the catches, which fluctuated from about 300 to 1400 barrels of whale oil per ship per year. There was a slow decline in the sixties and seventies in number of ships engaged, reflecting a fairly consistent decline in the average catch of oil, though bone was brought back in larger relative quality. No ships went out after 1880.[17]

---

stance will be discovered that will supersede the use of whale oil. It has already become too dear for the purposes of illumination, and even in Nantucket the inhabitants have had to resort to gas. The whaling business has become so uncertain, requires so large an outlay of capital, and its prosecution is attended by so many hardships and personal dangers, that no persons will ever engage in it who are not driven to it by the stern necessities of life." (October 9.)

[15] In 1870 five ships claimed San Francisco as home port. By the end of the century it has risen to be the second largest port of the languishing industry, sending out over 30 ships at one time.

[16] P. 82.

[17] *Hawaiian Annual* for 1913, pp. 47–50, 63–68.

There had been also several brief ventures in whaling in contiguous Hawaiian waters. In 1847 James Hough was granted permission by the Office of the Interior to pursue whales between Oahu and Maui, casks to be furnished by the Government, and one-thirtieth of the oil taken to be given up to the Government. Hough caught one whale before he was discouraged out by the high cost of the business. In 1854 and 1858 requests were granted for taking whales in Maalea Bay and off the Island of Kahoolawe; but the ventures seem to have been fruitless. (From the Files of the Office of the Interior, 1847, 1854, 1858; in Maud Jones, "Whaling in Hawaiian Waters," *Paradise of the Pacific,* April 1938, p. 20.)

CHART 4

THE COURSE OF HONOLULU WHALING

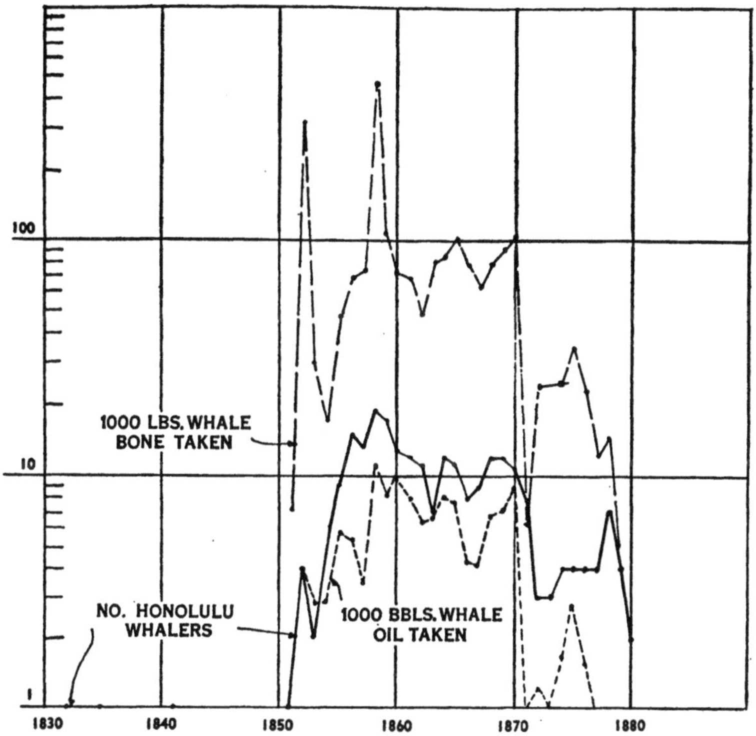

Data: *Hawaiian Annual*, 1913, pp. 63–68.

WHALING CREWS

The influx of thousands of independent-minded seamen during the fall and spring seasons continued to be a problem throughout the whaling trade years. They roamed the streets, and stormed through the town, looking for pleasure and excitement. If we allow 25 to 30 men to a ship, and consider the halcyon days when over a hundred ships lay in port, we arrive at an estimate of 2500 or 3000 men at one time in the small town of Honolulu and the village of Lahaina. They were sufficiently numerous and disposed to follow a common interest to burn down the Honolulu jail in 1852 (one of their number had been killed when unruly in jail) and to hold possession of the city for over a day.

Desertions were numerous, especially during poor seasons when little was due the men.[18] During the year 1845 when catches were small, 279 seamen are listed as deserters at Honolulu and Lahaina—between 2 and 3 per cent of the total in service in the industry. In that year 830 men, 6 to 8 per cent, managed to procure their discharge at Lahaina alone.[19] As time went on, and short-handed sailing from New England became common, the turnover at Hawaii was larger. Ten years later, the United States Consul thought that of the 8000 to 10,000 men then engaged in Pacific whaling, half were discharged and reshipped from Hawaii.[20]

A small fee and a bond was for a time required by the Hawaiian government in attempt to keep down the number of seamen discharged, but the charge was by no means always paid.

Native Hawaiians were shipped in relatively large numbers as whalers came to rely more on the Honolulu labor market for their men. No adequate figures are available, but in 1845 it appears that over 5 per cent of men in north Pacific whaling were Hawaiians.[21]

[18] They were paid on a "lay," that is a proportion of the total value of the catch, due when the voyage was completed.

[19] *Polynesian*, April 4, 1846, p. 196.

[20] Dispatches from Consul D. A. Odgen for 1855, National Archives.

The consuls compelled the masters to pay discharged men their share of the lay, or in earlier days three months' advance pay in accord with the United States Law of February 28, 1803. The masters objected (but without avail), arguing the men were by the articles to be paid only when voyages were complete. (Dispatches of John C. Jones to the Secretary of State, February 8, 1834; William Hooper to the Secretary of State, July 2, 1844, National Archives.)

Sick and destitute seamen were cared for by the consulate. Such expenses increased greatly as the trade grew in the forties, from an annual charge of $5690 in 1840 to $44,212 in 1846. (Dispatch of Consul J. Turrill, January 25, 1838.) But later disclosures indicate graft as one element in the increased expense. Masters were compelled to transport to the eastern seaboard derelict and disabled seamen, on request of the Consul. Payment of $10 was allowed, not suffieient as an inducement; and sometimes masters homeward bound avoided Honolulu for fear of having derelict seamen forced upon them. (Dispatch of William Hooper, October 10, 1842.)

[21] An estimate by the *Polynesian* (April 4, 1846) held that 700 natives were shipped during the seasons of 1845. It is unlikely that there were much over 10,000 men in the trade, 542 whaling ship arrivals being listed in the Islands for that year (p. 418).

In 1859 a law provided that permission of the governor of an island or his agent had to be secured before shipping any native, under penalty of $500 fine. Masters had to pay $2 if the native was shipped for less than 12 months, $4 if for over 12 months. (*Session Laws of 1859*, pp. 35–36.)

The effect of association with the seamen was not so deleterious as in earlier days. The natives were better adjusted to haole ways; and the larger body of reputable haole residents in some measure gave their own views and moral tone to the community.[22]

Agricultural and Commercial Effects of Whaling

During this period there were two factors tending to make a given number of visits more significant in absolute amount of induced economic activity. One was the growing length of voyages as whales became increasingly scarce and more time was required to procure a full cargo. A much greater proportion of fittings, repairs, and provisions had to be obtained away from the home port when the voyages were four or five years long than when they were two. Hence each individual visit tended to result in a greater volume of trade.

The second was growth of transshipping, a form of specialization of function indicating improved organization of the industry. Fast freight ships, often clippers, transported oil and bone round the Horn to the East Coast;[23] and the slower whalers went back to the hunt. Apparently this was done occasionally in the late forties; and was a settled routine by 1851 when a million gallons of sperm and whale oil were transshipped. The maximum volume of transshipping ever attained was realized only two years later, in 1853, when nearly four million gallons of oil are listed. Transshipping resisted the decline of whaling after 1859, over 1.8 million gallons being carried as late as 1869.[24] The practice brought ships to Honolulu more often, with a tendency toward sustained demand for provisions and fittings. And opportunity was offered for supplementary export of minor Island products, such as hides

[22] There are reported to have been 1572 non-Hawaiian residents in 1850, 2816 in 1860, 10,477 in 1878. (Romanzo Adams, *Interracial Marriage in Hawaii* (New York: 1937), p. 8.)

[23] The most valuable shiploads of whale products so transported were worth several hundred thousand dollars. The clipper *John Land* sailed in 1857 with a cargo, mostly whalebone, valued at $636,000. (*Pacific Commercial Advertiser*, November 5, 1857.)

[24] The opening of the Panama Railroad in 1855 furnished the possibility of an additional combination. The Railroad organized a regular semimonthly service of cargo ships from its eastern terminal; and in 1858 was advertising at Honolulu its facilities for through shipment of oil to New York. (*The Friend*, January 1858.)

The opening of the first transcontinental railway in 1869 offered another route; but the industry was then in advanced decline.

and goatskins,[25] which would not have justified transport in their own right.

An index of the importance of the whaling trade to agriculture is given by a comparison of "domestic produce exported" with estimates of "domestic produce supplied to ships." [26] Produce

CHART 5

DOMESTIC PRODUCE SUPPLIED TO SHIPS,
COMPARED TO DOMESTIC PRODUCE EXPORTED

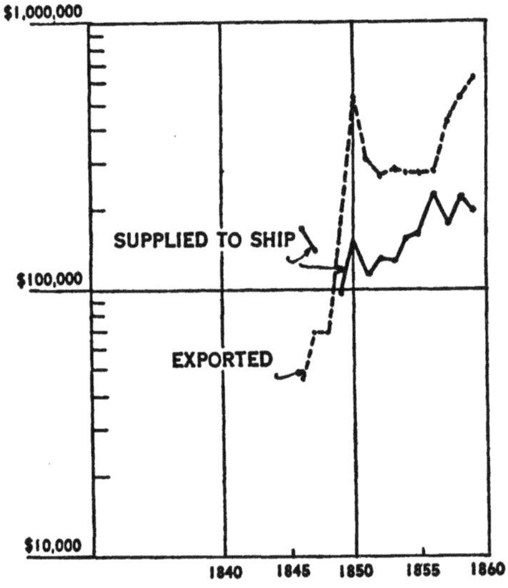

Data: Appendix III, see notes following Columns (6) and (12).

sold to ships went in substantial proportion to merchant ships as well as whalers; but the error does not seem disastrous when we

[25] Josephine Sullivan, *History of C. Brewer & Co.* (Boston: 1926), p. 26.

[26] Chart 5. These series are begun with 1846 because of lack of any creditable data from preceding years. Figures are available back to 1836, but there are omissions and cause for doubt in poor correspondence with numbers of visits of ships. (Tables in the *Polynesian*, September 12, 1840; September 4, 1841; January 18, 1845; March 7, 1846. The series given are from Customs Reports printed in the *Polynesian*, January 30, 1847 (corrected for a misprint by comparison with table of R. S. Kuykendall, *The Hawaiian Kingdom, 1778–1854*, p. 305); January 19, 1850; February 1, 1851; February 7, 1852; January 29, 1853; February 4, 1854; February 17, 1855; February 16, 1856; January 31, 1857; January 23, 1858; January 22, 1859; January 28, 1860. The series ends with the 1859 report. Figures for domestic produce exported are from *Report of the Minister of Finance* (1862), Table C, Archives of Hawaii.

consider that commercial visits were in large part derivative from the whaling trade. A like qualification is required for the series "domestic produce exported": domestic exports were not independent of the whaling trade.[27] Both errors lead to the biasing upward—from the point of view of our interest in them—of both series; and hence our qualms at a comparison between them are somewhat lessened.

The 1846 and 1847 values indicate the chief dependence of Island agriculture on the whalers for an external market, two or three times as much being sold to the whalers as was exported. (The period 1849–1851 is a non-homogeneous section of the whole series, for during the Gold Rush there was a temporary but violent demand for foodstuffs from California.) Through the fifties the shipping trade was in money value of about half the importance of the export market; and already by 1858 had begun its abrupt decline to insignificance.

The whalers demanded general garden produce, fruit, and meat; and so gave the last continued stimulus to diversified agriculture.[28] Beef, sweet and Irish potatoes, and firewood were brought to the ships in the largest money volume; but many other products were sold, among which fowls, turkeys, hogs, pumpkins, melons, onions, yams, coconuts, limes, oranges, bananas, pineapple, molasses, and sugar were the most valuable. The temperate-zone produce among these, which grew meagerly in the low warm plains and valleys, was cultivated on the slopes of several of the mountains. The flanks of Haleakala thrived with temperate crops.

Farming organization was not stabilized: the kuleana of the native produced for the market in competition with larger farms and plantations of the nobility and the foreigner. A plantation type of organization became dominant only with the rise of sugar.

The whaling trade was dominantly important to the merchants. During the two seasons when whalers were in port, "business was brisk and profitable, though as fickle and haphazard as the search for whales." [29] In 1847 and 1848 the uncertain nature of the business was emphasized when fewer whalers appeared than had

[27] P. 81.

[28] The demand from California gave such incentive, but was spent in hardly more than the three years 1849–1851. See Chapter X below.

[29] Josephine Sullivan, *History of C. Brewer & Co.*, p. 96.

been anticipated, and unsold stock overlay the market. The United States Consul thought in 1857 that "whalers are in fact the life of business here, and without them it would not be worth the attention of any three of the principal business foreigners of the Islands" [30]—so echoing the judgment of Wyllie in 1844.

Honolulu had originally been the favored port, but during the middle of the whaling period 1840–1855 Lahaina often surpassed it in number of recorded visits. Honolulu had the advantages of being a safer harbor, and more convenient for repairs.[31] Lahaina was an open roadstead and exposed to blows from the south; but charges there were lower.[32] Hilo was the third most frequented port, and visits were occasionally made to a few others. United States consulates were set up at Lahaina in 1850 and at Hilo in 1853.

Visits of whalers were favored through the privilege of free import by them of up to $200 of goods;[33] and later through specially low charges for imports of up to $1200 in value. Nevertheless frequent complaints came from the whalers as to the inordinate costs of refitting at Honolulu.[34]

Hawaii's orientation toward the whaling trade was unsatisfactory because whaling was not dependable—not because, as was sometimes argued, whaling failed to develop Island resources, for it did furnish a substantial impulse toward diversified agriculture, deficient in volume only when compared with the eventual sugar industry. When the whaling fleet left the Islands following 1859 the effect on prices and business activity was drastic. The missionary J. S. Emerson portrays those saddened days:

> All our means to help out our family support are suddenly cut off, as the whaling fleet has left the Islands. Beef which sold for $18 or $25 per head two years ago cannot now be sold for $10; within a few days Mr. Chamberlain

[30] Dispatch of Consul Anson Chandler to the Secretary of State, dated June 30, 1857. National Archives.

[31] Honolulu papers commented unenthusiastically on the qualifications of their competitor, San Francisco, as a whaling resort. (*Pacific Commercial Advertiser,* October 9, 1856; *Polynesian,* October 30, 1852.)

[32] They were estimated in 1846 by the Collector of Customs to be less than one-third of those at Honolulu, for an average whaler $16 as against $52. (William Patty in the *Polynesian,* December 31, 1846.)

[33] *Laws of 1842,* p. 183.

[34] See Starbuck, *History of American Whale Industry,* p. 112. The *Polynesian* argued that Honolulu charges were much below those of San Francisco; in one actual case, only one-seventh. (October 30, 1852, p. 98.)

has sold his whole herd of good cattle at $3.50 per head, and he threw in the calves. Samuel has slaughtered many of his poorer cattle mainly for the hides, and horses cannot be given away unless they are pretty good; at present there is almost no money in the land. So we are driven into close quarters . . . Mrs. Emerson has lost the twenty pounds of flesh she gained and usually is busy eighteen hours out of the twenty-four.[35]

In 1862, the scarcity of whalers appearing permanent, several of the business houses closed up and left the Islands; and with cattle and staple products comparatively worthless, a large part of agriculture was in an uncertain state of transition. Experiments were made toward raising sheep, and toward expansion of rice production. But with the passing of whaling went the last effective impulse toward general farming. The end of the whaling trade diverted attention and resources to sugar, in which technical progress and politics were to prove there lay greater advantage.

[35] Letter quoted in O. P. Emerson, *Pioneer Days in Hawaii* (New York: 1928), p. 206.

CHAPTER X

THE CALIFORNIA GOLD RUSH

THE FLOCKING of multitudes to the gold claims of California brought a brief but spectacular boom to merchandising and agriculture in Hawaii. Demand was bunched into a three-year interval, from the fall of 1848 through part of 1851, though it continued at a higher level after 1851 than it had been before 1849.

The timing was opportune: new demand took up the gap left by a contraction of whaling visits to their lowest level until 1861, when final decline was well under way. Trade had been in the doldrums for several months, the market glutted with imported merchandise—English, American, and Chinese—waiting for whalers that did not arrive. "Suddenly all the merchants were deeply engaged in the transshipment of goods to San Francisco. Clothing, shovels, pickaxes, flour, bread, boots, shoes, and such articles as were suitable for a mining population were in demand." [1] Stocks of such goods were completely exhausted by the surge of demand which reached the Islands in late 1848.

A still larger impression was made on agriculture. Diversified production of staple foods was stimulated as it had not been before, and was not to be again. The effect was portrayed in April 1850, at a meeting of the newly formed Agricultural Society:

> Our coffee and sugar no longer remain piled in our warehouses. Our fruits and vegetables no longer decay in the spot where they were grown. We are not even compelled to seek for them a market, but clamorous purchasers come to our very doors and carry off our supplies with an eagerness that has caused us to feel a scarcity ourselves, and we are assured for not only all these, but for any other products of the soil that we will raise, a steady and increasing demand that may be relied on from our enterprising neighbors.[2]

The hopes for continuity of demand were badly founded; but the temporary stimulus was tremendous. Visits by merchant ships give one index. Numbers rose abruptly, from 90 in 1848,

[1] Josephine Sullivan, *History of C. Brewer & Co.*, p. 96.
[2] *Royal Hawaiian Agricultural Society Transactions*, vol. 1, no. 1.

to 180 in 1849, 469 in 1850, and 446 in 1851. In the three following years, with diminution of demand, the numbers were 235, 211, 125.[3] The volume of visits for 1850 and 1851 was not surpassed until half a century afterward. (Chart 1, p. 79.) The price differential back of this activity was often extravagantly wide: in 1849, before trade relationships and supply had opportunity to adjust themselves to new conditions, Irish potatoes sold for $27 a barrel in San Francisco, for $2 in Hawaii. Price fluctuations were extreme in San Francisco, in accord with changing fortunes on the gold claims, and the changing volume of supply contracted for and of speculative imports. In Hawaii prices rose and fluctuated likewise, but in lesser degree.[4]

The response of agricultural production can be in part traced through the period of inflation.

EXPORTS OF SELECTED AGRICULTURAL PRODUCTS*

	1848	1849	1850	1851	1852	1853	1854
Irish Potatoes, bbls.	F	0.9M	52.0M	43.9M	8.2M	15.5M	7.6M
Sweet Potatoes, bbls.	F	0.3M	9.6M	56.7M	6.1M	9.0M	3.8M
Onions, bbls.	NSI	NSI	0.3M^{P}	1.2M	F	F	F
Pumpkins	NSI	NSI	4.7M^{P}	13.6M	29.2M	20.9M	3.5M
Oranges	NSI	NSI	118.0M^{P}	F	15.0M	124.0M	13.0M
Sugar, tons	0.3M	0.3M	0.4M	F	0.4M	0.3M	0.3M
Molasses, gal.	29.0M	41.0M	129.0M	44.0M	62.0M	76.0M	68.0M
Fowls	F	F	0.5M^{P}	5.0M	4.5M	2.0M	2.0M
Turkeys	F	0.5M	0.2M^{P}	0.8M	1.5M	0.6M	1.7M
Coffee, lbs.	58.0M	28.0M	194.0M	27.0M	117.0M	50.0M	90.0M
Tallow, lbs.	F	F	3.7M	4.6M	5.3M	16.5M	15.4M

* Explanation of Symbols: F, few or none; NSI, not separately itemized; M, thousand; ^{P}, partial figure.

Other products exported were swine, cattle, mules, hay, bananas, pineapples, yams, lumber, dried pork, fish, barreled beef, coconuts, eggs, melons, flour.

Sources: *Polynesian*, January 20, 1849; January 19, 1850; February 1, 1851; February 7, 1852; January 29, 1853; February 4, 1854; February 17, 1855.

Some of these exports went elsewhere than to California; but the shifts of demand there are the only important influence.

[3] The Honolulu market was unusually dull from mid-1851 to mid-1852. The desire of merchants to obtain funds to discharge merchandise debt which they had unwisely incurred led to a pronounced shift in rates for foreign exchange. That on eastern United States was about par, instead of the usual 15–20 per cent premium. (R. C. Wyllie to Minister of Foreign Affairs of Denmark. MS. letter of July 17, 1852. Archives of Hawaii.)

[4] William Shaw, visiting the Islands in 1850, notes the distress of people who, like the missionaries, lived on a fixed income. (*Golden Dreams and Waking Realities* (London: 1851), p. 253.)

Despite faulty data the table illustrates the diversity of influence on agriculture of what has been looked on as an unqualified stimulus. Tallow, an export complementary to the whaling demand for beef, was depressed compared to earlier and later volume. Coffee pursued its irregular course, reflecting mainly difficulties of production.[5] Produce whose supply could not be immediately increased (fowls and turkeys) responded with a lag. The variance of sugar and molasses will be commented on later.[6] In a few products, above all Irish and sweet potatoes, supply mushroomed extravagantly.

The center of potato production was the Kula section of the slopes of Haleakala Volcano on Maui, a stretch of fertile land 12 miles long on the side of the mountain between 2000 and 5000 feet of elevation. The riches hoped from potato production there led the natives to call it "Nu Kalifonia": government land was sold in small sections to the natives at $3 an acre; and strangers hopefully came there from Wailuku, Lahaina, and Hamakua to try their hand.[7] Potatoes were also grown elsewhere in the Islands, but in smaller volume.

With worsened prices and drought, there was a slight drop in potato exports in 1851, though export of other crops generally increased (especially sweet potatoes, which came into a high peak). With the fall of 1851 the boom was over: competition from the Oregon country (especially in potatoes) pushed Hawaii out of the market. In addition California was beginning to grow some foodstuffs itself.[8] Even so, the volume of general agricultural exports had been raised to a consistently higher level. In certain lines exports continued in fair volume: over 2000 barrels of sweet potatoes were sent out in 1855, and nearly 2000 as late as 1859.[9] The cattle industry diverted 25 tons of fresh and salt beef to export in 1853, and was still exporting nearly as much in

[5] Pp. 161–164.

[6] Pp. 177–179.

[7] *Polynesian,* November 24, 1849 (letter of "Rusticus") and January 5, 1850, quoted in Kuykendall, *The Hawaiian Kingdom,* p. 321.

[8] The effect of the competition is illustrated by a typical price situation faced by Island growers by the middle of the fifties: "The new crop of Koloa potatoes are ready for market, but the low prices in San Francisco must prevent any shipments at present. Sweet potatoes are dull, at 2¢ to 2½¢ per pound . . . The Molokai and Niihau potatoes recently shipped over have proved a failure (through spoiling). (*Polynesian,* February 16, 1856.)

[9] *Polynesian,* February 16, 1856; January 28, 1860.

1860. The volume of these and other goods varied greatly from year to year, with the season, and with California prices.

The export of 453 barrels of flour in 1855, and some wheat, flour, and bread thereafter were indirect results of California demand, and testimony to one more experiment in agricultural production. The eclipse of potato demand led to hopes being turned to wheat growing, especially on Maui where a little wheat had been raised before 1840. Export of flour in 1855 reflects the completion of a flour mill in Honolulu to process the new Island crop. By 1857 wheat growing seemed an assured industry to J. F. B. Marshall of the Agricultural Society: "A nobler culture could not have been undertaken. All honor to the brave pioneers who have carried forward this most praise-worthy enterprise to success."

But already nemesis was in plain view in comparative flour prices at San Francisco and Honolulu. In March 1857 sales were made in San Francisco at $11 and $13 a barrel, and about the same time in Honolulu at $17. Hawaii could not compete with a stable wheat-growing industry on the mainland, and certainly could not compete in view of the "mining" of the land for wheat production then beginning in California. However, a small volume of wheat was exported for several years.

We have not mentioned one other effect of the Gold Rush, the exodus of labor and incursion of prospectors. The "California fever" struck Hawaii no less than the East Coast. Haoles, especially skilled laborers, left in quantity; and the wages of the remainder rose abruptly toward $10 a day as going wages for craftsmen. Kanakas also left in numbers for California, and penetrated into the mining region of southern Oregon in remembered numbers.[10] Sometimes plantations were hard hit by the disappearance of their working force, not recovering for several years.[11] And during the winters of 1850 and of several following years,

[10] G. V. Blue, "Early Relations Between Hawaii and the Northwest Coast," *Hawaiian Historical Society Reports*, 33, p. 20. For report of Hawaiians earlier on the Coast, see *Bulletin of U. S. Ethnology*, no. 39, 1910; R. C. Wyllie in *The Friend*, September 4, 1844, p. 79.

[11] Pp. 326–7, 355. An owner of a Hanalei, Kauai plantation wrote in 1853: "A couple of years must elapse before (our plantation) re-attains the prosperous state it was in in 1849 and 1850 when all our natives left us, smitten with the California fever." Royal Hawaiian Agricultural Society *Transactions* (1853), p. 50.

there was a reverse migration of gold seekers to Honolulu, often pale, worn-out and sick men, to spend the several pounds of gold they might have collected, or attempt to regain their health. There were gambling and revelry by night, and expensive goods in shop windows to tempt away their dust. Prices of certain commodities increased considerably during the term of their visits. Board and room rose from $3 to a height of $20 a week.[12]

[12] William Shaw, *Golden Dreams and Waking Realities*, pp. 250–251, 253.

CHAPTER XI

MINOR INDUSTRIES

Cotton

From 1812 until after the Civil War there was persistent and repeated hope as to the possibilities of cotton growing. In 1812 Captains Winship and Davis must have considered cotton a promising product, else they would not have sought a monopoly of its export. Some cotton is reported exported about 1817 and in 1823, and it was being grown by the natives in the middle twenties; but lack of an effective machine for cleaning it from the seed, and heavy rains in 1827, stopped cultivation for a time.[1]

The missionaries, with memories of New England home spinning and knitting, had high hopes for home manufacture of cotton. In 1835 a teacher brought by the mission from Boston for the purpose began teaching a class at Wailuku, Maui, to card, spin, knit, and finally weave, introducing the domestic wheel and loom to the Hawaiians. In five months the class wove 90 yards of stout cloth. On the same Island a haole, Charles Smith, was encouraged to begin a cotton plantation. The native governor Kuakini in 1837 built at Kailua a stone factory for weaving cloth. It was functioning in 1838 with two hand-operated looms and most of its twenty spindles.[2] But the native workmen were dissatisfied, and interest in cotton soon flagged. Imported cotton goods were superior in quality and cheaper in price.

Some little cotton continued to be grown in an experimental fashion.[3] The Sea Island (long staple) variety was being grown in the middle fifties, rising to a luxuriant height of twenty feet.[4]

[1] Letter of Richard Charlton, British Consul, to Captain Waldyman, dated August 8, 1830. Archives of Hawaii.

[2] *Sandwich Islands Gazette*, September 15, 1838; *Pacific Commercial Advertiser*, April 30, 1857.

[3] A cotton gin was imported in 1841 of capacity 400 pounds of cotton daily. *Polynesian*, July 1841.

[4] Sea Island Cotton preferred for fineness and length of fiber was grown almost exclusively in Hawaii during the Civil War; but since then three medium or short staple varieties have been tried: the southern upland, Egyptian, and Caramonica. F. G. Krause, "Cotton Culture in Hawaii," *Hawaiian Annual* (1911), pp. 58–67.

The exceptional yield of 1000 pounds per acre was reported.[5] Hawaii had certain advantages over southern United States in cotton growing: cotton could be picked ten months out of twelve, and need be planted only once in five years, where in the South there was a brief picking season, and annual planting. The editor of the *Advertiser* in 1857 concluded that the only difficulty was lack of capital and experience, and that soil and climate were uniquely advantageous to its growth, though the harvested cotton should be exported and no attempt again be made to manufacture it into cloth.[6] The Agricultural Society was underwriting experimentation in cotton growing three years later.[7]

The boom in cotton came during the Civil War, when price rose astronomically as exports of the South were cut off, though the necessary lag in expansion of production blocked taking full advantage of the price rise. There was no organized or scientific treatment of production problems; but individuals expanded output wonderfully under the price stimulus. Some 600 pounds were exported in 1862;[8] and in 1863 (the first year when it is itemized in Customs House tables) 3122 pounds were sent out. The quantity declined a little in 1864, then rose rapidly to its maximum in 1866 of 22,289 pounds. From then on export dropped steadily, to 2355 pounds in 1874, and none in 1875.[9]

The competition of the reviving southern production and the increasing "opportunity cost" of not growing sugar were too much for the cotton grower. Cotton shrank to its present status of submarginal industry; potential, but impracticable unless there should be a drastic change in relative prices.

[5] E. A. Oudinot, in Royal Hawaiian Agricultural Society *Transactions*, 1856, p. 104.

[6] April 30, 1857.

[7] The Royal Hawaiian Agricultural Society, from whose *Transactions* we have often quoted, was founded in 1850. It was chiefly active during its first five or six years. The booming whale trade was a constant obstacle against interest in permanent agricultural development.

[8] *Pacific Commercial Advertiser*, October 2, 1862.

[9] The government tried to encourage cotton and woolen manufacture by a law of 1870 remitting duties on machinery and building materials for textile mills; also by promising a bounty when a given quantity of manufacture should be completed, and other advantages. (*Session Laws of 1870*, p. 34.)

A survey of production possibilities in 1871 was highly optimistic—even with the final collapse in progress. (*Pacific Commercial Advertiser*, February 25, 1871.)

COFFEE

Coffee cultivation is another industry for which from time to time high hopes have been held. But the industry has limped along uncertainly in the face of continued adversity. The two main limitations on its expansion have been high labor and other costs, and bad seasons and disease. The chart of export volume (page 163) portrays not only the violent fluctuations due to the latter—increases of five times and decreases to one-eighth being not atypical—but also the decisive pressure toward contraction brought by the great expansion of the sugar industry following Reciprocity (1876). The expanding sugar industry raised land rents and wage rates, and also offered hope of greater profits.[10]

Coffee was first planted in 1817 by the Spaniard Don Paulo Marin in his garden in Honolulu. Eight years later John Wilkinson planted coffee trees along with cane in Manoa Valley. He was a young agricultural scientist brought over from England by Governor Boki for the specific purpose of getting sugar and cane production under way. The seeds, brought in with Wilkinson on the *Blonde*, were obtained at Rio de Janeiro.[11] Other seeds were imported by Richard Charlton, the British Consul, from Manila, and planted about the same time in Manoa. There was possibly still another introduction from Manila, or Batavia. The Manoa plantings grew well, but were not cared for: natives came in and picked a few pounds of coffee at a time.

Slips from Manoa were set out in several other places, notably about 1828 or 1829 in Kona, Hawaii. They were carried there by the missionary teacher Samuel Ruggles, and "grew and produced largely." Natives cultivated the plants crudely and on a small scale, without concern for technical niceties of planting, cultivating, pruning, and hulling. The irregular and rich slopes of Kona, with their moderate rainfall and temperature, have ever since been identified with coffee growing.

Large-scale systematic growing was begun from 1835 to about 1845 in Kauai, where four plantations were devoted to its growth. The Ladd Plantation at Koloa, which we remember chiefly as the first ultimately successful sugar plantation, had 5000 coffee trees growing by 1836. Much larger were the two plantations at

[10] Pp. 179–181.
[11] *Hawaiian Annual* (1876), p. 46.

Kanalei, those of Bernard and Rhodes, and Charles Titcomb. Here 100,000 trees were growing by mid-1844,[12] and a year later the area under cultivation was expanded to take up nearly the whole valley. The fourth was begun at Wailuku, but was soon abandoned. On other Islands, Oahu, Maui, and Hawaii (at Hilo and Kona), there were also plantations begun in the forties, but of smaller scale than those at Hanalei.[13]

The prospects must have seemed bright to have induced the rapid spread of cultivation through the Islands. But there were many troubles to face. Those encountered at Hanalei are representative. Labor was a principal one; natives were "pretty independent";[14] and chiefs were still not always coöperative. In May 1847 when the plantations were getting hopefully under way, a two weeks' heavy rain flooded the trees, and loosened a landslide of trees, rocks, and earth which crushed several hundred trees. The flight of labor to California during the gold fever made men harder to get and more expensive for several years after 1848. There are some hints of lack of coöperation from missionaries. The drought of 1851, extending through the Islands generally, was catastrophic in its effect, cutting exports to one-eighth of their value during 1850. The blight (due to a species of aphis, or plant louse) appearing shortly afterward was a final blow on some plantations; and persisted as a severe drag on the whole industry. The *Advertiser* reported in 1858 one plantation on which there would as a result of the blight be hardly enough berries to pay for the cleaning;[15] and Charles Hall, who had a large plantation at Kona, testified sadly that his crop of 18,000 pounds in 1858 (when the blight had not yet reached him) was reduced in successive years to 12,000, and 5000, until in 1861 he actually had to buy coffee for his own use.

These large plantations were as atypical of coffee (and still are), as they are typical of sugar. Cultivation was usually on a

[12] Dispatch of U. S. Commissioner George Brown to the Secretary of State, July 1, 1844. National Archives.

[13] Wyllie wrote in 1846 that there were eight plantations; two large ones on Kauai, three small ones on Kauai, two on Maui, and one on Hawaii. (R. C. Wyllie's *Answers to Questions put by Mr. Dudoit, Consul of France,* dated April 22, 1846.) In 1847 he presented the bright prospects of high returns from coffee as one reason for establishing alodial land tenure. (*Reports of the Minister of Foreign Affairs,* 1853–1862, p. 62.)

[14] Dispatch of U. S. Commissioner George Brown cited above.

[15] *The Pacific Commercial Advertiser,* October 14, 1858.

small scale. Especially after the rise of sugar, coffee growing was able to survive only on the basis of use of home labor, removed by immobilities of location, training, and habit from the competition of the cane fields. Coffee culture was predominantly by natives, with either seed or slips planted in localities that trial had

CHART 6

COFFEE EXPORTS

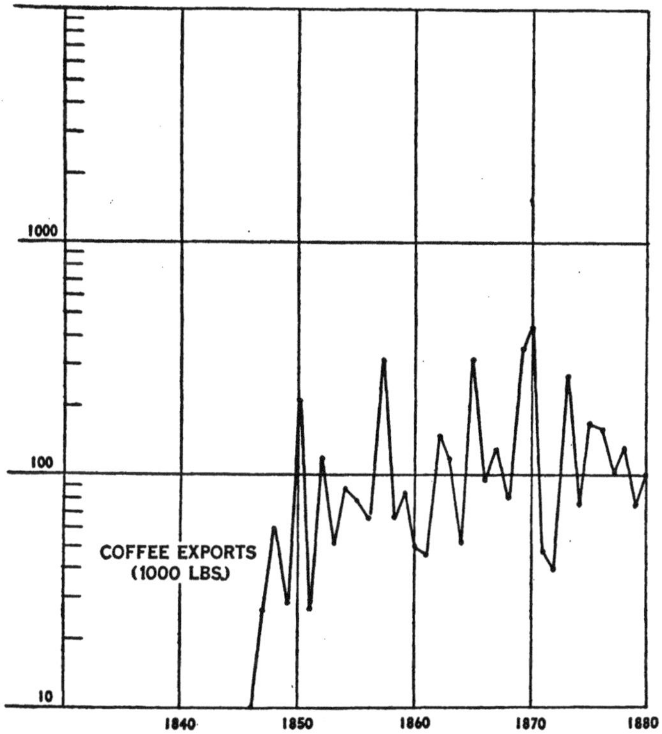

Data: Appendix III, Column (9).

shown favorable, and left to mature without attention until it was time to pick the berries. The husk was cleaned off by primitive methods; and consequently had not the clean appearance requisite for good prices on the market. And sometimes there was objection to the flavor of Hawaiian-grown coffee.

The determinant nature of alternative opportunity in sugar is shown in the decline of coffee exports in the 1880's to their lowest level since exports were first listed in 1845.[16] Coffee has continued since as a minor Hawaiian industry, sometimes advocated as the potential basis of a farming community of small, independent producers,[17] to offset the socially questionable plantation system of sugar. Often it has been the source of worry as a sick industry, with blight, low prices, mortgages, and foreclosure dogging the weary steps of the Japanese and Hawaiian grower in Kona.

RICE

Rice cultivation got under way as a significant enterprise only with the collapse of whaling. Unemployed agricultural resources sought another productive use, and many of them found it in rice. There were in Hawaii many areas especially suited to rice growing: swampy lands near the sea, and taro patches—some in use and some deserted—which with their existing banks and irrigation channels could be quickly made ready for rice growing.

Rice had been cultivated before. At least as far back as 1838 some rice was grown on Oahu, and the *Sandwich Islands Gazette,* always enthusiastic about new developments, welcomed the dawning prospects of bountiful rice fields.[18] But for twenty years little was done. The general obstacles to all production during that time are sufficient explanation: insecure terms on which land could be held, absence of markets, and the short term interest of the early foreign residents.[19]

Cultivation on any scale awaited experimental plantings of the Agricultural Society up Nuuanu Valley in 1858, with seed paddy[20] procured from the East Indies. But the season was unfavorable. Since rice mills and polishers were unknown at that time,

[16] Home consumption must be added to these figure to obtain total production. This amounted in the early 1870's to about 200,000 pounds. Since home consumption was relatively steady, its addition would not affect appreciably the validity of comparisons among export data for years not too far apart.

These exports went primarily to the Pacific ports of the United States during the final years of our period, 1860–1876. Generally Atlantic ports of the United States took second place, sometimes British Columbia. Germany is the only other market worth noting. (*Hawaiian Annual,* 1876, p. 52.)

[17] Department of Foreign Affairs booklet, *Coffee, the Coming Staple Product* (Honolulu: 1896). Here coffee is advertised as the ideal field for immigrants with small capital.

[18] November 3, 1838.

[19] P. 98; also *Hawaiian Annual* (1877), pp. 45–46.

[20] Unhulled rice.

the crop was taken to the then existing flour mill, and hulled between the mill stones. "The unpolished rice, small in grain, was so dark and looked so unmarketable an article that the press took little interest in the introduction of rice culture." [21] And the whaling trade was still booming at this time.

The experiment was repeated in 1860 with seed paddy from Charleston, South Carolina. Though the immediate crop after a stormy and cold season was poor, a replant of four pounds from its product by Dr. S. P. Ford in a taro patch near his home grew to a prodigious harvest of 1163 pounds. Less than a quarter acre had been planted: the yield was at the rate of 7260 pounds per acre.

The whaling fleet had vanished; interest in the new crop grew intense. There ensued a speculative fever that compares with stock market booms and the Holland tulip fever. Rice cultivation spread like an epidemic. Since taro patches which could be flooded were peculiarly adapted to rice growing, they were made use of generally as rice paddies. Many people—among them a Judge Montgomery who distinguished himself by his total loss of judicial calm—pulled up growing taro to replant with rice. A taro famine resulted; and since taro remained the mainstay of native diet, not easily substituted for by other foods, its price rose astronomically until it "was worth nearly its weight in money." The natives suffered. During the next year, with many people repenting of their first year's excitement, and finding returns from rice disappointing and taro dear, there was a shift back to taro production. Taro became cheap, and rice again offered the best return.[22]

Chinese rice farmers were beginning to produce at this time. The first Chinese contract laborers, released from their plantation obligations in 1857, were free to continue plantation work, or find what employment they could elsewhere. Some had formerly been rice farmers in southeastern China near Hong Kong, and congenially started growing rice in taro patches and swampy lands near the sea not suited to cane. By 1860 there were 700 free and contract labor Chinese in the Islands; by 1866, 1200.[23]

[21] *Hawaiian Annual* (1877), p. 46.

[22] *Hawaiian Annual* (1877), pp. 47–78.

[23] James Chun, in *Honolulu Star Bulletin*, March 4, 1929; Coulter and Chun, *Chinese Rice Farmers in Hawaii*, p. 9.

The home market was correspondingly expanded by the taste of the Chinese for rice. In 1867 about a million pounds of rice was consumed in the Islands. There was being exported at the same time, mostly to California, a little more than a million pounds of rice and paddy combined. California consumption is

CHART 7

RICE AND PADDY EXPORTS

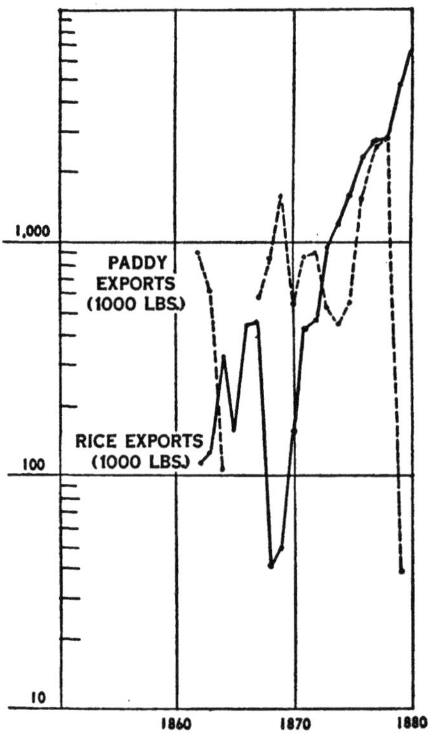

Data: Appendix III, Columns (10) and (11).

explained partly by the rising tide of Chinese workers there (in 1860 there were 35,000; in 1880, over 75,000);[24] and partly by the disaster of the Civil War to southern rice production (187 million pounds being produced in the South in 1860, only 74 million pounds in 1869).[24]

The Chinese continued to supplant Hawaiian and haole culti-

[24] Coulter and Chun, *op. cit.*, p. 14.

vators, and output of rice expanded fairly steadily after 1862. There were three groups of producers: (1) Small independent farmers, whose families helped in the cultivation. They were financed from their own savings, by private borrowing from friends and relatives; and—a considerable proportion—by borrowing from local grocery stores, often without any written token of debt. (2) These farmers were outnumbered in the early years by huis, groups of eight to fifty men organized together under leadership of a promoter.[25] (3) Finally, there were a few large Chinese companies. Leong Pak On was the largest Kauai grower; Ho Yee controlled production at Pearl City and Waimanalo;[26] and Sing Chong[27] produced half the Oahu output, having 4000 acres under cultivation.

The problem of labor supply was important for large-scale producers at the seasons of planting and harvesting. The labor market at Honolulu supplied that Island, and sometimes in part Kauai and Hawaii, though there were local markets on each island. The rate of pay in the middle seventies is reported at about $12 a month and bed and board,[28] paralleling sugar plantation wages, and an extraordinary increase from the level of a few years before.[29]

The major part of the production was on Oahu (with two-thirds of output) and Kauai. A small additional amount was grown on Hawaii and Maui. The Chinese took over former taro patches as the industry expanded, though hundreds remained unused for want of reliable irrigation—a continued decline in water flow in the streams was a hindrance of the time. The Chinese expanded the land available in the patches by cutting away the old Hawaiian paths between them until the strip of earth left was narrow and precarious. Swamp lands and salt marshes, of which there were many near the coast unsuited to cane, were converted in quantity to rice fields, notably at Waialua, Oahu

[25] Pp. 137–138.

[26] His name became so identified with high quality that it is used now as a brand name.

[27] The company was founded in 1868 as a partnership. It became agent (factor) for other producers as well, and through its dominant size considerably influenced the price of rice for many years. (James Chun, "Cultivation of Rice," *Honolulu Star Bulletin*, March 4, 1929.)

[28] Coulter and Chun, *Chinese Rice Farmers in Hawaii*, p. 16.

[29] P. 107.

and Mana, Kauai.[30] Location of the industry was determined by the presence of the irrigable taro patches and marsh lands.

Two crops were harvested during the year, the first in late June or early July, and the second in October or November. Fertile, well-watered land produced a crop of 2500 to 3000 pounds of paddy an acre, which, selling at 2 cents a pound, represented a gross income of $50 or more.[31]

Due to lack of local hulling and polishing machines, paddy in the first few years had to be shipped to San Francisco, where it was sometimes long delayed before milling, with consequent charges for storage. In 1862 Dr. Ford brought in a small rice mill, and a little later Colonel Prendergast set up an effective polisher.[32] By the early 1880's Hooper and Son were milling on a large scale, about 60,000 bags a year.

The continuation of the rice industry during the rest of the century, with expansion to a maximum in 1887, and not too sharp decline afterward, reflects advantageous use of the skill and habits of the Chinese, and of wet areas and small tracts of land unsuited to cane.

LIVESTOCK

Introduction of cattle and other livestock by Vancouver and later visitors, and the early activity of supplying meat to whaling and trading ships, have been mentioned.[33] Beef cattle were driven to the port villages on hoof, and slaughtered as needed. Sometimes they were shipped alive to Lahaina from Hawaii ranches. Two breeds of cattle were thriving on Hawaii in the thirties, identified as the "wild Mexican" and the "Australian tame English" breeds.[34] Spanish or Mexican cowboys, "paniolos," had been brought in by 1830 to chase on horseback, and lasso or kill the wild cattle. By the late thirties, hunting of wild cattle had proceeded so industriously that the king laid a *kapu* on killing wild bullock, effective from 1840 to 1845.[35]

During the decade of the forties, numbers of cattle increased

[30] Coulter and Chun, *op. cit.*, p. 11.

[31] *Pacific Commercial Advertiser*, February 25, 1871.

[32] *Hawaiian Gazette*, August 19, 1865. Other mills followed: *Hawaiian Gazette*, October 7, 1867; *Pacific Commercial Advertiser*, September 27, 1873.

[33] Pp. 68–69, 81–82.

[34] S. E. Bishop, *Reminiscences of Old Hawaii* (Honolulu: 1916), p. 39.

[35] *Polynesian*, September 4, 1841, p. 51.

rapidly: some were owned and branded by chiefs and haoles, and many were unclaimed, especially on Hawaii. The cattle destroyed lauhala trees (with whose leaves native houses were lined, and mats were made), trampled over cultivated land, and ate growing crops. An urgent practical question came to be how to reconcile the diverse interests of agriculture and grazing. The natives were not in the habit of fencing land, and means of fencing were scarce.

Missionaries were especially conscious of the distress the natives were suffering, and reported that in at least two areas, Waimea, Hawaii, and Kahuku, Oahu, native people were actually driven away from their homes by the depredations of the cattle, and that elsewhere they were discouraged from cultivating the land.[36]

J. S. Emerson wrote from Waialua, Oahu:

> The result at the present time is 100 or more acres of choice land for tillage now given up, and the people plant neither corn, beans, potatoes, or anything of the kind, to any extent, lest they be destroyed by the cattle. These cattle, by which the agricultural interests of this whole district are wholly prostrated, are on the whole the greatest evil from which we are now suffering as a people.[37]

As time went on the evil was mitigated by fence building, and by transition of interest from stock raising to sugar-cane growing. But in the meantime severe damage was done.[38]

The absence of winter, with its need for accumulation of fodder and protection against weather, was a special advantage to the

[36] Reverends R. Armstrong and J. S. Emerson, in *Answers to Questions put by R. C. Wyllie* (Honolulu: 1848), p. 41.

[37] At Kahuku, Oahu, "the depredations of (a haole's) herds and flocks on their small homesteads became unbearable; but they appealed in vain for the protection of their beloved hala trees . . . and patches of vegetable . . . There was no redress, and with the fading of the lauhala forests, the people also disappeared, and the once populous district of Kahuku became a lonely sheep and cattle ranch . . . Sometimes (cattle) would eat the very thatch off the sides of the native huts. It was impossible to restrain them save by constant watchfulness, and if a man caught or hemmed an animal, legal steps would be taken against him." (O. P. Emerson, *Pioneer Days in Hawaii* (New York: 1928), p. 136.)

In the fall of 1846 a law was passed by which the owner of cattle trespassing on cultivated ground was made liable to a fine of $5 for every offense. The fine was reduced to $1 in 1848. (*Statute Laws of Kamehameha III*, vol. II, p. 72; *Laws of 1848*, pp. 12–13.) The laws were not enforced.

[38] V. William H. Lee, Address before the Royal Hawaiian Agricultural Society, in the Society's *Transactions* (1851), vol. 1, no. 2, p. 6.

graziers in the Islands. Judge Lee, the President of the Agricultural Society, thought in 1851 that livestock raising was the most successful enterprise yet undertaken at the Islands: "The owner of a small herd is sure, with a reasonable degree of care and attention, to become wealthy in a few years." [39]

Rapid increase in number of cattle between 1850 and 1870 indicates the healthy state of the industry. In 1846 Wyllie had estimated total cattle to be 35,000,[40] 25,000 of which were wild. Such wild cattle were killed in numbers in the fifties and sixties,[41] but they increased nevertheless. The official census of 1866 gave the number of beef cattle at 59,913, with possibly 40,000 more running wild,[42] three times the Wyllie estimate for 1846.[43]

The only continuous measure of the size of the cattle industry which we now possess is the record of exports. (Chart 8.) Beef, omitted from our chart, was exported in significant quantity only during the Gold Rush and for a few years afterward. No acceptable series exists for supply of beef to whalers and traders. Hide and tallow exports vary greatly in quantity during the late thirties, the forties, and the fifties. Causes for the variance lie in the fortunes of hunters, the rate at which contracts were issued by the government and king, and the fluctuating state of the whale trade. At first hides were sent in large part to South America, later nearly exclusively to California, when the population mushroomed there after 1847.

Measured by the record for hide exports, the industry reached maturity in the early 1870's; and from then to the end of the

[39] Lee, *op. cit.*

[40] This checks with an estimate in 1851 of 40,700. (Charles R. Bishop in the *Polynesian,* August 14, 1852, reported in L. A. Henke, *Livestock Industry of Hawaii* (University of Hawaii, Research Publication no. 5, Honolulu: 1929), p. 22.)

[41] The arrangement at Waimea, Hawaii, in 1859 was typical. The Government and King, joint owners of wild cattle, sold or leased right to slaughter to private individuals, who maintained an agent at Waimea, paying hunters at the rate of $1.25 for each bullock hide, and $1.00 for each cow hide, properly dried and delivered. Since the hides of wild cattle were unbranded, they were worth more than tame hides. Though payment was made for meat, too, cattle were hunted almost solely for their hides. (*Pacific Commercial Advertiser,* August 11, 1859.)

[42] *Pacific Commercial Advertiser,* February 25, 1871.

[43] Breeds of tame cattle were rapidly improving in 1850 and after. The Agricultural Society was a prime mover. A Durham bull was imported in 1854; and the Society recorded that it imported Devon cattle in 1855: "a bull calf, a cow named Edith, and a bull named Herod." (*Transactions,* 1854, vol. 2, no. 1, p. 79.) Dexter and Shorthorn cattle were brought in in the early 1860's. (L. A. Henke, "A Survey of Livestock in Hawaii," pp. 8–15.)

CHART 8

EXPORTS OF HIDES, GOAT SKINS, AND WOOL

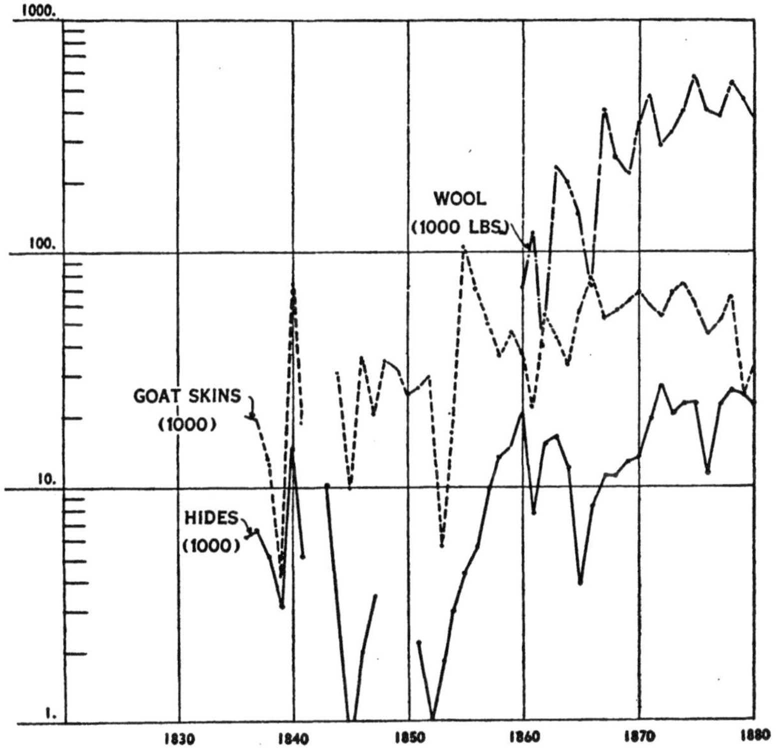

Data: Appendix III, Columns (13), (14), and (15).

century it distinguished itself by its even course. In only two years up to 1898 did numbers fall below 19,000 or rise above 29,000.[44] One chief reason was that livestock slaughter was no longer complementary to the undependable fortunes of the whale trade. A second reason was the fixed capacity of the limited amount of range land to support herds. Rational use of the range meant concern to prevent over-grazing. On the other hand, roughness of terrain, and especially lack of adequate rainfall and economic impossibility of irrigation, ensured against use of the range by the expanding sugar industry. Such blocks to the more extensive use of the land by sugar were most effective on Hawaii, on whose immense mountain slopes cattle reigned supreme.

[44] *Hawaiian Annual* (1900), p. 25.

The sheep and goat industry followed something of a parallel course. There was concern in 1853 as to the quality of the breed of sheep, the original Saxons and Merinos having deteriorated.[45] Importations of Merinos had by 1871 led to a high quality of animal in the best flocks; though it was estimated very roughly that 201,000 sheep all together, about half, were running wild. An index to the industry is given by the export of wool. The goats left by Cook and Vancouver had multiplied immensely, especially on Hawaii, though a smaller proportion of the total was by 1871 running wild than was true of sheep. Goatskin exports, noted occasionally in our records in the 1830's, continued throughout the century, reaching a maximum in the twenty years following 1860, during which time the California market offered a high demand; and sugar and other Hawaiian industries had not expanded sufficiently to cut down on supply.

Other Products

Many other products entered in small amounts into Island consumption, or were exported. Among them were kukui oil (listed in exports occasionally 1836–1858), tobacco (exported in occasional small quantity), bananas (listed first in exports in 1851, and steadily until after 1862), and, finally, *Pepeiao Akua* and *pulu*. Pepeiao Akua,[46] a fungus gathered from the decaying trunk and limbs of kukui trees, was shipped as a food to Chinese in San Francisco, and later to the Orient. It met a fluctuating market, but figures in the export tables for a third of a century, 1852–1885.[47] Pulu is listed consistently 1851–1881. It was the mossy substance that envelops the fronds of the pulu fern; and when dried in the sun made an excellent filler for mattresses and pillows. During the high tide of the industry in 1860 and for a few years after, native families were going on expeditions of weeks into the forest to collect it, undergoing privations reminiscent of sandalwood days.[48]

[45] Royal Hawaiian Agricultural Society *Transactions*, vol. 1, no. 4, pp. 10 11; L. A. Henke, *op. cit.*, pp. 16–17.

[46] *Hirneola polytricha.*

[47] *Hawaiian Annual* (1914), pp. 201–203.

[48] *Pacific Commercial Advertiser*, February 25, 1851; Ethel M. Damon, *Father Bond of Kohala* (Honolulu: 1927), p. 157.

CHAPTER XII

THE RISE OF SUGAR

We have often referred to aspects of the sugar industry, whose extraordinary expansion after the Reciprocity Treaty with the United States in 1876 boomed it into being the dominant, nearly the all-important, Island industry. Two phases of the expansion of sugar force themselves to our attention. One is the continuing technological advance, which, with mechanical innovation in the factory and the field, and with scientific analysis and experiment, raised the industry to exemplary efficiency. The other is the reversion, in the plantation system, to a structure of production much resembling the old feudal order. To a partial extent, our story of these hundred years has come full circle.

Likenesses to feudalism lie in (1) the paternalism of the plantation management to its laborers, with an economic and social hierarchy from executive down to unskilled labor; (2) social inferiority and isolation of those workmen, set off from the rest of the community by lack of skill, low earnings, and difference of race; (3) the peon status of the workmen (up to Annexation in 1898), legally enforced in accordance with the labor contracts. The plantations were impelled to this arrangement in order to secure continuity of service.

Factors logically associated with the rise of the plantation system elsewhere in the world were here to be found also: a quantity of arable land; market and production conditions favoring the cultivation of one or two crops in which there is much routine, non-skilled work to be done; and last the possibility of obtaining unskilled labor of low living standards.

The chief problems that Hawaiian sugar met were (1) the obtaining of a stable market, an adequate supply of capital, and an adequate supply of labor; and (2) technological and biological obstacles to production. In addition there were the problems of (3) effective fertilization and irrigation, which became important when, under the hot-house stimulus of Reciprocity, there was intensive cultivation of the limited good land, and expansion into previously submarginal areas.

The Founding of the Industry

Sugar cane was growing naturally on the Islands by the time of discovery, at elevations of from sea level up to 3500 feet. It must have been brought in by the early Hawaiians on their voyages, though as long ago in Hawaiian history as their traditions extend it had been known to them. There were five varieties. The most common, a white cane resembling the Tahitian, was cultivated in the early days of the industry.

The first sugar making is credited to a Chinese who in 1802 brought with him, on a ship trading for sandalwood, a vertical mill and boilers. He set up his apparatus on Lanai, ground off a small crop, and made sugar; but he took himself and his mill back to China the next year. There were several attempts during the 1820's. An Italian, Lavinia, made sugar in 1823, having natives crush the cane on poi-boards with stone beaters, and boiling the juice in a copper kettle. Two mills were set up at the same time on Maui, at Wailuku and Waikapu. Interest in rum making explains several agreements for manufacture of sugar and rum in 1823–1826. There is record of the landing of a sugar mill in 1826,[1] possibly in connection with 100 acres of cane set out in 1825 at Manoa Valley by John Wilkinson,[2] under the patronage of Governor Boki. Only one crop of sugar was taken off, the field being then allowed to run to weeds from lack of care.

Lack of knowledge of sugar making dogged the industry for many years, but at no time more acutely than in these late twenties. A journal of the time gives example:

> February 20, 1829—Dr. Serriere attempted to cut a load of cane at Manoa, in order to make sugar; hope he will succeed better than he has with rum.
>
> February 25—J. C. Jones and I went up to see the sugar mill . . . Got the mules in to grind, and after some coaxing they went very well. Afterwards it was found that the mill was going wrong side foremost; shifted, and found a great difference. At 8:00 no sugar. Mr. Jones is of my opinion that Dr. S. knows nothing of distilling or sugar making.[3]

[1] *Journal of Stephen Reynolds*, quoted in the *Hawaiian Annual* (1909), p. 159.

[2] P. 161.

[3] "Journal of One of Honolulu's Pioneer Merchants," *Hawaiian Annual* (1901), p. 85.

Early Plantations

None of these ventures were of commercial importance. The first systematic sugar plantation was that of Ladd, Hooper, and Brinsmade, all from New England, at Koloa, Kauai, in 1835. They had come in 1833 with intent toward merchandising, but not having found the hoped-for profits, decided to try also the sugar business, and succeeded in leasing 1000 acres of land for sugar and silk culture. Obstacles were great. The local chiefs, jealous at seeing their lands alienated, forbade sale of all provisions to Hooper, the resident agent. He was almost starved into submission . . . "A greater obstacle lay in overcoming the repugnance of the natives to regular and protracted labor, and their utter ignorance of tools . . . Indigenous canes abundant in the vicinity of Koloa were *kapued* by the chiefs, and a nursery was started only after prolonged resistance to the *kapu*."[4] Lack of effective equipment was a constant deterrent. At one time, for want of oxen, forty kanakas were hitched to a plow. Their first two mills, one of wooden rollers, one of iron, proved ineffective, and the entire works, buildings, and machinery were abandoned.[5] No sugar was produced the first year, only molasses and syrup; and in succeeding years up to 1842 the sugar was hardly merchantable. The partners continued hopeful—Hooper wrote in 1839, "It wants only enterprise, capital, and perseverance." New capital was raised by selling an interest, and in 1841 an improved imported mill was set up at Waihohonu, at an estimated cost of nearly $16,000.

The problem of a market was as serious as that of production, and up to 1843 the partners were compelled to ship their sugars on their own account to Valparaiso, Sydney, and eastern United States (California being sparsely settled).[6] The resources of the firm finally being exhausted after a loss of some $30,000, their property was sold at sheriff's auction in 1845. The plantation continued in other hands.

[4] A. C. Alexander, *Koloa Plantation* (Honolulu: 1937), pp. 4–5. Hooper wrote after a year there, "I have had more annoyance from the chiefs and difficulties with the natives than I had thought it possible for a white man to bear" (p. 6). The King sent a representative in 1839 to try to bring the chiefs to order.

[5] R. W. Wood, "The Manufacture of Sugar," in Royal Hawaiian Agricultural Society *Transactions* (1850), vol. 1, no. 1, pp. 67–68.

[6] R. W. Wood, *op. cit.*, p. 68.

Ladd & Company's venture was a pronounced stimulus to ventures in sugar. The *Gazette* in 1838 was enthusiastic over the 2½-ton crop of sugar the Company had produced from a single acre.[7] There were reported then in operation, or soon to be, twenty-two mills for crushing cane. Several missionaries had such mills in 1838, on Kauai, Oahu, and Maui. They encouraged cultivation of cane, both for helping the natives toward economic independence, and for supporting the schools.[8]

These mills were evidently of the crude vertical type. There were two vertical rolls, powered by a horse or bullock. The cane was fed by hand, stalk by stalk. Some mills, all those of Ladd & Company, were run by water power. They were small and light: the wooden rollers which Aiko, the Chinese sugar maker, installed at Kohala in 1841 were two and a half feet high, and eighteen inches in diameter.[9] Iron three-roller mills were just being introduced, and they weighed less than a ton apiece complete.[10] Three such iron mills were in operation, or were being set up by 1841.[11] All these primitive mills together, wooden and iron, were estimated in 1842 to be able to turn out 1000 tons of sugar; but it was not until eighteen years later that such an amount was actually produced. The juice was often boiled down in nothing more elaborate than whaling "trying out" pots, used on shipboard for rendering whale blubber.

Such equipment represented only a small investment of capital. It was fairly portable, and changed hands with some frequency. The early industry had then extreme flexibility: "Mills were established, produced sugar for a few years, and then were abandoned or moved to new sites if conditions warranted. This was

[7] "In the West Indies we have been informed 2 tons of Sugar to an acre is considered a good crop . . . 2½ tons . . . is most decidedly a heavy quantity: The Sandwich Islands are looking up! . . . At Maui some lots of sugar have been made of good quality. At Honolulu there is now a sugar mill, of rude construction, worked by a single mule . . . We called at the mill with a friend the other day and felt our heart hop like a rubber ball to witness this foundation stone of Sandwich Island prosperity. The time *is coming*,—Aye! it has almost come, when the level of commerce, poised on the fulcrum of industry, shall lift these dear islands 'sky high'!" (*Sandwich Islands Gazette*, March 17, 1838.)

[8] *Sandwich Islands Mirror*, May 15, June 15, 1840.

[9] Thomas G. Thrum, "Notes on the History of the Sugar Industry," *Hawaiian Annual* for 1875, p. 37.

[10] Lorrin A. Thurston, in the *Pacific Commercial Advertiser*, July 2, 1906.

[11] *Polynesian* (July 1841).

not always desirable for it tended to divorce mill operations from field practises, hindered the development of a settled agriculture, and perpetuated makeshift methods."[12] Other influences tending toward a migratory industry were the inability of producers to own land, and the common reliance on native wild cane.

At Kohala, where Aiko made sugar for a time under agreement with Governor Kuakini, planting was done by natives in the old fashion. With an *oo* or native hand spade, they scraped off the grass, making the smallest hole possible for the slip.[13]

Often share agreements were formed between the chiefs and mill owners, the chiefs to assure the growing of cane by their tenants, the latter to see to the making of sugar. A typical contract of the sort was made in 1843 at Waimea, Hawaii:

> That Kuakini shall plant sugar cane at Waimea and when the same shall be ripe, shall carry or cause the same to be carried to the Sugar Mill of A. H. Fayerweather at Waimea, and shall furnish men to do all the labor for same including the grinding, and shall furnish firewood for boiling the same. That A. H. Fayerweather shall furnish a mill for grinding the aforenamed cane, a Sugar Maker, and all the tools for making the sugar and molasses; and the sugar and molasses proceeds of the aforementioned cane shall be shared equally between the said Kuakini and A. H. Fayerweather, one half to each.[14]

The quantity of exports (Chart 9) shows a rapid rise in the early years,[15] from a reported two tons in 1837 to 288 tons in 1840. The drop to 30 tons in 1841 may have been partly due to lack of market,[16] since there was hope, followed by disappointment, that France would admit sugar advantageously. By 1846, when 150 tons are listed, Wyllie reported eleven "establishments

[12] William H. Taylor, "The Hawaiian Sugar Industry" (unpublished dissertation, University of California library), p. 9.

[13] Thomas G. Thrum, "Notes on the History of the Sugar Industry," pp. 34–41. The homemade carts which carried the sugar over the hills to port at Mahukona had wheels made of cross sections of koa logs! For all this the plantation made money, until the avaricious successor to Governor Kuakini increased the rents to such a level that Aiko gave up in disgust.

[14] Dated December 5, 1843. Archives of Hawaii.

[15] Detailed statistics of *production* were not issued until 1877, when the Hawaiian Sugar Producers' Association began publishing them.

[16] R. C. Wyllie said five years later that lack of a market was the great obstacle the industry faced, more weighty than lack of machinery, capital, or labor. (*Answers to Questions put by Mr. Dudoit, Consul of France,* April 22, 1846, MS. in Archives of Hawaii.)

for the manufacture of sugar and molasses" on the Islands, two on Kauai, six on Maui, and three on Hawaii.[17]

From 1848 on for some five years the Industry went through a critical period. The settlement of California was both a stimulus and a depressant. It did of course hugely increase demand; and the unprecedented price of ten cents a pound was realized in 1850, to be compared with the three cents a pound of 1843.[18] But it also exacerbated the chronic problem of labor scarcity, since the natives emigrated in quantity to the gold fields in 1848. Some estates were abandoned, and all were threatened with ruin.[19] The critical stringency of labor supply was relieved, save on the largest plantations, by 1853; but the difficulty of getting *enough* labor remained, and is one of the causes of the unsteadiness of output from 1853 to 1855.

Other difficulties were a general drought over the Islands in 1851, and low prices in the California market in 1851–52, the latter partly as a result of disappointments on the gold claims, and partly a consequent of the bad reputation Hawaiian sugars had earned in 1850, when, under the stimulus of high prices, planters had shipped out accumulated low-grade sugars from previous years.[20] Only ten tons were exported in 1851.

In consequence of labor scarcity, drought, and low prices, the number of plantations dwindled to the year 1857, when only five remained. There was first of all Koloa, where fruits of Ladd & Company's pioneer efforts were being reaped by a Dr. Wood, who had managed the plantation with nearly consistent success since 1847.[21] A second on Kauai was at Lihue, with a record (due mainly to irrigation expense) of five straight years of loss. These were the two largest of the five, each valued at about $100,000,

[17] *Ibid.*

[18] Dispatch of William Hooper, U. S. Vice Consul to the Secretary of State, July 26, 1843, National Archives; A. W. Parsons, in the Royal Hawaiian Agricultural Society *Transactions* (1850), p. 77.

[19] R. H. A. S. *Transactions* (1853), p. 49.

[20] Before, in 1849, Hawaiian sugar had a price advantage of 2 cents or more a pound on the California market, because of its superior quality compared with competing sugars from Manila and South America. Afterward, for several years, it was placed "almost on a par with Manila sugar." (Josephine Sullivan, *History of C. Brewer & Company* (Boston: 1926), p. 108.)

[21] It was already prosperous in the year of high prices, 1850, when $20,000 gross income was reported, with expenses of less than half. A. C. Alexander, *Koloa Plantation* (Honolulu: 1937), p. 50.

and with 4000 and 2000 acres, respectively, of cane and pasture land. There were two smaller plantations on Maui, the East Maui and the Brewer, each valued at about $50,000. At Hilo on Hawaii, Aiko had set up another plantation, after withdrawing from his disappointing venture at Kohala.[22] The amount of sugar produced annually is not given for Lihue plantation; for the others it is respectively 200–350, 150–170, 150 and 100 tons. The plantations which had survived the wringer were the large ones, incomparably larger than the mill and field units of twenty years before. The unified plantation had replaced the system of central mills to which individual cultivators brought their cane.

Large and centralized units were favored by several associated economies: (1) the more fully mills were utilized, the less their fixed charges weighed on the product. With prolonged periods climatically possible for planting and cutting cane, there was clear advantage in having large acreage per mill, for harvesting could be spaced so that the mill was kept busy much of the time the year round. (2) There was rapid technical development in the industry during these years; hence advantages from specialization were becoming more significant. Only when the number of men employed was great could individuals acquaint themselves well with special phases of the progressing trade. (3) Separation of management of mill and fields was obsolescent since better cane could be grown under the direction of the haole than individually by the traditionally minded native; and since the use of one mill by a number of small producers led, unless cutting was well planned as to time, to a period of delay between the cutting of the cane and its crushing at the mill. The juice in the cane quickly deteriorates in any such period of delay.

Expansion After 1857

The number of plantations increased rapidly following the low point of 1857, though output had already been rising since 1855 on the plantations that lasted through the time of stress. Two new plantations were begun in 1857, those of Samsing & Company, and Utai & Company, both near Hilo; and in 1858 three more, the Makee and Haiku plantations of Maui, and the Metcalf plantation at Hilo.[23] Technical improvements encouraged both

[22] Pp. 176, 177; *Pacific Commercial Advertiser,* April 2, 1857.

[23] Thomas G. Thrum, "Notes on the History of the Sugar Industry," pp. 34–41.

large and small ventures.[24] There were 22 plantations in operation in 1861, and output was skyrocketing.[25]

The industry had always responded sensitively to the stimulus of higher prices. In 1840–1849 the average price had been 6.85 cents per pound, and in 1850–1859, it was 6.95 cents. With the Civil War, prices in the North rose extravagantly due to cutting off of supply of Louisiana sugars and inflation of the currency. In 1863 the price was 10.55 cents; the next year it reached a peak of 17.19 cents. The average annual price continued over 10 cents until 1873.[26]

Under such circumstances a drought on Maui in 1862 and the failure of two sugar brokers in 1865 [27] were only minor incidents. The area cultivated increased from 2,750 acres in 1853 to nearly 22,000 in 1882.[28] Twelve years of the fifteen from 1860 to 1875 show record crops, as exports rose from 572 tons to 12,540.[29] Comparing average exports for two-year periods (to minimize chance fluctuations), 1859–60, with 1864–65, with 1869–70, and with 1874–75, we obtain successive increases of 763 per cent, 43 per cent, and 34 per cent.

Boom prices of the Civil War had furnished the major stimulus; but the industry was continuing to expand against the pressure of declining prices as the Civil War inflation ended. Naturally

[24] Pp. 181–185.

[25] In 1876, 35 were producing; and the maximum number of 72 was reached in 1890. Since that time the numbers have dropped as holdings have been consolidated under the "Factors."

[26] New York wholesale raw sugar prices, annual averages. Source: Hearings before the Committee on Ways and Means, House of Representatives, V, 2893–2895; in William H. Taylor, "The Hawaiian Sugar Industry," pp. 167–169; Josephine Sullivan, *History of C. Brewer & Company*, p. 124.

[27] C. W. Brooks & Co., of San Francisco; and Walker, Allen & Co. of Honolulu. Also there was stiff opposition of interest from this time on for some years between the San Francisco and Pacific Refinery and the Hawaiian producers. This refinery took the bulk of the Hawaiian sugars; but its effort to take advantage of its monopsonistic position by specification as to grade and price of sugars was opposed by the Hawaiian industry. Later Hawaiian producers came to own a large part of the refinery stock, and opposition ended.

[28] The main production center shifted from Kauai to Hawaii in this time: Kauai had nearly half the output in 1853; Hawaii had gained about the same proportion by 1882. (*Personal Reminiscences of William Cooper Parker*, Cambridge, Mass.: 1891, p. 107; Royal D. Meade in the *Honolulu Star-Bulletin*, March 25, 1909, p. 1.)

[29] Local consumption, and sales to shipping, furnish an indeterminate addition. One estimate for such addition (about 1860) runs a little under 3000 tons. (Lorrin Thurston, "Sugar, its Status and Development," *Pacific Commercial Advertiser*, July 2, 1906.)

9-cent prices were less pleasant than 17-cent prices, but the industry had survived its youthful testing, and had proved its ability to survive. It is not possible to take seriously the legend that Hawaiian sugar was in the doldrums, or declining, until rescued by the Reciprocity Treaty.

CHART 9

SUGAR AND MOLASSES EXPORTS

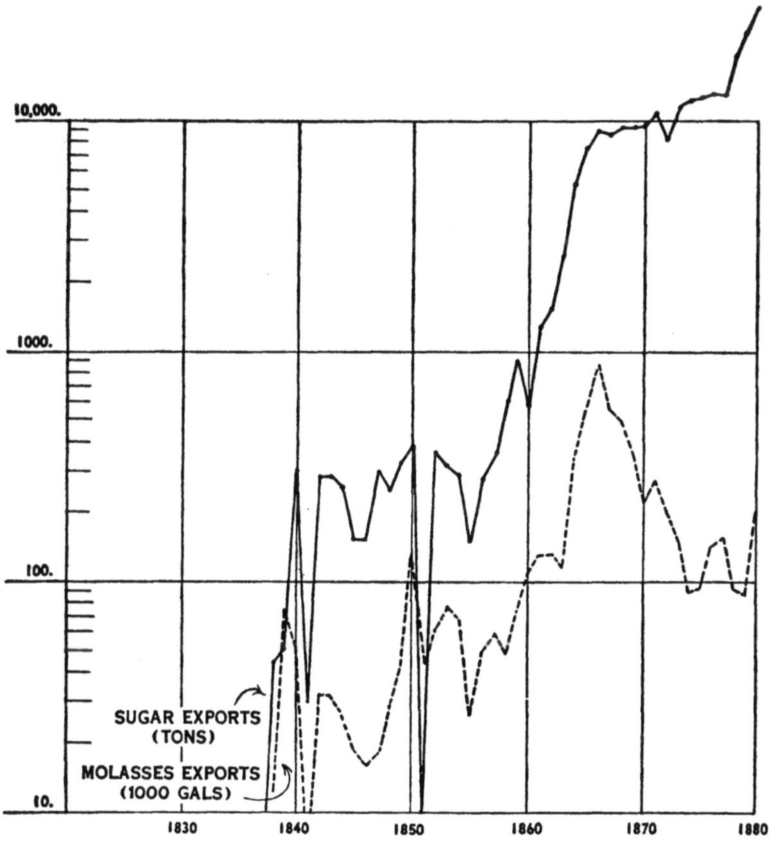

TECHNICAL ADVANCE

A committee of the Agricultural Society wrote in 1850 without compliment of the technical deficiencies of the early planters:

> It is a fact worthy of remark, as your committee believe, without a single exception, that all the plantations that have been commenced at these Islands, have been so commenced by persons possessing neither experience in the business they were undertaking, . . . nor the requisite . . . knowledge of the soil, to carry it through to a successful result.[30]

But technical progress was a characteristic of the Hawaiian sugar industry from the early days down. We have mentioned before the small vertical wood and iron mills of the 1830's and 1840's. Simple two-roller wood mills were being supplanted in the forties, but many still served in the late forties and even in the fifties. The horizontal mill imported at Koloa in 1841 was then the best in the Islands; but size increased and design improved rapidly enough so that twelve years later it appeared antiquated and inefficient, "an immense amount being lost through evaporation during the grinding of the cane." [31] Though efficiency of mills increased thereafter, enough juice was left in the crushed cane for it to be too damp to burn even in 1868 and later. Modern mills have been developed to express 98 per cent of sugar content.

A corresponding evolution took place in the power used for grinding. At first a bullock or horse had been hitched to the end of a long pole whose fulcrum was one of the rolls. Of the 22 mills in 1838, 20 were run in this fashion, two by water. But water power was coming in: Ladd & Company anticipated hopefully the efficiency of their 1841 imported mill powered with a pitch-back water wheel. Of the five plantations in 1857 three used water power, two moderate sized ones used "mule power." [32] One of these, Lihue, was already using steam as an auxiliary, and two years later used it regularly. By 1861 steam was replacing water generally: 9 mills of the 22 were using steam, 12 were using water power, and only one was using animal power.[33] Steam was quickly found effective also for boiling the juice and finishing.

The most distinguished advance probably took place in this process of crystallization of sugar—here especially technical in-

[30] *Transactions* (1850), p. 7.

[31] G. W. Bates, *Sandwich Island Notes* (New York: 1854), p. 172; Royal Hawaiian Agricultural Society *Transactions* (1853), pp. 49–51. The Society was useful during its active life 1850–1857 in spreading information of superior techniques.

[32] Thomas G. Thrum, "Notes on the History of the Sugar Industry," pp. 24–41.

[33] *Ibid.*, Josephine Sullivan, *A History of C. Brewer and Company*, p. 124.

eptness was penalized. The earliest process for recovering sugar from the cane juice involved simply successive boilings in open try-pots bought from visiting whalers. When the resultant syrup was thick enough, it was cooled until sugar had crystallized out, and the mixture of sugar and molasses put in boxes or barrels, through which holes had been bored to let the molasses drain. The remaining sugar, after a week or several weeks, was still imperfectly and unevenly dried.[34] The large proportion of molasses obtained in this process was not originally an objection; for the early industry relied much on selling thick syrup to whalers, presumably for rum making.[35]

During the forties a Frenchman (Prevost), who had experience on the Isle of Bourbon, introduced new methods into the boiling, clarifying, and granulating of sugars; and their quality was somewhat improved. A major advance occurred in 1851 when D. M. Weston adapted a centrifugal device to sugar drying. It was phenomenally successful, increasing quality without decreasing quantity,[36] doing well in a few minutes what the old method had done badly in weeks.[37] Almost as notable was the "vacuum pan," which, by using a partial vacuum, enabled the juice to be concentrated at a much lower boiling temperature than before, increasing quantity of recovery, and quality. It was first used in 1861–62, at Kaupakuea (later Pepeekeo) and Lahaina plantations.

An index to the efficiency of recovery of raw sugar is given in the ratio of molasses to sugar (though this measure is not significant until after the forties, when the whaling demand for syrup, and hence the incentive to produce it, had declined). The lower the ratio, the larger the proportion of sugar recovered. It will be seen (see Chart 9) that the ratio undergoes a sharp drop after the middle 1860's, indicative of the spreading of the new methods.

But the vacuum pan was expensive, and hence available chiefly

[34] Thomas G. Thrum, *op. cit.*, pp. 34–41; Josephine Sullivan, *op. cit.*, p. 107.

[35] G. W. Willfong, "Twenty Years' Experience in Cane Culture," *Planters' Monthly*, I, pp. 147–152.

[36] It was in part in consequence that Hawaiian sugars regained in the middle fifties the good reputation they had lost in 1850. *Pacific Commercial Advertiser*, April 2, 1857.

[37] The centrifugal was used first at Hana, East Maui, in 1852. Weston in 1853 established the Honolulu Iron Works, which drifted into sugar-mill construction gradually through repairing parts. Its presence, and Weston's skill, facilitated mechanical improvements in sugar manufacture.

to large plantations. Small ventures were encouraged about the same time by the introduction of a simple "sorgum pan" for crystallizing, since it required only small capital outlay.

Another useful innovation of the time was the "trash house," to hold and air bagasse (crushed cane, from which juice had been pressed out) until it was dry enough to be effectively burned for power. The mills left so much juice in the cane—about half—that the bagasse had to be dried out before it could be burned. (Now trash can be burned direct from the mill; and hence the trash house is no longer needed.) Willfong of Kohala first thought of the device about 1868, and it quickly spread through the Islands.

Improvements took place also in the field. At first joints from poor native varieties of cane had been used as "seed." Two tons of cane an acre were considered a good yield, though sometimes as much as four tons were realized.[38] One step toward higher yields was taken in 1854 with the importation of a better variety of cane from Tahiti. It was called Lahaina cane, from the port at which it was brought into the Islands. Soon it displaced native cane; and one of its descendants, "H-109," has under ideal conditions of growth produced up to 100 tons of cane an acre, or 14 tons of raw sugar.

Water supply was in many areas a stringent limitation on cane growth, even in the earliest days when only the most productive land was used. But with contiguous mountain ranges and summits drenched with rain as they intercepted the trade winds, and sending their streams coursing to the sea, plantations usually found irrigation possible. Father Rice on Kauai was possibly the first to ditch and tunnel mountain water, to fields at Lihue. At Koloa in the early fifties George Dole diverted a stream to the plantation. The first project of any size was the development in 1856 of Father Rice's small ditch to tap Hanamaulu stream near its source, at an outlay of $7000. Soon after, this too was extended and enlarged.[39]

From this time on there was a considerable amount of small-scale irrigation. It must have been practiced before 1870 on the

[38] G. W. Bates, *Sandwich Island Notes*, p. 172; Josephine Sullivan, *History of C. Brewer & Company*, p. 109; Royal Hawaiian Agricultural Society, *Transactions* (1853), pp. 49–51; *Sandwich Islands Gazette*, March 17, 1838.

[39] Ethel M. Damon, *Koamalu* (Honolulu: 1931), p. 71. Thomas G. Thrum, "Notes on the History of the Sugar Industry," pp. 34–41.

comparatively dry land near Lahaina. The three plantations at the foot of the Iao valley in Maui were irrigated by 1868 from the Wailuku river: Willfong reported that division of water between them during the dry season caused law suits and much quarreling.[40]

Benefits from irrigation were being demonstrated; but projects up to 1876 did not involve heavy outlay, or involve resourceful engineering. The first major project was the Hamakua ditch on Maui,[41] carried through 1876–1878 under stimulus of the Reciprocity Treaty. The object was to water the sun-baked plains at Haiku, Paia, and Grove Ranch plantations where former operations had not been profitable, and where without water little could exist save "the razor back hog, prickly pear, and wild indigo." The completed ditch from the wet windward slope of Haleakala Volcano was 17 miles long, crossing gorges up to 450 feet in depth. The daily capacity was a flow of over 40 million gallons. Though reported cost of the finished project was $80,000, over three times the original estimate, it paid wonderfully well; and it was the first in a series of major irrigation projects that changed barren hot central Maui into a splendidly productive agricultural area.[42] The Maui conditions and water resources were typical of those of many other Island areas; and progressive planters elsewhere followed the Hamakua example.

The Factors

The early Ladd & Company plantation at Koloa led also in this, that it was financed and partly conducted from a central agency at Honolulu. Until the Civil War boom such an arrangement was not general: independent farmers or plantation companies financed themselves as they were able, and negotiated directly with firms in the United States or elsewhere for purchase of equipment and sale of sugar.

[40] G. W. Willfong, Twenty Years' Experience in Cane Culture," *Planter's Monthly,* I, pp. 147–152; in H. A. Wadsworth, *Historical Summary of Irrigation in Hawaii* (University of Hawaii Miscellaneous Publications), pp. 143–145.

[41] The project was carried through by H. P. Baldwin and S. T. Alexander.

[42] Afterward, the Spreckels, Lowrie, Koolau, and other ditches paralleled that of Hamakua. The Spreckels ditch followed first, 30 miles long, of 50 million gallons daily capacity. (H. A. Wadsworth, *op. cit.,* pp. 143–145; Lorrin Thurston, "Sugar, its Status and Development," *Pacific Commercial Advertiser,* July 2, 1906; *Hawaiian Annual* (1878), pp. 39–41.)

The factors who grew to dominance after this time were agents of the plantations for obtaining tools and supplies, floating loans, and selling sugar. The early spread of the factor system is explained readily by the advantage of specialization. Plantation managers were fully occupied with technical and administrative problems, and found it convenient not to burden themselves with commercial ones as well. Heavy fixed investment to look after, variable growing seasons, and rapid technical evolution were a sufficient preoccupation. The Honolulu general merchants were, in contrast, equipped to deal with commercial contacts; and the departure of the whalers in 1859 had left them at loose ends. Some of them had besides accumulated considerable capital from their trading operations; and capital for expansion was a continuously urgent need of the plantations.[43]

Probably the earliest of these factors was Hackfeld & Company,[44] which around 1850 secured the agency for Koloa and East Maui plantations. In 1863 C. Brewer & Company had charge of getting supplies, markets, and capital for three plantations, and finding the business "more profitable than whaleships," was interested no further in cultivating the whale trade.[45] Already the purveying of capital was a preëminent part of the business.

The vital lack of capital, and the superior access which the commercial houses had to capital, gave them a strategic advantage in their dealings with plantations. Also prolonged dealing with one factor gave a "conjuncture value" to its services, since that factor was best acquainted with the plantation's particular needs and routines. The control of the factors increased through the century. A near crisis from acute stringency of capital during the vast expansion following 1876, and several later depressions in which plantations were faced with either bankruptcy or the necessity of turning stock over to their factors have led to the complete domination of the sugar industry by the largest factors.[46]

[43] The best thermometer of capital need is the interest rate, the "coefficient of tension" of an economy, which was usually at 12 per cent or higher. Pp. 197–198.

[44] The present "American Factors," organized in 1918, is successor to Hackfeld & Co.

[45] Josephine Sullivan, *History of C. Brewer*, p. 124.

[46] Recently over 95 per cent of sugar tonnage has been handled by the "Big Five." These are American Factors, Ltd., already mentioned, Alexander and Baldwin, Ltd. (of the Hamakua ditch, organized as a firm in 1894), Castle and Cooke, Ltd. (founded 1851), Theo H. Davies & Co. (founded as Starkey and

The Plantation System

Basic causes favoring the rise of the plantation system were suggested briefly before.[47] Less abstractly, the development progressed naturally out of local circumstances. A paternalistic concern for the kanaka of the thirties and forties was necessary, both because he had little thought for the morrow, and because of the desirability of isolating him from the claims of his chief. Later, imported labor lacked local ties and adjustments, and required looking after for its shelter, food, and other supplies. Since the efficient size of the productive unit was large, small farms did not persist; and the large-scale producer found it more convenient to have its workers live on his land, rather than away in private settlements from which daily transportation was required. And perhaps something of the missionary sentiment of obligation to care for the flock remained, represented in paternalistic and detailed rules for employee behavior.[48]

The plantation system developed and spread, with its isolated compact communities. The employees were housed by the Company, amused by Company-planned recreation, cared for by Company doctors, kept in order by Company police. They bought their food at Company stores, and sent their children to plantation schools. All about them was the plantation atmosphere, and the dominance of plantation authority. What had begun as a simple economic relationship came to be one of status: the plantation manager was the lord of his demesne, accountable only partially to the political authorities—especially during the hollow façade of native monarchy in the late nineteenth century. Nor was the plantation manager completely accountable even to the Company executives, who were distant in Honolulu and isolated from the plantation's daily requirements. Beneath the manager came widening strata of sub-lords, or lesser officials with, as we descend the scale, their lessening degrees of responsibility, and concomi-

---

Janion, 1845), and C. Brewer & Co. (successor to James Hunnewell's store of 1827). For comment on the later position of these factors, A. W. Lind, *An Island Community* (Chicago: 1938), pp. 178–186; William H. Taylor, "The Hawaiian Sugar Industry," chap. III, pp. 62–89; U. S. Bureau of Labor, Bulletin No. 66, Report on Hawaii (1906), pp. 450–451.

[47] P. 173.

[48] File No. 51, Interior Department, Archives of Hawaii, has examples of remarkably minute rules. Also Ethel M. Damon, *Father Bond of Kohala* (Honolulu: 1927), p. 87.

tant repute, privilege, and pay. At the base was the mass of unskilled laborers, with a minimum of status, and simple and heavy duties.

The haole had eliminated the native hierarchy only to establish a new one, with gradations from the executives of the Factors down to unskilled labor. Of course the new system did grant much greater mobility among social classes than had existed under native feudalism. And the new system had its rigors tempered by much greater humaneness. But still, at any one period of time, economic dominance was so complete as to have nearly full reflection in political and social dominance.

Labor Supply

The obtaining of a sufficient supply of laborers was a chief obstacle of the industry from the beginning. Constant pressure for additional labor led to recruited immigration up to 1876 from south China, the South Sea Islands, and Japan.[49]

Despite the severity of population decline in the earlier years, the trouble with native labor was rather qualitative than quantitative. Hooper wrote from Koloa plantation in 1838 in wrath and despair: "I consider the results of the experiments we have been making for three years past prove the complete worthlessness of Sandwich Islanders as laborers on a farm."[50] The plantation had been employing 400 kanakas, whom he rated equal to "10 white men (poor) or 2½ smart Yankees." Fifteen years later Bates noted as emphatically the proficiency of the kanaka in evading work:

> No beast of prey watches his victim with a closer scrutiny than the kanaka watches his employer. In his presence he makes every effort to appear active and useful; but the very minute he disappears it is a signal for a general cessation of work, and one keeps a "look-out" while the group indulges in every variety of gossip. On the reappearance of their master, the sentinel gives the alarm, and every man is found to be at work as though he meant never again to lay down his tools. The owner may have watched them

[49] Since that time there has been, in addition, recruiting by Government agents in Siberia, Mongolia, the Philippines, continental United States, Puerto Rico, the Azores, Portugal, Spain, Italy, greater Germany (including Austria), Poland, Norway, and Russia.

[50] A. C. Alexander, *Koloa Plantation* (Honolulu: 1937), p. 22.

through a clump of foliage; but they will swear him out of the use of his eyes, and insist on it he was altogether mistaken.[51]

Several laws in the forties reflect labor scarcity. We have before spoken of the legal threat to put idlers to work on public projects.[52] By the Organic Act of 1846 the Minister of the Interior was authorized to seize vagrants and apprentice them for not over one year, two-thirds of the wages to go to the vagrant, one-third to the government. The 1846 law relating to the shipping of natives on whaling ships has labor scarcity implications also: permission had to be secured, and a bond of $100 per man deposited.[53] The gold fever led to a law of 1850 banning the enticing of labor to California. It states rather naïvely: "Whereas, the native population is diminishing," and "the want of labor is severely felt by planters and other agriculturalists, the price of provisions being enhanced," and "whereas many immigrants had migrated to California and there died in great misery," —that any native subjects must obtain the express permission of the King before migrating.[54] In 1850 there were also legalized two new forms of labor contract, apprenticeship and indentured service. Under the second contract a person might contract himself for a period of not over five years, and could be compelled to serve double the time of any absence without leave.[55]

The importation of foreign labor had already been considered. Ladd & Company in 1843 obtained the permission of Kamehameha III to import Belgians, in numbers to be specified by the Government.[56] Chinese immigrants had earned a fine reputation as effec-

[51] G. W. Bates, *Sandwich Island Notes,* p. 126.

[52] Pp. 118–119.

[53] *Laws of 1846,* section VI.

[54] Katherine Coman, *History of Contract Labor in the Hawaiian Islands* (New York: 1903), pp. 7–10.

[55] The provision suggests the similar penalty upon the bond servant of early Virginia. Safeguards under the Hawaiian law provided that contracts were not assignable, that they were to be canceled in case of death of the master, and that the laborer could not be held for debt contracted while in service. For minors the term could not be increased as a penalty for absence, for more than one year beyond the original term. The minor was also protected by provisions for education, and for explicit agreement as to payment at the end of his service. (Katherine Coman, *op. cit.,* pp. 8, 18–21; W. W. Goodale, "A Brief History of Hawaiian Unskilled Labor," *Hawaiian Annual* for 1914, p. 186.)

[56] W. W. Goodale, *op. cit.,* p. 181. None were actually imported.

tive workers;[57] and, besides, their habits of life were economical. Planters were discussing their introduction at the end of the forties. The matter of labor supply became critical as the gold rush drew away workmen; and a principal motive for the formation of the Agricultural Society in 1850 was to facilitate such importation should it come to seem feasible.[58] Finally Captain Cass of the bark *Thetis* was engaged to bring in coolies from China. In 1852, 280 arrived, under conditions of five years' service at pay of $3 a month in addition to food, clothing, and shelter.[59]

In general they were satisfactory labor: the president of the Society congratulated the country on obtaining "quiet, able, and willing men." The coolies were generally found to be cheaper than native labor, and far more "certain, systematic and economical." [60] They continued to be imported, the largest numbers being brought in just following reciprocity:

	Arrivals	Departures	Excess Arrivals[61]
1852–1865	1,306	——	1,306
1866–1874	641	365	276
1875–1887	25,497	10,196	15,301

As their contracts expired, the Chinese, like other races later, displayed an objectionable tendency from the point of view of the plantation owners not to renew them, and to drift into towns, where they entered "into distressful competition with the whites and Hawaiians as merchants, storekeepers, mechanics, and artisans." [62] Some of the coolies were badly chosen,[63] but as Prince

[57] "The Chinese portion of the population . . . include many of the most industrious, enterprising, and persevering of the inhabitants." (*Sandwich Islands Gazette,* March 17, 1838.)

[58] *Transactions,* 1850, p. 8.

[59] With cost of recruiting and transportation a little over $50, and maintenance per man estimated at $5 a month, total cost to the planter would have been about $9 a month.

[60] Josephine Sullivan, *History of C. Brewer,* p. 110.

[61] About 7000 additional were imported up to 1894. For 1852–1863, 54 women listed are included. After 1865, individuals in Hawaii were not permitted legally to import labor, but the law was often violated. (Records of the Collector General of Customs, in the *Hawaiian Annual,* 1894, pp. 72–74.)

[62] *Hawaiian Annual* (1894), p. 73.

[63] "[The coolies] are too vicious and ignorant to do anything with . . . If the material was required for a gang of pirates and cutthroats, I could recommend them strongly." (Letter from J. S. Low, manager of Princeville Plantation, to

Liholiho concluded tersely and brutally: "With all their faults, and a considerable disposition to hang themselves . . . they are procurable . . . they have been procured . . . their wages are reasonable . . . you can calculate on retaining them for a certain term . . . the climate suits them . . . they are handy in the house and in the fields." [64]

The flood of Chinese entering after 1875 (they were one-fifth of the population in 1889) gave rise to legislative restrictions in 1883 on their continued entry. The social objection against overwhelming the Island population with one foreign group worked in the same direction as the economic incentive of the plantation managers. For the plantations had an interest in securing a labor supply of mixed races which could less readily unite over issues of wages or work conditions.

Following 1850 immigration commissioners were sent into many parts of the world, seeking competent labor that would work at the lowest wage possible, and, as a lesser motive, would assimilate with the declining native race. Several attempts were made to bring in Polynesians from the South Seas,[65] but they did not make satisfactory workers. The only other importation in our period was that of 148 Japanese in 1868;[66] but Portuguese (1878 and later), and Japanese (beginning in 1885) were later imported in large numbers. South Sea Islanders were introduced in modest quantity 1878–1885.[67]

The business of obtaining labor was often denounced as man stealing, or "black-birding." Trickery and kidnaping may have been occasionally practiced in getting Chinese coolies about 1860 and after, for there was sometimes unregulated importation in defiance of the laws. We have report of one recruiter in the South

His Majesty's Board of Immigration, Interior Department, file No. 51, 1866, Archives of Hawaii.)

[64] About 1855. Quoted in Coman, *History of Contract Labor,* p. 25.

[65] In 1852 Kamehameha III sought to move north the whole population of Pitcairn's Island; but the project failed since the British Consul required that they enter as British subjects. A few came in 1865. The largest importation (126) in our period came in 1869, under a legislative subsidy of $36,000 for the purpose.

[66] Their contracts ran for three years only, with pay at $4 per month per man.

[67] Total introductions up to 1900 under the auspices of the Agricultural Society 1852–1864, and the Board of Immigration afterward (not counting individual entries, either on the worker's own account or under contract to a planter—the latter was illegal after 1865), were: Chinese, 34,309; Japanese, 65,034; Portuguese, 10,835; South Sea Islanders, 2444. A few Germans, Norwegians, and Galicians were also brought in. (Coman, *History of Contract Labor,* p. 63.)

Seas who, having received on board natives defeated in war with another tribe, gave them their choice of signing for Hawaii or of being released to the waiting head-hunters on shore.[68] In general careful supervision by the Board of Immigration of recruiting and transportation kept the trade on a fairly high level,[69] negotiations as to conditions of work and level of pay being carried on with governments of relatively advanced areas, such as Japan and the Madeira Islands, and standards of fair dealing being set up with reference to backward areas, such as the South Seas.[70]

Within the Islands, procedures and abuses were sufficient to lead to a reform crusade. In the earlier days contracted laborers were disposed of in accordance with the choice of plantation managers, after they arrived. Workers were inspected and examined with respect to teeth, health, and build, as in the slave trade. Flogging was not an uncommon punishment on the plantations. The reform movement in the Islands was sufficient to lead in the period 1872–1884 to increased safeguards for the laborer: contracts had to be acknowledged by both master and worker before an officer of the government, flogging was banned, extension of the term as a penalty for desertion was prohibited, penalty for misusage of the worker specified, a nine-hour day established where length of the working day was not otherwise agreed on, and sanitary standards set up for plantation camps. It will be remembered that the laborer had not at any time been legally bound to the plantation: in case of the death of the master, or sale of the plantation, he was released from his contract.

There was no clear preference in these later years for any one foreign nationality, even had it been desirable to the plantation or government that one nationality be imported to the exclusion of all others. Each group in turn, as it became acclimated to the local environment, grew less docile; and, as its contracts expired, tended to move to town into higher-paid occupations of higher social standing. Chinese, Japanese, and Portuguese successively fell into the bad graces of the planters for these reasons.

We note significantly, as evidence of native adjustment to wage work at fixed hours and of general improvement in morale, that

68 Lind, *An Island Community*, pp. 196–197.

69 Coman, *History of Contract Labor*, pp. 15–16.

70 In 1880 the Reverend H. Bingham was sent as a special investigator to see to the adherence to Hawaiian laws in that region, and to recommend improvements.

by the 1860's the native Hawaiian had lived down his reputation of being a wretched worker, and was conceded superior to imported labor.[71]

The inflow of new labor was not sufficient to prevent a continuing rise in wage levels. In the late 1840's the average was 15½ cents a day,[72] plus grass houses, (often) taro patches, and an outlay of 6 to 10 cents per working day for food supplied by the employer.[73] An extraordinary wage rise 1850–51 during the California exodus to as high as 50 cents a day for native labor was short-lived. By 1853 or 1854 native labor could be hired "without trouble" for 25 cents a day. Free coolies were less, about 18 cents, though the latter did "the most work and (gave) the most satisfaction." Contract coolies, the first of whom had now been imported, were paid at the daily rate of 11 cents.[74] In all cases board, quarters—and with the latter, import costs—had to be added.

By 1863, with the sugar boom, $8 to $10 a month plus food is given as a reasonable cost of labor.[75] The stimulus of Reciprocity is reflected in the comparatively high levels of 1888–1890: $15.58 to $19.53 a month for contract labor, and $17.47 to $22.25 for free labor.[76]

[71] Letter of S. N. Castle, dated July 23, 1869, in Ethel M. Damon, *Father Bond of Kohala* (Honolulu: 1927), p. 191; Report of the Committee on Labor, Planters' Labor and Supply Company, in *Planters' Monthly*, November 1882.

[72] Wages are from an average of six areas. (*Report of the Minister of Foreign Affairs, 1853–62*, p. 64.) Koloa paid 12½ cents through the decade, but had a strike in 1841, and was having "labor trouble" in 1850. (A. C. Alexander, *Koloa Plantation*, pp. 37, 51.)

[73] *Answers to Questions Proposed by R. C. Wyllie* (Honolulu: 1848), pp. 3, 4.

[74] Royal Hawaiian Agricultural Society *Transactions* (1853), pp. 49–51; G. W. Bates, *Sandwich Island Notes*, p. 172. In 1856 the total cost of natives and coolies, including all costs, was thought by Wyllie to be about 33 cents a day ($9 per month), which he compared favorably with an estimated 37½ cents a day cost of keeping slaves in the southern United States—depreciation and interest on the capital investment being extra! (*Transactions*, 1856, quoted in the *Pacific Commercial Advertiser*, July 19, 1916.)

[75] G. W. Willfong, in the *Planters' Monthly*, December 1882, pp. 225–230. Workers were tempted from one plantation to another during the sixties by advances, or promise of higher wages. (W. W. Goodale, "A Brief History of Hawaiian Unskilled Labor," *Hawaiian Annual*, 1914, p. 184.)

[76] Estimates of the Board of Immigration, reproduced in Coman, *History of Contract Labor*, p. 23. Commutation was, as before, in addition. The lower pay for contract labor may logically be explained in that they were first arrivals, hence unskilled; or those less able workers who could find employment only under contract. About one-fourth of the workers were by 1882 "free," engaged by the month.

Contract labor was justified by the problems of location and industrial need of the Islands. From the point of view of the plantation, if men were to be imported at all, there needed to be assurance of having them stay long enough to compensate for importation cost. Such assurance could be given only by a financial pledge or personal obligation; and the former was out of the question.

But living conditions, and remuneration on the plantation could easily, in view of the bounding prosperity of sugar, have been attractive enough to induce voluntarily continued service after the contracts had expired. Hence there need not have been renewed resort to areas of the world with low living standards to take the places of earlier immigrants as they fled from the plantation to better occupations in the towns.

Severe disadvantages of the system were that the employer could not discharge those who turned out to be lazy, stupid, or vicious; nor could he give the incentive of extra reward to the able and willing. The latter was a disaster as well for the workers. Other disadvantages for them were the social atmosphere of peonage, of penal enforcement of contract, and the opportunity sometimes taken advantage of by employers to keep their laborers in poverty and compel them to recontract.[77] But it is clear that a labor contract to Hawaii was on the average a road to economic and social advancement not obtainable in the laborer's homeland.

(Report of H. M. Whitney before the Planters' Labor and Supply Company, *Planters' Monthly,* November 1882, p. 190.)

The whole institution of contract labor was made illegal with Annexation in 1898.

[77] W. W. Goodale, "A Brief History of Hawaiian Unskilled Labor," p. 186.

CHAPTER XIII

GENERAL DEVELOPMENTS

ECONOMIC CHANGE from 1844 to 1876 was dominated nearly completely by land reform, whaling, and sugar. After 1860 an intelligible account can be given in terms of sugar alone. We note that in this period tenuous trading connections were supplanted by a steady effort toward development of Island resources, with an efficient productive mechanism evolving on the Island plantations. Honolulu was changing into a commercial and administrative city—trade alone could not have justified its growth. The grass shack was obsolescent. The natives were becoming adjusted to the new order in which the ways of the haole were dominant. By 1876 importations of labor were in prospect which would make the foreign part of the population preëminent in numbers, as sections of it already were economically and politically.

MERCHANDISING AND COMMERCE

The chief commercial development is the transfer of interest of the large mercantile houses from whaling to sugar; the use of their accumulated capital on the plantations; and the beginning of extension of their control through the industry. This we have already discussed.[1] The five firms whose successors handle over 95 per cent of sugar exports had all been set up by the end of our period.[2]

"Reëxport" commerce at Honolulu diminished drastically in significance during these years. Where in the middle forties "domestic exports" (that is, exports of domestically produced goods) were only a tenth to an eighth of "gross exports," in the early seventies they were around nine-tenths. The increase portrays the shift of activity from intermediary commerce to sugar exports. The reëxported goods in the forties had been mainly British,

[1] Pp. 185–186.

[2] Only one did not originate as a Honolulu store, or, as then called, "mercantile establishment." Alexander and Baldwin had begun as a plantation development on Maui, with their first big venture the building of the Hamakua irrigation ditch.

United States, and Chinese merchandise. Lima and Valparaiso in South America were intermediate supply ports for some of this merchandise. Lumber and fish entered the trade from the Russian settlements and the Oregon area. Two and three decades later there was a focusing of commerce to a far greater degree than before on the California and Oregon coasts as population there increased. Trade with the Orient diminished relatively; and South American trade nearly stopped.

Expansion of commerce as the plantations grew was accompanied by need of improved transportation. The first steamer for inter-island communication was introduced in 1853, an "old and shaky boat," lost afterward off Kauai. In 1859 a franchise for such service was gained by "The Hawaiian Steam Navigation Company." It brought in the steamer *Kilauea,* which ran for many years between the Islands. Regular transpacific steamer calls were begun only in 1870 with the commencement of a British run between San Francisco, New Zealand, and Australia, with calls at Honolulu.

Roads within the Islands improved slowly, despite the continued assessment of a road tax. On Oahu in 1853 there was a passable road toward Ewa and Waianae; but only horse trails extended to Waialua and over the Pali to Kaneohe.[3] By 1875 a road around Oahu was traversible by carriage, but there were only short ones elsewhere in the Islands. Traveling was generally by horseback.[4]

Money, Prices, and Banking

No general issue of coins was made in our period. Not until 1880 was a law for national coinage enacted.[5] A great variety of coins continued in circulation, with the Spanish gradually giving way to British, and especially American, coins, as trade relations with the West Coast grew all important.

The quantity of money in the hands of the general population increased slowly. By 1850 transactions throughout the Islands were being carried on frequently with money as one consideration; though of course barter continued, with imported merchan-

[3] S. E. Bishop, *Reminiscences of Old Hawaii,* p. 61.

[4] H. M. Whitney, *The Hawaiian Guide Book* (Honolulu: 1875), pp. 30, 121.

[5] In 1846 the minister of finance had been authorized to issue a copper coin, but apparently finally did not, though the coins are spoken of as ordered. (Report of Minister of Interior, May 21, 1845, April 28, 1847; Dispatch of Anson Chandler, U. S. Consul at Lahaina, to the Secretary of State, June 30, 1857.)

dise exchanging for beef, pork, poultry, goatskins, hard poi, vegetables, and the like, as well as for money. Small coins were not viewed with favor by the natives—in 1857 they were refusing dimes and half dimes.[6]

With respect to price changes: we have already spoken of the rapid inflation of land values,[7] and steady increase of wage rates.[8] Comparison of prices for consumption goods 1844–1875 shows only a moderate rise in most items.[9] Often there is no significant change when allowance is made for some probable variance in quality of the goods.[10] While no close estimate of change in economic "welfare" can be ventured, because of alteration in living habits over the time, the relatively stable prices of consumption goods and rapidly rising wages (for labor) and land values (for landowners) prove a sharp upward movement in real income.

The legal interest rate, binding where there was no stipulation otherwise, was 12 per cent a year;[11] but at times when the chronic stringency of capital became acute, the market rose much higher. During 1850–51 the rate was as high as 24 to 36 per cent;[12] and it was above 12 per cent also in the piping days after 1876.

The extraordinary rates of 1850–51 induced the first serious

[6] Dispatch of Anson Chandler cited above.

An instance of the operation of Gresham's law is noted in 1872. An act making the silver half dollar legal tender in payment of debts was followed by disappearance from circulation of gold. (A. F. Judd, *An Essay on the Hawaiian Currency and Silver Question,* Honolulu: 1884.)

[7] P. 137.

[8] Pp. 107, 193.

[9] *The Friend,* September 1844; *Polynesian,* January 9, 1847, March 6, 1847, January 17, 1857; *Pacific Commercial Advertiser,* May 27, 1857, July 2, 1906; *Report of Hawaiian Immigration Society, 1874,* p. 20.

H. M. Whitney gives sample prices in Honolulu for 1875, which may be compared with those from 1844 (above, p. 107): flour, 4 cents a lb., beef and mutton, 5–8 cents a lb., potatoes, 2½ cents a lb., eggs, $2.50–$4.16 per hundred, milk, 6–8 cents a quart, sheep $1–$2, goat 50 cents–$1, rent in Honolulu for foreign style house, $200–$600 annually, depending on the dwelling. Prices out of Honolulu were much lower. (*The Hawaiian Guide Book,* Honolulu: 1875, p. 118.)

[10] There was of course the short-lived inflation in prices of foodstuffs 1849–1851 when California demand was high; and also the price rise during the Civil War, especially in goods whose southern supply was shut off. Chief among these latter were rice and sugar, goods produced in the Islands, whose price rise was hence more significant in raising local income (the level of total consumption), than in diminishing consumption.

[11] R. C. Wyllie, in *The Friend,* May 1844; *Civil Code of 1859,* p. 357.

[12] R. C. Wyllie, *Capital and Banking,* paper read before the Agricultural Society, June 1, 1852, Miscellaneous Correspondence, 1852, Archives of Hawaii; Dispatch of Charles S. Punker, U. S. Consul at Lahaina, to Secretary of State, April 1, 1851, National Archives.

proposals to start a bank, and so economize on the community's monetary capital. R. C. Wyllie often advocated setting up a bank, pointing out in 1852 that several of the planters had gone bankrupt since the last meeting because they had no place to resort to for advances, when they were under pressure—even though they held good security.[13]

An act to charter a "Pacific Bank of Honolulu" passed the House of Representatives in June 1854, but was rejected by the House of Nobles.[14] Already an agency for a famous bank of the American West, Page, Bacon & Company of San Francisco, had been carried on by a Honolulu merchant; and a separate branch office was in existence from 1854 to December 1855, when disaster struck the home office.[15]

The first permanent bank was that of Bishop & Company, opened August 12, 1858, as a partnership between Charles R. Bishop and W. A. Aldrich. Sums up to $300 were receivable, with 8 per cent interest paid if they were left deposited three months. Larger sums were to be received under special agreement. Thirty days' notice was required of intent to withdraw money.[16] The bank was successful from the beginning, nearly $5000 in deposits being received the first day. The high demand for money capital put a premium on a means by which it could be mobilized.

A second Hawaiian bank, Claus Spreckels & Company, was opened seventeen years later, in May 1885.

[13] "Will anyone tell me that the Planters on these Islands can look to anything but certain ruin with labor at 50¢ a day and money at 3% a month. To avert that fatal consequence . . . I conceive of no expedient equal to the establishment of a bank." (*Op. cit.*)

He itemized here the specific values a bank would have in Hawaii: (1) a place of security for deposit and safekeeping of money, a more efficient device than to fortify and guard the house of every merchant and private capitalist; (2) a place of safe deposits for jewels, bills, deeds; (3) a place to draw together small sums of money which would otherwise remain idle, and so economize on monetary capital; (4) a means of transferring money, and of keeping accounts straight; (5) a means of reference as to the reliability of its customers; (6) an encouragement of habits of frugality; (7) a source of funds for persons who wish to engage in trade and commerce.

[14] Cecil G. Tilton, *History of Banking in Hawaii* (Honolulu: University of Hawaii Press, 1927), pp. 39–42.

[15] A charter given it in 1855 authorized it to issue notes. It was to handle money of the kingdom without charge, and the petitioners were personally liable. (Tilton, *op. cit.*, pp. 43, 46–47.)

[16] Advertisement and editorial in *The Friend,* August 1858; Tilton, *op. cit.*, pp. 50, 51, 56, 66.

GOVERNMENT REVENUE

We may briefly summarize changes in tax laws during the period. The framework of the laws of 1840 was continued, but gradually modified. (1) With respect to the poll tax, men continued to pay $1 per annum,[17] but the tax on women and girls was repealed in 1852.[18]

(2) The land tax was stated in terms of money only in the general tax law of 1846, with levies ranging from $10 for large estates (ahupuaas) to $1.50 for small estates (ilis). The amounts could be reduced at the discretion of the assessor.[19] In 1850 this and all other classes of taxes save the labor tax came to be payable in money only.[20] The feudal tradition of land tenure had led to obscure demarcation between taxes and rent, with a resultant implication that land obtained in fee simple ought to be free from all taxes.[21] A selfish pressure lay in the political power of the new large-scale holders of lands.[22] All land taxes were abolished in 1852.[23] They were restored in 1859 only under the compelling need for more revenue. The rate was ¼ per cent on assessed value (later specified as eight times the rental value),[24] the same rate as was applied to personal property, unless "specifically exempted." The rate was raised to ½ per cent in 1870 on both real and personal property,[25] to ¾ per cent in 1876,[26] and to 1 per cent in 1886.

[17] Over age 20, 1846–1859 (*Session Laws of 1846,* pp. 165–166); between ages 17 and 60, after 1859 (*Civil Code,* 1859, pp. 105–106).

[18] *Session Laws of 1852,* p. 23.

[19] *Session Laws of 1846,* pp. 165–171.

[20] *Session Laws of 1850,* p. 168.

[21] This was promised specifically to alodial holders of certain classes of land; and to all fee simple holders 1846–1850. (Acts of April 27, 1846 and August 7, 1850. See *Session Laws of 1850,* p. 192.)

[22] The Minister of Finance had argued that a property tax, owing to the peculiar state of the Islands, would be a difficult and expensive one to collect. G. W. Bates tartly commented that "it might have been much less difficult and expensive if the minister himself had not been in possession of huge estates." (*Sandwich Island Notes,* p. 320.)

[23] By resolution of the King and Nobles, July 1851, approved by the Legislature, June 1852.

[24] *Civil Code of 1859,* pp. 105–106.

[25] *Session Laws of 1870,* p. 33.

[26] An exemption to kanakas who held small homesteads (kuleanas) specified the tax to be on only the excess of value over $300; but tax assessors might at their own discretion raise the nominal valuation so that the small owner paid as before. (W. R. Castle, "Taxation in Hawaii," *Hawaiian Annual,* 1892, p. 68.)

(3) The labor tax, set in 1840 at 3 days a month, or 36 a year,[27] was reduced in 1853 to 6 days a year, and in 1874 to 4 days.[28] It could be commuted by a payment of $3 in 1853, and of $2 after 1859.[29]

There were a few other taxes of significance. Chattel taxes began with the law of 1846, with specified rates on horses, mares, cattle, dogs, and cats, and *ad valorem* levies on other property.[30] There was complete exemption for families having two children. A school tax of $2 for each adult male continued for many years after 1850.[31]

The inequity of these laws is evident. The poor kanaka earning $60 a year might be forced to pay almost or even entirely as much as a minister of the Crown at $4000 a year, or a prospering merchant.[32] Nominal land taxes, or none, encouraged the accumulation of land for speculative purposes, and its withholding from cultivation.

The tariff came to be differentiated, and followed a rising trend. The levy of 3 per cent *ad valorem* of 1842 [33] was raised to 5 per cent in 1845,[34] the maximum allowable under treaties with France and Great Britain. Higher tariffs were sought several times on alcoholic liquors imported; but such efforts for a number of years met effective opposition from French and British representatives. The 1855 act classified articles into four groups according to their usefulness, with duties of 15 per cent, 10 per cent, 5 per cent, and 0 per cent.[35] There was a heavy charge on wines and strong liquors. The Code of 1859 returned to the general tariff of 5 per cent, with higher duties on wines and spirits, where no existing treaty was contravened, and increased special charges on sugars, molasses and syrup, and coffee.[36] A duty on rice followed in 1864.[37] By 1875 most foreign goods were scheduled in the 10

[27] See p. 110; also *Session Laws of 1846*, pp. 165–171.

[28] *Session Laws of 1874*, p. 13.

[29] *Civil Code of 1859*, pp. 105–106.

[30] *Session Laws of 1846*, pp. 165–171.

[31] *Penal Code and Laws of 1850*, pp. 134-141.

[32] Especially was this true before 1846; and afterward if their assets were held in the form of cash, or (1852–1859) in land.

[33] *Laws of 1842*, p. 123.

[34] *Polynesian*, June 7, 1845.

[35] Act approved May 14, 1855. *Polynesian*, June 16, 1855.

[36] *Civil Code of 1859*, section 516, pp. 116–117. The first tariff on sugar, molasses, and coffee had been levied in 1852. (Tariff Act of July 6, 1852.)

[37] *Session Laws of 1864*, p. 12.

per cent bracket, though there was a free list for goods considered especially useful. Around 1850 the tariff was bringing in about two-fifths of total government revenue. The reliance on it increased somewhat during succeeding years due to higher rates.

Total revenue from taxes increased phenomenally after government organization in the forties. In 1842 when the Hawaiian government first began to keep something like systematic accounts, total receipts were about $41,000.[38] In the two-year fiscal period 1874–1875 receipts were a little over a million dollars. The Government debt grew nearly as fast. In 1843 it amounted to $30,000,[39] but was soon paid off. The first permanent debt of $22,000 in 1856 had grown to $335,050 in 1874–75,[40] a disproportionate part of the increase having taken place in the years just preceding.

The Royal House had come to be dependent for income on appropriations of the legislature. Kamehameha III in 1853 addressed the House of Representatives hopefully:

> I desire the representatives of the people to investigate the question whether I have legally or not lost my right to the special appropriation of ten thousand dollars for a yacht . . . Another question I have to submit to you. The appropriation for the necessary expenses of my household expired the 1st April . . . I thank my grateful people for . . . ten thousand dollars granted in 1852 in payment of my debts.[41]

The Government itself was hard pressed for revenue in the late sixties and early seventies prior to Reciprocity. The falling price of sugar at the end of the Civil War compelled retrenchment.[42]

Social Conditions; Population

The numbers of foreigners were greatest on Oahu and Kauai. With them came their views and habits of life. In 1847 Honolulu was already a town with 40 stores and warehouses, 5 markets,

[38] *Report of Minister of Finance* (1851), p. 13.

[39] R. C. Wyllie, in *The Friend,* May 1844.

[40] *Hawaiian Annual* (1906), p. 29.

[41] Address of May 9, 1853, quoted in G. W. Bates, *Sandwich Island Notes* (New York: 1854), p. 43.

[42] Two impressions from intelligent observers are the reports of Captain William Reynolds, U. S. N., Commanding U. S. S. *Lackawanna,* dated June 16, 1868, to the Secretary of the Navy, MS. in U. S. Naval Archives; and Rear Admiral A. M. Pennock, Commanding U. S. Naval force on North Pacific Station, dated February 15, 1873, dispatch to Secretary of the Navy, MS. in U. S. Naval Archives.

and over 1300 houses, five-eighths of which were of foreign construction.[43] Most of the people seen about the streets were natives. The women generally wore loose sack-like dresses, or "Mother Hubbards," which the missionaries had deemed suitable. The men were not permitted in the settlement without trousers: when they went out they took them off, and tied them around their necks, the upper part hanging gracefully behind.[44] The kanaka was coming gradually to conform to European dress, thought, and methods of production. Among the natives were excellent blacksmiths, carpenters, tailors, and capable house servants; but most of them earned their way by unskilled labor, or individual farming.

By 1875 Honolulu was an active little commercial city with a population of nearly 15,000, one-fifth of whom were foreigners. The native usually wore light European clothing in town. People of many lands and tongues jostled each other in the streets. There, as also in Hilo and Lahaina, wooden houses were replacing the remaining grass shacks. There was a hotel of 42 rooms, stone wharves, six churches, ten lodges, many stores, a hospital, a substantial jail, a customs house, a post office, and a brass band which played every Saturday.[45]

But to a number of isolated areas and valleys the foreigner came infrequently, or hardly at all; and there the native caught his fish and grew his taro as in former days. So far as he had wants the native economy could not supply, a day's work now and then sufficed to bring in a bit of wages—work perhaps on the government road, or perhaps for another native who had some plantation money to pass on. These isolated rural retreats remained, with the ghosts of the old culture—tabus, religion, and ancient tradition—hovering over them. They exist even now in dry or rough terrain, or small areas hard to get to: on Niihau; on parts of Molokai; near Hana and at Waipio and Kau on Maui; and Kau and part of Kona, Hawaii.[46]

Where foreigners were numerous, the psychological dominance of the foreign culture, both in its commercial and religious phases, was becoming complete. In 1854 the King, tired of his shad-

[43] *The Friend,* January 1, 1847.
[44] Frederick Walpole, *Four Years in the Pacific* (Paris: 1850), p. 267.
[45] H. M. Whitney, *The Hawaiian Guide Book,* pp. 6–15.
[46] See A. W. Lind, *An Island Community,* pp. 101–103.

owy power, said he would "rather command a fine clipper ship than reign over all the Islands of the Pacific." [47] The growing acclimatization of the Hawaiian to commercial environment and regular daily work is shown by a clear preference for them, about 1870 and after, above workers of any other race.[48]

Emerson wrote several years earlier of the change already apparent in the natives and in the Hawaiian scene:

> The spirit of servile obedience has to a great degree departed; now if men move at all they move from some other motive than the mere will of a chief. There is now more cheerful, productive industry, more comfort and wealth, obtained more honorably and intelligently, and more equally divided. There is more independence, less hypocrisy . . . Yet with this freedom comes more immorality, profanity, stealing, and litigation.
>
> Many now own their homesteads, and plows with which they cultivate their lots. The fields of waving grass and shrubbery, which fifteen or twenty years ago covered our hills and plains, with but here and there a flock of goats to revel in their luxury, are no longer to be seen. Horses and cattle have reduced their rank pasturage, and where formerly there were only taro, potato, and banana patches, there are now fields of cane, wheat, corn, rice, and coffee. Twenty years ago wooden or stone houses were quite rare; but now such buildings are common, and the grass hut is disappearing.[49]

Although there is evidence of social acclimatization there is none of physical adjustment to the new conditions—specifically, of increasing resistance of the native to disease—until about 1890. Up to that time the population drop was, with remarkable consistency, 50 per cent every 36 years. Several epidemics were disastrous—in 1848–49 one-tenth of the population, by report, died from measles and whooping cough, and other diseases; and smallpox swept several areas in 1853–54, in 1872, and 1881.[50] After 1850, part-Hawaiians increased rapidly in numbers until by 1900–1910 their absolute increase was equal to the absolute decrease of the pure-blooded native. The foreign segment of the population increased even more swiftly as labor was imported.

[47] Letter of David L. Gregg to Thomas L. Harris, Honolulu, February 3, 1854; Report of the Historical Commission, 1924, p. 21.

[48] Letter of S. N. Castle, July 23, 1869, in Ethel M. Damon, *Father Bond of Kohala* (Honolulu: *The Friend*, 1927), p. 191; "Report of the Committee on Labor," Planters' Monthly and Supply Company, in *Planters' Monthly*, November 1882.

[49] John S. Emerson, "Journal" for May 1852, in O. P. Emerson, *Pioneer Days in Hawaii* (New York: Doubleday Doran, 1928), pp. 182–183.

[50] Thomas G. Thrum, "Hawaiian Epidemics," *Hawaiian Annual* (1897), pp. 95–101; Lind, *An Island Community*, p. 98; O. P. Emerson, *op. cit.*, pp. 180–182.

CHART 10

THE TREND OF POPULATION

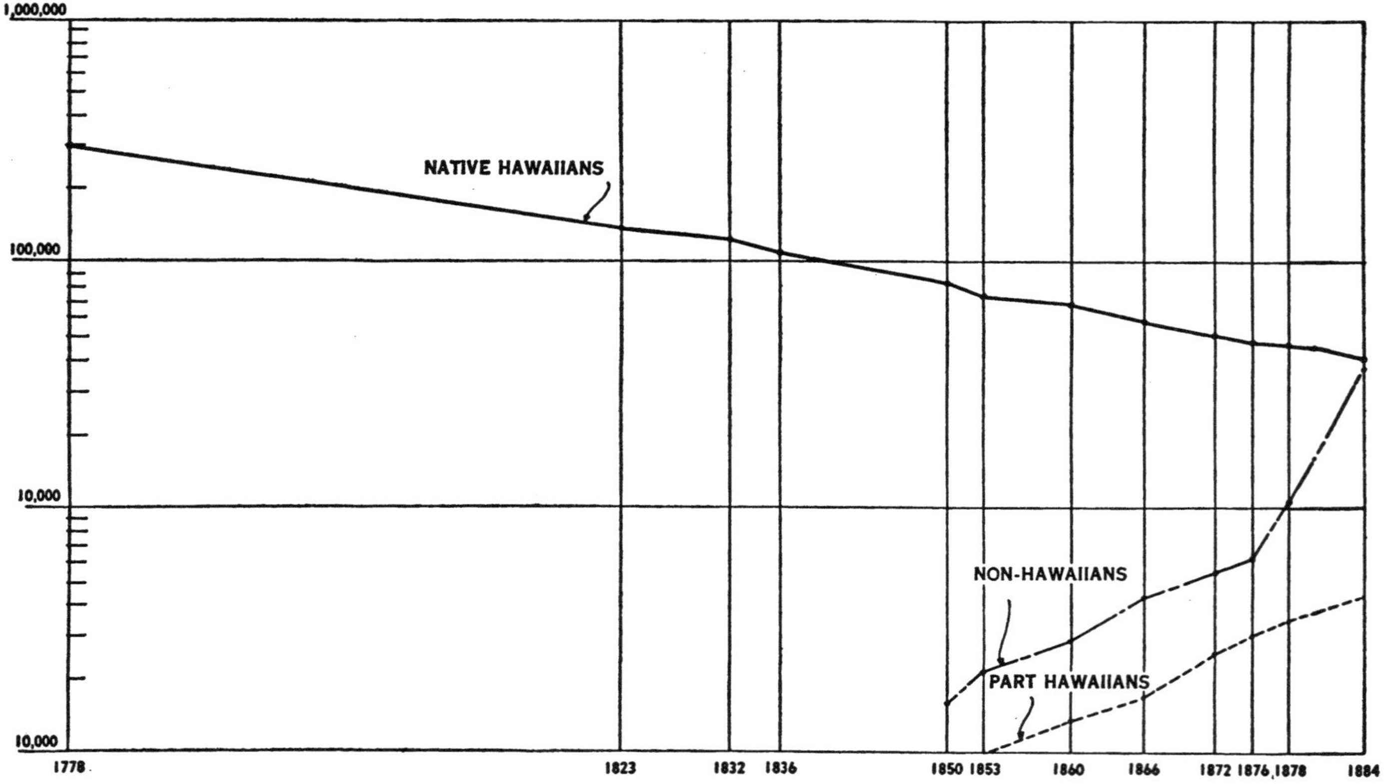

Data: Romanzo Adams, *Interracial Marriage in Hawaii* (New York: 1937), pp. 8, 9.

Apologia

Each historic process is unique. A study of the past can be justified through our gaining knowledge of the unique local circumstances; but one searches too for threads of general meaning in the mass of specific facts. We first came on the Hawaiian economy in a form as fully internally caused as we can find in any century, in any area of the world. Its feudal structure and its rigid traditional economy directed toward subsistence were the product of centuries of isolated development within the limit of Island resources.

Here is suggested the "natural" character of a feudal order, which has evolved independently out of different cultural backgrounds in several parts of the world.

After 1778 we follow a process of external causation and adaptive reaction, as an expanding western economy and culture absorbed Hawaii into its network. Up to the 1840's there was precarious, short-term, and shifting connection to the outer world. The white traders sought what plunder they could get from commercial contacts, effecting little permanent improvement. They expected to stay only a time in the Islands, and then retire with their gains to their northern homes. The native race was in sharp eclipse, declining in numbers and decaying in culture and morale. Techniques of production were improving rapidly; but the society was disintegrating nevertheless. Here is an extreme case where the optimum rate of technical progress is far less than an "economic" analysis only would recommend, for against the increase of real income is to be debited social costs of adjustment. Those costs are great where the improved techniques, coupled with an alien civilization, run sharply counter to deep-rooted habits of life. The effect of a "higher" culture impinging on a lower can be catastrophic if the induced rate of change is fast, even when the invasion is peaceful and humane, as in Hawaii.

The Land Reform of the forties was the major explicit breach in the native defense of its feudal order, foreshadowing complete victory of foreign economic ways. The meagerness of grants to commoners, contrasting with altruistic intents and proclamations, indicates that benefit to their morale was greater than the "real" benefit; but that such a reform could be carried out at all is encouraging evidence for the possibility and effectiveness, where need is felt and prestige of the innovators is adequate, of consciously planned and peaceful long-range social adjustment.

As markets developed along the borders of the Pacific, there was rapid change in the types of products and services the Islands supplied. When we try to interpret the shifting course of experiment in commerce and agriculture, there is evident the commonsense usefulness for the short run of the concept of "opportunity cost"—that is, of the attractiveness of alternative opportunities. In the longer run the quantity of all resources expanded in response to economic stimulus. Quantity of productive land, of capital equipment, and of labor were relatively fixed in the short run, but divertible by changes in demand from one channel of use to another; in the longer run the total quantity of each responded with more or less elasticity to stimulus, and labor responded remarkably.

Economic power, political authority, and social prestige moved into the hands of the white invaders as the century progressed. It is hard to imagine any healthy and dynamic society, essentially "capitalist" or not, in which the same sort of conquest would not have taken place. The most alert and able, themselves apostles of the recognized superior economy and society, and well adjusted to the coming order, must have succeeded to the seats of authority unless the bonds of tradition had paralyzed change. By 1876 the haole merchants and planters and missionaries had reformed the Island economic structure essentially after their own image. Their plantations, stores, steamships, churches, and weekly brass band were drowning the traditions of the past. Hawaii was bound tightly in the expanding commercial network of the world; and Hawaii's future was the future of its plantation economy.

SECTION IV

POSTSCRIPT ON RECIPROCITY

CHAPTER XIV

THE RECIPROCITY TREATY AND ITS AFTERMATH

THE INCENTIVE of Hawaiian sugar producers toward negotiating a reciprocity treaty well justified the efforts they made toward it. The United States tariff on sugar from 1846 to 1861 was 30 per cent *ad valorem*. Afterward to 1890 it was stated in terms of cents per pound, rising with the Civil War need for revenue to 3/4 cents a pound,[1] and declining afterward as the price of sugar declined.[2] Removal of the tariff through the period would have amounted to a bounty of 30–45 per cent to sugar producers, depending on the grade of sugar, and current price, and the tariff. Responding to local pressure, the Hawaiian government attempted to negotiate a reciprocity agreement with the United States in 1848, 1852 (when the Senate was apparently favorable), 1855, 1867–1870, and 1874–1875, when the Treaty was finally achieved.

The interest of the United States in such a treaty was primarily political. Through the forty years preceding, the Islands had been uneasily maintaining their independence against the jostling for commercial and political advantage of representatives of five nations. There had been threat of Spanish rule in the early days when Spain held Mexico and California;[3] and fear toward the end of the forties of attack by filibusters from California.[4] In 1839 Captain Laplace of the French frigate *Artemise* threatened the King with war if the government did not mend its ways with respect to treatment of French Catholic missionaries, and deposit $20,000 as security for future behavior. Captain Paulet of the British Navy in 1843 compelled a deed of cession of the Islands to him, and wielded complete authority for five months. The Anglo-French accord of 1843, recognizing Hawaiian independence, was a self-denying ordinance that could have been altered in

[1] Act of June 30, 1864.

[2] Act of July 14, 1870.

[3] Martinez' MS. "Journal," p. 211, Archives of Hawaii.

[4] R. C. Wyllie to Captain Bailey, commanding U. S. S. *St. Mary's*, San Francisco. (Copy in Hawaiian Historical Society Library.)

the future by agreement between the two parties. A French force in 1848 took possession of the fort and government buildings for several weeks.

The circumstance that many of the threats and acts against independence represented the unauthorized opinions of hotheads, generally to be sharply contrasted with the fairness of the policy of the home government, did not greatly reassure the Hawaiian King and ministers. In 1849, after the French foray, Kamehameha III authorized his commissioner to the United States, France, and England in secret instructions to sell the Islands "in case . . . our Royal Domain is exposed to further hostile attacks."[5] In 1851 the U. S. representative, Luther Severence, was given a deed ceding the Islands to the United States—in a sealed packet to be opened only in case the French definitely attacked the Islands again.

Enough has been listed, of all that might be listed, to indicate Hawaii's precarious sovereignty. The United States was well aware of the situation, and successive Presidents indicated their interest in seeing Hawaiian independence maintained.[6] Predominance in Hawaii of American shipping, merchants, missionaries, and advisers in the Government ensured a continuous partiality for closer contact with the United States rather than with any other country.[7]

The market in Hawaii was too insignificant to serve as adequate

[5] Instructions dated September 7, 1849. "A Suppressed Chapter of Hawaiian History," *Hawaiian Historical Society Publications* (1908), p. 11.

[6] "Hawaii's near approach to this continent and the intercourse which American vessels have with it—such vessels constituting five-sixths of all who annually visit it—could not but create dissatisfaction on the part of the United States at any attempt of a third power . . . to take possession of the Islands." (President Tyler's Message to Congress, December 31, 1842.)

President Johnson recommended a reciprocity treaty in 1868: ". . . the United States would be unwilling to see the Islands pass under foreign control . . . A reciprocity treaty would be a guarantee of the good will and forbearance of all nations until the Islands shall of themselves, at no distant day, voluntarily apply for admission into the Union." (Message to Congress, December 9, 1868.)

[7] Of goods imported 1845–1859, \$8.6 millions came from the U. S., \$2.9 millions from Britain, \$2.3 millions from all other countries. (*Report of Minister of Foreign Affairs,* 1860, p. 7.) In 1872 14.4 million pounds of sugar were sent to the U. S., 2.6 million pounds to all other markets; in 1875 23.8 million pounds to the U. S. to 1.3 elsewhere. (*Hawaiian Annual,* 1876, p. 57; 1877, p. 49; William H. Taylor, "The Hawaiian Sugar Industry," p. 15.) Of the estimated total value of the sugar industry in 1883, \$15.9 millions, Americans owned \$10.2 millions. (Laughlin and Willis, *Reciprocity* (New York: 1903), p. 74.)

incentive to the United States to negotiate a reciprocity treaty. The Hawaiians, made conscious of this by their lack of success in 1855 and 1867, undertook a campaign of a political character in the 1870's, which finally secured them their hoped-for reward. The argument was that the Islands were about to drift under British influence. Three evidences were adduced: (1) The Islands were under the pressure of deflation induced by decline of Civil War prices to normal levels. The Government was increasing its debt, in part by a large loan from an Englishman. It was feared that a default on payment might lead to the holding of the Islands by Britain as indemnity.[8] (2) Report also came to Washington that there was a movement to import Hindu coolies to Hawaii as plantation labor, with British consent and under British supervision; and (3), that the Hawaiian planters, having found they could sell their sugar to better advantage in free trade ports of Australia, were planning to send their whole 1875–76 crop there. If Island trade were diverted to Britain, Hawaii would come under British influence, and probably ultimately become a British dependency.[9]

These arguments are no more than superficially plausible. The threat of an immanent shift of trade, the most persuasive of all, seems likely to have been "propaganda." The trend of trade in the seventies argues strongly against such a possibility:

EXPORTS OF SUGAR FROM HAWAII
(in million pounds)[10]

To:	1872	1873	1874	1875
The United States	14.41	14.83	18.19	23.76
British Columbia, Australia, and New Zealand	2.57	8.28	6.23	1.22
All other ports	.02	.02	.14	.10

[8] Chalfant Robinson, *Two Reciprocity Treaties* (New Haven: 1904), p. 121. Also A. M. Pennock, Rear Admiral commanding the U. S. Naval Force on North Pacific Station, in a dispatch to the Secretary of the Navy: "It is believed by many . . . that . . . revenue from all available sources will be unable to continue the government for a longer period than two or three years. All thinking men have arrived at the conclusion that something decisive must be done to avoid incurring a foreign debt, which would ultimately place the Islands at the mercy of that Government whose citizens shall hold the claim." (Dated February 15, 1873, U. S. Naval Archives.)

[9] Robinson, *op. cit.*, p. 123.

[10] *Hawaiian Annual* (1876), p. 57; 1877, p. 49. See figures and analysis in Taylor, "The Hawaiian Sugar Industry," p. 15.

In the Congressional inquiry into the treaty and in the debate, fear of foreign domination took the leading role. "The arguments for the treaty were of a negative character. The danger of British influence in the Islands seemed to be of greatest weight." [11] In the background were the expanding population of Australia, and the developing British trade network in the Pacific. The majority report of the Ways and Means Committee favoring the treaty,[12] touched on commercial aspects negatively, urging that loss of tariff revenue was negligible, and that trade might be encouraged to offset any such loss. Their case relied chiefly on assurance that the Islands would not fall to another foreign power. The minority attacked the commercial effect of the treaty, showing that the small amount of Hawaiian sugar imported could not cause the price of sugar to drop to consumers, that tariff revenue would be lost to the government, and that indirect trade benefits were problematical. They had no trouble in proving the proposed treaty a bad business proposition. The arguments of both sides were right. The final affirmative vote showed that Congress felt political gain weighed heavier than commercial loss.[13]

The Treaty came into effect September 9, 1876.[14] It provided for free entry into the United States of fifteen tropical products, of which the most important were sugar, molasses, and rice. In exchange Hawaii was to admit free agricultural equipment and hardware, machinery of all kinds, grain and breadstuffs, building materials, and cotton and woolen goods. But the important imports of clothing and liquors were omitted from the list.[15]

[11] Laughlin and Willis, *Reciprocity*, p. 77.

[12] Reports of Committee, 1873–1876, 44th Congress, 1st session, no. 116; comments in Laughlin and Willis, *op. cit.*, pp. 76–82; Robinson, *op. cit.*, pp. 124–132.

[13] "The Hawaiian treaty was negotiated for the purpose of securing political control of the Islands, making them industrially and commercially a part of the United States, and preventing any other great power from securing a foothold there, which might be adverse to the welfare and safety of our Pacific coast in time of war . . . As political supremacy in the Islands must inevitably follow the commerce, it was recognized that this country must make favorable concessions to them, or else let them follow the inevitable tendency and drift slowly into the status of an English colony." (Report of the Committee on Foreign Relations of the U. S. Senate, 1894, p. 103.)

[14] It was to run for seven years. The discussion over renewal, beginning in 1883, was concluded affirmatively only in 1887. The new treaty, including rights for a naval coaling and repair station at Pearl Harbor, was in force till Annexation in 1898, though its benefit to sugar producers was canceled 1890–1894 by the McKinley Act abrogating duties on sugar from any source.

[15] The text of the treaty is given in Laughlin and Willis, *Reciprocity*, pp. 473–474; and in Robinson, *Two Reciprocity Treaties*, pp. 197–199.

The anticipation of Congress that the Treaty would secure Hawaii against drifting into the sphere of influence and control of another power was justified. Closer commercial connections led to Annexation in 1898. But the argument that the commercial loss must always remain small because of limited area and declining population in the Islands was not realized. When the Treaty was being discussed in Congress in 1875, the imports of Hawaiian sugar (12,500 tons) were only 1 per cent of U. S. consumption. But well over 10 per cent (222,000 tons) was being furnished by 1898, as the lure of high profit had induced introduction of contract labor, and intensive and extensive cultivation of land.[16] Exports from the United States to the Islands rose also, though not so extravagantly.

Since Hawaiian sugar remained, despite expansion, a small part of the consumption of the United States, price did not fall appreciably because of the increased import from Hawaii. With respect to the price paid by refiners for raw sugar, the practice was earlier developed by competition (and later maintained by custom as sugar refining became cartelized) of paying the going world price plus duty. Hence the whole benefit of tariff elimination came to the Hawaiian planter.[17] The Treasury Bureau of Statistics calculated the amount of bounty so transferred as shown in the table below.

This bounty does not represent additional profit to the planters to the extent they were induced to expand their acreage to include poorer land, or utilize expensive equipment and heavy fertilization to increase their crops.

The era after Reciprocity was in Hawaii one of booming expansion, as $50–$60 a ton, the former duty, was added to the then

[16] Increase in rice exports was still more extraordinary, until sugar expansion effectively bid away land and labor from rice production. The volume was 787 tons in 1875, 6085 tons in 1882. Exports were irregular afterward, and declining in the nineties. The rapid early increase is explained in that rice production was a young industry, its opportunities just being explored.

[17] "The United States Treasury lost very considerable amounts; so much sugar came in that would have been taxed. The consumers in the United States did not get the benefit. The price of sugar did not fall, nor could it have been expected to fall . . . The effect of the Reciprocity Treaty was to include the Hawaiian planters within the pale of the protective system. They were put in the same position as the planters of Louisiana. Or, to state the outcome in other terms, the United States gave a bounty of about two cents a pound to sugar growers of Hawaii." (F. W. Taussig, *Some Aspects of the Tariff Question* (Cambridge, Mass.: 1915), pp. 59–60.)

BOUNTY TRANSFERRED

	Sugar Imported (million pounds)	Total Value of Sugar and Molasses (million dollars)	Estimated Duties Remitted (million dollars)
1877............	30.6	2.1	.99
1878............	30.4	2.3	.99
1879............	41.7	2.8	1.27
1880............	61.6	4.2	1.88
1881............	76.9	5.0	2.43
1882............	106.2	6.9	3.31
1883............	114.1	7.4	3.55
1884............	125.1	7.1	2.96
1885............	169.7	8.2	3.94
1886............	191.7	9.2	4.44
1887............	218.3	9.3	5.02
1888............	228.5	10.3	5.00
1889............	243.3	12.1	5.21
1890............	224.5	11.6	4.80
1891............	307.3	13.2	5.54*
1892............	262.6	7.4	*
1893............	288.5	8.5	*
1894............	324.7	9.4	*
1895............	274.2	7.4	*
1896............	352.2	11.3	4.54
1897............	431.2	13.2	5.27
1898............	499.8	16.7	13.08

* Duties remitted calculated only to April 1, 1891, when all sugar was admitted free.

The above table is adapted from Monthly Summary, Commerce and Finance, Treasury Bureau of Statistics, November 1899, p. 1375. All final numerals are carried to the nearest unit.

received price of $120–$135.[18] The bonus amounted in some years to over 100 per cent of the price otherwise realizable. The industry had already survived its infancy, and was expanding healthily, as we have shown, despite falling prices after the Civil War. Now sugar was as profitable as gold mines were only hoped to be. The earth was scoured for cheap labor; land already in use was cultivated more zealously. About 20,000 acres of new land were brought into use in six years. Heavy applications of

[18] Report of Commission appointed by the Secretary of the Treasury to Investigate Alleged Frauds under the Reciprocity Treaty, 1883; in George S. Boutwell, *Remarks before Committee on Foreign Affairs of the House of Representatives* (Washington: G. P. O., 1882), p. 14.

fertilizer were made, and water came to be pumped from artesian wells, carried by tunnel through mountains, and flumed overland as far as 30 miles. There were 20 plantations in 1875; five years later[19] there were already 63. Planters and businessmen generally in the Islands might have written at the bottom of their accounts for the year when Reciprocity came into effect as did P. C. Jones of Brewer & Company, "So ends the year 1876, Praise God." [20]

What shall be our judgment on the Reciprocity Treaty? Economists have unanimously condemned it. Professor Taussig made it the text of a favorite lecture:

> So far as the planters had to turn to poorer sources of supply, or pushed their plantations to extra yield by high cultivation, they were led to make that disadvantageous application of labor and capital which is the more ordinary consequence of a protective duty. The higher price of sugar enabled the planters to carry on some sugar growing which they could not have carried on without the bonus. It is impossible to determine how large a part of the sugar growing of the Islands was in this sense wasteful.[21]

This is a static economic logic, concerned with maximizing aggregate world output, and looking toward world allocation of resources as the means. It assumes costs and prices represent social values; that is, that "social net revenue" equals private net revenue; and it neglects certain dynamic considerations, such as rates of technical change, and the possibility of development of monopolistic or monopsonistic situations. But following out such channels of thought does not lead one to a different conclusion from that of Taussig.

We may look at the matter from the more limited viewpoints of Hawaii and the United States. Reciprocity was not an unalloyed joy to the Islands, for to be weighed against the increase of income to the planters and its percolation down to other groups are (1) the risk factor involved in making Hawaii dependent on one crop; (2) probable encouragement to concentrating control of the industry into the hands of a very few "factors"; (3) problems of social adjustment and, in general, the questionable desirability of

[19] A financial crisis resulted from the demand of plantations for capital. The Hawaiian government came to the rescue of the industry, and lent it money for a season.

[20] Sullivan, *op. cit.*, p. 142.

[21] *Op. cit.*, p. 64.

developing a heterogeneous population, as men of many lands were imported to labor on the plantations.

For the United States there was loss to the Treasury to be balanced against political gain. The United States could have made the best of both worlds, economic and political, by a firm extension of the Monroe Doctrine without tariff concession, as the minority of the Congressional Committee had recommended.

APPENDICES

APPENDIX I

Notes on Special Phases of Whaling

(A) Whale Products

Up to about 1860 sperm oil was the most valuable of the whale products. A single whale yielded as much as 100 barrels. Formerly most of the oil was used for sperm candles, but toward the end of the nineteenth century it came to be used chiefly for fine lubricating purposes. In some uses it has not yet been excelled.

"Whale oil" includes oil from all other varieties of whales, and also from the blackfish, porpoise, and walrus. A "right whale" may yield up to 230 barrels of oil. Whale oil, in the early days used in the evil-smelling whale oil lamp, came to be utilized later in leather tanning, preparation of coarse woolen cloths, manufacture of soft soaps, and in coarse paints and varnishes. Its use as a heavy lubricating oil was important before petroleum came on the market in quantity.[1]

Whalebone was thrown away in the early nineteenth century when its value was as low as 7 cents a pound. It became in the late nineteenth century the most important product of all, its price rising to $4 to $5 a pound. The difference in price trend between oils and bone after 1864 is due to a combination of the factors of joint production, and of petroleum competition: with increasing use of petroleum, whale oils irregularly declined in value; and the lessened supply of bone led to a great rise in its price.

Whalebone comes from the "right" or "sulphur-bottom" whale, occurring as several hundred blades of up to 15 feet in length, hanging down on each side of the whale's tongue. Its value lies mainly in its property of retaining any desired shape, once softened in hot water or by open heat. It seems first to have been used for women's stays, then in parasols and umbrellas, in upholstery, in fishing rods and whips, springs, wheels, and shafts. The original use—corsets and stays—took most of the output at the end of the century, though there, as elsewhere, steel, celluloid, rattan, and other materials served as increasingly adequate substitutes. In the twentieth century a price decline carried its value down to a negligible figure.

[1] Tower, *History of the American Whale Fishery*, p. 94.

(B) Whales

Two varieties can be taken as types: the sperm, and the bowhead, a variety of the "right" whale. The sperm whale is distinguished by a long narrow jaw, and, above the mouth, a very bulky mass consisting of portions called the "case," "junk," and "white horse." In the "case" was a reservoir of liquid spermaceti of up to 30 barrels in quantity, which had only to be bailed out and headed up. This is the oil mentioned above, considered of unique merit to the present time for oiling watches and similar fine machinery. The length of a common sperm whale was 40 or 50 feet.

The bowhead was a thicker and shorter whale. The portion below the mouth, the "lips," was, by contrast with the sperm whale, thick and rich in oil.

Sperm whales were especially numerous along the Chilean coast, and in the "Offshore Grounds" to the west, before those areas were exhausted; but they were also widely distributed throughout the world in tropical and subtropical waters. Only rarely were they found in Arctic waters.[2]

The various types of right whales frequent temperate seas of the north and south hemispheres, into the Arctic and Antarctic regions.

(C) The "Lay"; Food

Whalemen were paid by a "lay," or fractional part of the net proceeds of a voyage. The captain, mates, boat steerers and coopers received lays varying from 1/8 to 1/100; able and ordinary seamen, stewards, cooks, and blacksmiths received from 1/100 to 1/160; and green hands and boys, from 1/160 to 1/200.[3] Thus for a voyage of the ***Benjamin Tucker*** of New Bedford, returning in 1851, net proceeds were $45,682, and a seaman with the relatively small lay of 1/260 received $175.70.

Hohman estimates that the average wage of the whaling foremast hand during the mid-nineteenth century was $3 to $8 a month, in addition to board and quarters, but without subtracting the cost of outfit and slop-chest articles, which were often sold to the crew at 100 per cent profit.[4] Pay was below that of merchant ships, and that of comparably skilled occupations ashore.

The fo'c's'le, or quarters of the seamen, located forward of the foremast, was usually cramped and stinking. Men and their gear were crammed tight in a narrow space. As to food, scarcity and poor quality were commonly complained of. For breakfast the foremast hands

[2] J. T. Jenkins: *A History of the Whale Fisheries* (London: Witherby, 1921), p. 20.

[3] Hohman: *The American Whaleman* (New York: 1928), p. 217.

[4] *Ibid.*, p. 238.

might receive salt beef or pork, hard bread, coffee, and molasses; for dinner, hard bread and salt pork or beef; and for supper the same "salt horse," hard tack, and tea or coffee. "Duff," something of a delicacy, was made of flour, lard, and yeast, with sometimes salt pork fat chopped and added.[5]

(D) Whale Catching, "Cutting in" and "Trying out"

At sea, life aboard ship varied from complete inactivity, for weeks on end, to labor almost day and night while a whale was being converted into oil. It was natural that in reaction from this life the sailor when on land was apt to throw himself into drunken sensuality, so long as the money held out.

At all times, so long as a cask remained unfilled, a lookout was kept at the masthead. When "a blow" was sighted, boats were lowered away, and rowed or sailed to the whale. The whale was quietly approached from his right rear, if possible, out of his range of vision. At the mate's command "Give it to him," the boat steerer plunged the harpoon up to the hilt into the whale, generally at the neck or somewhat back. A second harpoon was thrown if possible.

The whale might "sound" (dive), or "run" (swim along the surface), or even sometimes rush upon the boat and attack it with open jaws. If he sounded, the line attached to the harpoon ran out from its keg at such speed as to set fire to the loggerhead, and water was heaved on it. The whale would not stay more than an hour or so in the depths. Returning to the surface for breathing, he would be set on again.

When dead the whale would be towed to the ship—often a weary pull for the oarsmen of several boats in line—and tied alongside to windward if possible, below the "cutting-in frame," a platform built out from the edge of the ship. If it was a sperm whale, the lower jaw was detached, and the junk (above the jaw) hoisted aboard.

The next step was the "cutting in" proper: the thick "blanket," or blubber, was spaded clear from the carcass in a spiral fashion. A block and tackle was attached to the forward end of the blanket. As the windlass crew heaved, the "blanket" rose higher and higher, the cutters plied their spades, and the whale rolled over and over.

When all the blubber was off, the carcass was turned loose to the numbers of sharks sure to be about. Work was carried on at top speed to finish before sharks should have torn the blubber to shreds, or the weather turn foul.

The blanket was cut into smaller sections, "horse-pieces," and then minced into "books" or "bible pieces," on the same principle as farmers nowadays cut up hog lard. Then it was "tryed out" (rendered) in a

[5] Hohman, *The American Whaleman*, p. 131.

deck furnace, containing two large kettles for the purpose. When the bible pieces had given up their oil, they were used as fuel. The whaler was proclaimed over the horizon, merchant vessels claimed, by the peculiar stench from the "trying out;" and marked by its blackened sails and smoke in daytime, and illuminated masts and rigging at night.

The oil was thoroughly cooled on deck, and stowed away.

(E) Sample Entries from a Whaling Log Book

Behring Straits of Ice Cape

September 9, 1851, Tuesday

Begins with fine weather and plenty of polar whales ensight. lored three boats. Capt boat struck and killed and sunk him took the ship along side of him holed him up and commence cuttin him in middle A strong wind from SE at 11 the peas tore of and the flook chane parted and lost about twenty lbs oil at 12 wone ship at daylight plenty of whales ensight lored the Boats Larbord Boat Struck Killed took him along side commence cuttin North Lat obs 70 10.

(Log Book of the *George and Mary* of New London, in Arctic Ocean Whaling. Archives of Hawaii.)

September 15, 1852, Wednesday

Begins with fine clear pleasant weather light Breeze from SE heading NE by E 12 ships Ensight Standing the Same Saw one whale did not loar. Middle hours fresh Breeze latter part Raised whale loared the Boats BB struck Killed took him along side at 12 35 Ships Ensight 5 boiling one cutting. North Lat by Obs 68 10 Long by Ac 169 30.

(Log Book of the *George and Mary*.)

(F) Abridged Whaling Instructions

Instructions to be Perused Frequently during the Voyage by the Captain and Mates

Cold Spring Harbor, Long Island
State of New York, July 21, 1847

To Captain Philader Winbert
Sir:

The ship "Richmond" of this place, fitted and supplied with everything deemed requisite for a Whaling Voyage, now lying in this harbor, is placed under your charge. You will take command of her and her crew and proceed to *the Pacific Ocean, to procure a cargo of whale oil* [written in].

The ship has been put in good order, and furnished with the necessary articles to keep her so and extras to guard against contingencies. We shall expect you to keep her in good order until the completion of the voyage; using diligence and economy and your best exertions to bring the voyage to a successful and speedy termination. The ship is supplied with a slop chest of clothing, and an invoice of other articles to supply the crew and to barter for recruits, besides which, you have *five hundred* [written in] dollars, in cash. Everything being provided for your safety and comfort and that of your crew, we shall expect you to prosecute the voyage until your ship is full or nearly so.

You are not to take any merchandise for sale on your own account, or for any other person, neither are you to allow it to be done by any of your officers or crew; nor are you to engage in any acts or trade inconsistent with a whaling voyage.

In the course of your voyage, it will be necessary to stop at ports or places, to recruit your vessel and refresh your crew, the selection of which must be left to your good judgment: in governing your decision, you will give particular attention to the safety of the harbors, and reasonableness of the prices of refreshments you may be in need of at the time, and where they will receive in exchange such articles as you may have on board to give, and where whaling vessels are received with favor without risk of capture or plunder or exposure of health.

You are carefully to observe all port regulations at the places you may visit. The charges at some places are high and unreasonable, the regulations strict and severe, you are to give particular attention to their laws, violating none, and to pay all dues and exactions that may be required; also to be careful that you are not the subject of imposition . . .

In foreign ports you will apply for advice and assistance where you can obtain them to best advantage. The United States Consuls are the proper persons to apply to; some of them charge high, still, you will find it generally expedient to call upon them. They are clothed in many cases with beneficent legal authority which no other person can exercise.

If you are obliged to discharge some of your crew abroad, from sickness, inefficiency, or other good cause, you will settle with them in full, according to the shipping articles and U. S. Laws, taking their discharge and the Consul's certificate of discharge and settlements, so as to prevent all difficulty and trouble in the United States when you return . . .

You will exercise prudence and economy in all your expenditures. A full account of all your disbursements, exchanges for recruits, and supplies for your crew, will be expected on your return, an account book is placed on board for the purpose. You will enter in full all settlements made with such of the crew as you may of necessity be compelled to discharge; all advances to the crew during the voyage; and if the advance is made in money, you will also enter the rate and amount of exchange . . .

The casks, before being filled with oil, you are to keep full of water, and salted, to prevent decay; and frequently coopered to prevent their leaking; when ready to be filled with oil, the water is to be entirely taken out and the casks cleansed, swabbed out, and re-coopered . . .

You will see that the blubber is properly tried, that the oil does not get burnt or discolored in boiling; and that the blubber does not become rancid before boiling; either injury is equally detrimental to its value and greatly injures its sale.

You will see that the bone be properly scraped and cured, and neatly bundled before arrival . . . It will be best to leave it open to dry as long as it will answer, before putting it up and stowing it away . . .

You are not to omit taking a whale when you can, even if you are obliged to suspend boiling or other duty.

You will avoid visiting other ships, or receiving company on board of your own to a prejudicial extent.

You are to maintain a strict discipline and energetic deportment on board, requiring every man to do his duty; to unite kindness and humanity in enforcing your orders, keeping your crew well supplied with provisions and other articles furnished for the purpose, and carefully guarding against desertion and improper absence from the vessel . . .

Recommending you to take all possible care of the ship and crew, and especially the health and safety of the latter, and to preserve peace and harmony with your men; we wish you a prosperous voyage and a safe return; and trust that a full cargo of oil and bone for the benefit of all concerned may be the evidence of your diligence, care, and skill, upon which a profitable result will greatly depend.

[From a copy in the Archives of Hawaii.]

APPENDIX II

Statistical Tables

These data are subject to varying degrees of doubt into the late forties, and even the fifties. Earlier figures are useful in following changing levels, not as indicating absolute quantities. Especially doubtful figures are enclosed in parentheses. Further comments follow the tables.

All data are carried to the nearest final digit.

	(1)	(2)	(3)	(4)	(5)	(6)
		Ship Arrivals		Gross Imports	Gross Exports	Domestic Exports
	Whalers	Traders	Nat'l Ships	(in thousands of dollars)		
1824	104	17*				
1825	78	18				
1826	138	37				
1827	98	23				
1828	157	37				
1829	173	32				
1830	157	39				
1831	159	37				
1832	198	37				
1833	189	35				
1834	—	31				
1835	—	33				
1836	—	39		($413.0)	($73.2)	
1837	129	32		($350.0)	($79.6)	
1838	148	23		($207.0)	($65.9)	
1839	116	33		($378.5)	($94.4)	
1840	86	31		($218.0)	($75.1)	
1841	133	31		($445.2)	($93.3)	
1842	172	46				
1843	383	37	11	$223.4		
1844	490	42	14	350.3	$169.6	
1845	542	41	14	546.9	269.7	$31.4
1846	596	53	17	598.4	682.9	46.5
1847	406	67	4	710.1	264.2	68.4
1848	309	90†	7	605.6	300.4	66.8

* Honolulu only through 1847.
† All ports after 1847.

	(1)	(2)	(3)	(4)	(5)	(6)
		Ship Arrivals		Gross Imports	Gross Exports	Domestic Exports
	Whalers	Traders	Nat'l Ships	(in thousands of dollars)		
1849	274	180	12	729.7	383.2	(185.1)
1850	237	469	12	1,035.1	783.1	536.5
1851	220	446	7	1,823.8	691.2	309.8
1852	519	235	3	759.9	638.4	257.3
1853	535	211	7	1,402.0	473.0	281.6
1854	525	125	16	1,590.8	585.1	274.0
1855	468	154	13	1,383.2	572.6	274.7
1856	366	123	9	1,151.4	670.8	(466.3)
1857	387	82	10	1,130.2	645.5	423.3
1858	526	115	10	1,089.7	787.1	530.0
1859	549	139	5	1,555.6	931.3	628.6
1860	325	117	10	1,223.7	807.5	480.5
1861	190	93	7	761.1	659.8	476.9
1862	73	113	6	998.2	838.4	586.5
1863	102	88	6	1,175.5	1,025.9	744.4
1864	130	157	8	1,712.2	1,662.2	1,113.3
1865	180	151	7	1,946.3	1,808.3	1,521.2
1866	229	150	3	1,993.8	1,934.6	1,505.8
1867	243	134	11	1,957.4	1,679.7	1,324.1
1868	253	113	7	1,935.8	1,898.2	1,450.3
1869	102	127	6	2,040.1	2,366.4	1,743.3
1870	118	159	16	1,930.2	2,144.9	1,514.4
1871	47	171	9	1,625.9	1,892.1	1,733.1
1872	47	146	7	1,746.2	1,607.5	1,402.7
1873	63	109	12	1,437.6	2,128.1	1,725.5
1874	43	120	13	1,310.8	1,839.6	1,622.5
1875	41	120	22	1,505.7	2,089.7	1,774.1
1876	37	141	14	1,811.8	2,241.0	2,055.1
1877	33	168	17	2,554.4	3,676.2	2,462.4
1878	27	232	11	3,046.4	3,548.5	3,334.0
1879	25	251	6	3,743.0	3,781.7	3,665.5
1880	16	239	15	3,673.3	4,968.4	4,889.2

Sources, and limitations, of data: Columns (1), (2), (3), 1824–1842, from a register kept by S. Reynolds, Merchant of Honolulu. Published in *The Friend,* May 1844. Column (1) is corrected by comparison with data of Kuykendall: *The Hawaiian Kingdom,* p. 307, which makes use of records of William Richards and E. Spaulding, in *Sailor's Magazine and Naval Journal* (New York), August 1834.

For 1843–1849, *Hawaiian Annual* (1876), p. 56.

For 1850–1880, *Hawaiian Annual* (1890), p. 25.

From all of these data a certain subtraction is necessary in order to get number of *ships,* to allow for those which touched more than once. In the case of whalers, this deduction is estimated to be about one-third.

Columns (4), (5), 1836–41, from records of Pierce and Brewer, approximate, and include imports to the port of Honolulu only. Exports are from all the Islands. Data for 1840 extends from January 1 to August 17; data for 1841, from August 18, 1840 to August 17, 1841. In the *Polynesian*, September 1840, p. 54.

For 1843–1874, *Hawaiian Annual* (1876). For 1875–1880, *Hawaiian Annual* (1883).

Column (6), 1845–1848, Exhibit of Minister of Finance, Table C, 1862, Archives of Hawaii.

1849–1880, same as Columns (4) and (5).

	Exports: (7) Sugar (tons)	(8) Molasses (thousand gallons)	(9) Coffee (thousand lbs.)	(10) Rice (thousand lbs.)	(11) Paddy (M lbs.)	(12) Salt	
1836						3520	bbls.
1837	2	3				2160	"
1838	44	12				1120	"
1839	50	75				(2160)	"
1840	288	52				(2880)	"
1841	30	6				(1800)	"
1842	286	32					
1843	286	32					
1844	257	27				2810	"
1845	151	19					
1846	150	16	10			8500	"
1847	297	18	26			15,549	"
1848	250	29	58			4570	"
1849	327	41	28			2866	"
1850	377	129	210			5750	"
1851	10	44	26			3769	"
1852	367	62	117			7118	"
1853	317	76	50			3509	"
1854	288	68	88			5041	"
1855	145	26	78			6328	"
1856	277	49	64			4691	"
1857	350	59	312			1550	"
1858	602	48	65			1125	tons
1859	913	75	83			884	"
1860	572	109	49			884	"
1861	1,281	128	45			762	"
1862	1,503	130	146	111	812	598	"
1863	2,646	114	113	123	598	656	"
1864	5,207	340	50	320	105	729	"
1865	7,659	543	311	154		120	"
1866	8,865	852	94	435		739	"
1867	8,564	545	128	442	572	107	"
1868	9,156	493	78	40	863	540	"
1869	9,151	338	341	49	1,587	1,152	"
1870	9,392	217	415	152	535	2,573	"

	Exports: (7) Sugar	(8) Molasses	(9) Coffee	(10) Rice	(11) Paddy	(12) Salt
	(tons)	(thousand gallons)	(thousand lbs.)	(thousand lbs.)	(M lbs.)	
1871	10,880	271	47	417	867	711 tons
1872	8,498	192	39	455	895	522 "
1873	11,565	146	262	941	508	445 "
1874	12,283	90	75	1,188	439	730 "
1875	12,540	94	166	1,574	556	96 "
1876	13,036	139	154	2,259	1,543	5 "
1877	12,788	151	101	2,691	2,572	322 "
1878	19,216	93	128	2,768	2,785	180 "
1879	24,510	87	74	4,793	39	50 "
1880	31,792	198	100	6,470		14 "

Sources, and limitations, of data:

Columns (7), (8), 1837–1841. Accounts of Pierce and Brewer, September 12, 1840, September 4, 1841. Data for 1840 are partly estimated; 1841 data run for a fiscal year other than the calendar year, August 18, 1840 to August 17, 1841.

1843–1868, *Hawaiian Annual* (1875), p. 37.

1869–1880, *Hawaiian Annual* (1900), p. 25.

Column (9), 1845–1856, *Pacific Commercial Advertiser,* April 2, 1857.

1857–1859, *Hawaiian Annual* (1875), p. 37.

Columns (9), (10), 1860–1880, *Hawaiian Annual* (1900).

Column (11), 1862–1880, *Hawaiian Annual* (1914), p. 202.

Column (12), 1836–1841, Accounts of Pierce & Brewer, the *Polynesian,* September 12, 1840; September 4, 1841.

1844, Collector of Custom's Report in the *Polynesian,* January 18, 1845.

1846, the *Polynesian,*	January 30, 1847	
1847	"	January 8, 1848
1848	"	January 20, 1849
1849	"	January 19, 1850
1850	"	February 1, 1851
1851	"	February 7, 1852
1852	"	January 29, 1853
1853	"	February 4, 1854
1854	"	February 17, 1855
1855	"	February 16, 1856
1856	"	January 31, 1857
1857	"	January 23, 1858
1858	"	January 22, 1859
1859	"	January 28, 1860

1860, *Hawaiian Annual* (1890), p. 24

1861–80, *Hawaiian Annual* (1900), p. 25.

	Exports: (13) Hides	(14) Goat Skins	(15) Wool	(16) Pulu	(17) Pepeiao	(18) Bananas
	(M's)	(M's)	(M lbs.)	(M lbs.)	Akua (M lbs.)	(M bunches)
1836	6.0	20.0				
1837	(6.5)	(19.6)				
1838	5.0	(13.0)				
1839	(3.0)	(4.3)				
1840	(14.7)	(72.7)				
1841	(5.0)	(18.8)				
1842						
1843	10.7					
1844	2.5	30.8				
1845	0.9	(9.9)				
1846	2.0	35.0				
1847	3.5	20.4				
1848		(34.0)				
1849		31.5	1.0			
1850		25.0				
1851	2.2	26.7	0.4	2.5		0.7
1852	1.0	29.8		25.1	4.9	1.5
1853	1.7	5.6	10.8	12.7	23.5	1.7
1854	3.0	17.0	12.8	34.0	10.3	0.6
1855	4.3	103.7	*	82.6	*	0.0
1856	5.4	70.9	*	*	*	0.1
1857	9.8	49.8	*	*	*	
1858	13.2	35.9	*	*	*	0.2
1859	14.6	45.3	*	*	*	
1860	20.3	37.3	70.5	649.2	178.8	
1861	7.5	21.9	119.9	530.8	278.3	
1862	15.5	53.1	40.4	738.1	301.4	0.1
1863	16.4	43.6	233.2	425.1	279.2	0.1
1864	12.0	32.3	196.7	643.4	368.8	1.9
1865	3.8	55.0	144.1	221.2	224.0	1.2
1866	8.3	76.1	73.1	212.0	120.3	1.8
1867	11.2	51.9	409.5	204.0	167.7	2.9
1868	11.1	57.7	258.9	342.9	76.8	4.0
1869	12.8	62.7	218.8	623.0	85.2	6.9
1870	13.1	67.5	234.7	233.8	42.0	4.0
1871	19.4	58.9	471.7	292.7	37.5	3.9
1872	27.1	53.6	288.5	421.2	32.2	4.5
1873	20.7	66.7	329.5	412.8	57.5	6.5
1874	22.6	72.0	399.9	418.3	51.0	6.5
1875	22.8	60.6	565.5	379.0	45.1	10.5
1876	11.1	45.3	405.5	314.4	35.9	15.0
1877	22.2	51.6	385.7	150.6	11.6	16.0
1878	25.3	64.5	522.8	212.7	22.4	13.4
1879	24.9	24.9	464.3	137.0	2.6	12.4
1880	22.9	31.0	381.3	44.8	14.8	19.2

Sources, and limitations, of data:

Column (13), 1836–1841, Accounts of Pierce & Brewer, in the *Polynesian,* September 12, 1840, September 4, 1841. (Approximate only.)

1843–1845, Report of Collector of Customs, the *Polynesian,* March 7, 1846; January 18, 1845.

1846–1860, *Report of Minister of Finance,* 1862.

1860–1880, *Hawaiian Annual* (1900), p. 25.

Columns (14) and (15) 1836–1841, same as Column (1)

1844, *Polynesian,* Jan. 18, 1845, p. 143.

1845–1846, *Polynesian,* January 30, 1847, p. 146.

1847–1859, same as Column (12)

1860–1880, *Hawaiian Annual* (1900), p. 25.

Column (16), 1851–1859, same as Column (12).

1860–1868, *Hawaiian Annual* (1890), p. 24.

1869–1880, *Hawaiian Annual* (1900), p. 25.

Column (17), 1860–1880, *Hawaiian Annual* (1914), p. 202.

Column (18), 1851–1858, same as Column (12)

1859, *Polynesian,* January 28, 1860.

1860–1880, *Hawaiian Annual* (1914), p. 202.

	(19) Government Revenue	(20) Total Internal Taxes	(21) Government Debt
		(in thousands of dollars)	
1842	($41.0)		
1843	(50.0)		$30.0
1844 } 1845	*		
1846	95.9		
1847	127.9		
1848	155.2		
1849	166.3		
1850	301.6		
1851	284.4		
1852	315.7		
1853	326.5		
1854	323.5		
1855	419.2		
1856 } 1857	†		22.0
1858 } 1859	‡		60.7
1860 } 1861	571.0		128.8

* March 31, 1844 to April 1, 1845, $64.1.
† January 1, 1856 to April 1, 1858, $638.0.
‡ April 1, 1858 to March 31, 1860, $655.9.

	(19) Government Revenue	(20) Total Internal Taxes	(21) Government Debt
		(in thousands of dollars)	
1862–1863	528.0	133.2	166.6
1864–1865	538.4	131.7	166.6
1866–1867	721.1	150.7	183.0
1868–1869	825.5	165.4	120.8
1870–1871	834.1	166.5	126.6
1872–1873	912.1	216.0	178.0
1874–1875	1,136.5	207.4	355.1
1876–1877	1,009.0	213.9	459.2
1878–1879	1,151.7	291.7	444.8
1880–1881	1,703.7	400.3	388.9

Sources of data:

Columns (19) and (20), 1842–43, R. C. Wyllie in *The Friend,* May 1844; *Report of Minister of Finance* (1851), p. 13.

1844–1859, "Exhibit" of R. C. Wyllie, F. O. and Exchange, Archives of Hawaii.

1860–1881, *Hawaiian Annual* (1906), p. 29.

Column (21), 1862–73, *Hawaiian Annual* (1875), p. 45.

1874–1881, *Hawaiian Annual* (1881), p. 15.

APPENDIX III

Glossary of Hawaiian Terms

Ahu—altar erected where the boundary of the ahupuaa intersected the main road, and upon which was deposited the yearly tax.

Ahupuaa—a division of an island, equivalent to a large estate, the basic land unit for the alii.

Aina—island, connotes "Land," place of food.

Aina loi—productive, watered area of land.

Alii—the chiefs, the chieftain class.

Atooi—old spelling of Kauai.

Auwai—irrigation ditch.

Hale—house.

Haleakala—the major mountain on Maui, 10,000 feet high ("House of the Sun").

Haole—white man or foreigner.

Heiau—old native temple.

Hilo—chief town on the Island of Hawaii, second in size to Honolulu; in 1936 the population was 15,885 (distorted name of a Polynesian navigator).

Holoku—"Mother Hubbard": a loose, sack-like dress developed by the missionaries for native women.

Honolulu—chief city of the group, on the Island of Oahu; in 1936 the population was 145,875 ("Fair Haven").

Ie—basket, a climbing plant.

Ili—the largest division of the ahupuaa, often extended to the sea.

Ili kupono—(or Ili ku)—an independent area of land within the ahupuaa, owing no fealty or taxes to the landlord of the ahupuaa.

Ili lele—an ili made up of several scattered pieces of land.

Kahuna—native witch doctor, priest, sorcerer.

Kailua—a village, and section, of windward Oahu (two sea currents); also a town and section of Kona.

Kalaimoku—a king's councilor.

Kanaka—man, native.

Kapu—"forbidden," tabu, originally a religious and political interdiction.

Kauai—northernmost of the main Islands ("fruitful season").

Kealakekua—name of the bay where Cook landed, and of the adjacent section of Kona, Hawaii ("pathway of the Gods").

Kihapai—a named and cultivated piece of ground smaller than the *pauku*.

Kihei—a shoulder cape, sometimes worn by men.

Kilauea—an active volcano on Hawaii ("rising smoke cloud").

Koele—patches of gardens cultivated by the common people for their landlords.

Kona—west; applied to the leeward section of any district or island.

Konohiki—the agent of a landowner, who looks after his estates, and collects his taxes; the head man of an ahupuaa, or a person who has charge of a land, with others under him.

Kukui—the candle-nut tree.

Kuleana—the smallest unit of land, the basic unit for the commoners.

Lahaina—a town on Maui, formerly a principal resort of whalers ("bay of cruelty").

Lele—jumps, used to refer to separated sections of the ili or Kuleanas.

Luna—above; a leader or official (used in many combined forms).

Mahele—the division of land between the king and chiefs, 1847–48. Sometimes applied to land distribution continuing to 1855 and after.

Makaainana—the common people, as contrasted with alii.

Makahiki—the time when yearly taxes were paid; also, year.

Makai—toward the sea, common indication of direction.

Mamane—a useful mountain acacia.

Mauka—toward the mountains, common indication of direction.

Maui—the second largest island of the group.

Mea-ai—food.

Moku or *Mokupuni*—island, connotes separation from other islands by the sea.

Moo—a division of the ahupuaa, like the ili—usually it did not extend to the sea.

Mooaina—(see Moo)—an arable portion of the ili, really a field division.

Nui—large.

Oahu—the most populous of the Islands ("gathering place").

Oloana—a vine from which fish line was made.

O-o—a primitive spade; made of a long stick of hardwood with a flattened point.

Owhyhee—an old spelling for Hawaii.

Pau—a form of dress used by women, consisting of a yard-wide strip of bark-cloth wound tightly round the hips, reaching from the waist to the knees; it also means done, finished.

Pauku—division of land smaller than a moo.

Poalima—area which were in later years cultivated on Fridays only. Poalima is the Hawaiian word for Friday.

Poi—a staple native food, made from the crushed and usually fermented pulp of the *taro*.

Tapa—(old spelling Kapa)—a native cloth, formed of the processed bark of the paper mulberry, and other plants.

Ti—a broad-leafed, low-growing plant, whose leaves the natives are reported to have used for weaving into cloaks.

Waikiki—("spurting water") a beach, and a part of Honolulu.

Wauke—the paper mulberry, whose bark was used for making *tapa*.

APPENDIX IV

BIBLIOGRAPHY

1. Books

Adams, Alexander, *Extracts from an Ancient Log* (1906). Taken from the log of Captain Alexander Adams.

Adams, Romanzo, *Interracial Marriage in Hawaii* (New York: The Macmillan Company, 1937).

Alexander, Arthur C., *Koloa Plantation* (Honolulu: Honolulu Star Bulletin Press, 1937).

Alexander, Mary C., *The Story of Hawaii* (New York: American Book Company, 1912).

Alexander, William De Witt, *A Brief History of the Hawaiian People* (New York: American Book Company, 1891).

———, *History of Later Years of the Hawaiian Monarchy and the Revolution of 1893* (Honolulu: Hawaiian Gazette Company, 1896).

Alexander, W. P., *Irrigation of Sugar Cane in Hawaii* (Honolulu: 1923).

Allen, Frederick H., *Commercial Aspects of the Hawaiian Reciprocity Treaty* (Washington: Thomas McGill & Company, 1883).

Anderson, Rufus, *The Hawaiian Islands* (Boston: Gould and Lincoln; New York: Sheldon & Company, 1864).

Andrews, Lorrin, *A Dictionary of the Hawaiian Language* (Honolulu: The Board of Commissioners of Public Archives of the Territory of Hawaii, 1922), revised by Henry H. Parker.

Bantwell, George S., *The Reciprocity Treaty in Hawaii* (Washington: Judd and Detweiler, 1886).

Bates, G. W., *Sandwich Island Notes* (New York: Harper and Brothers, 1854).

Baxley, H. W., *What I Saw on the West Coast of South and North America and at the Hawaiian Islands* (New York: D. Appleton and Company, 1865).

Bennett, C. C., *Honolulu Directory and Historical Sketch of the Hawaiian or Sandwich Islands* (Honolulu: C. C. Bennett (publ.), 1869).

Bennett, F. D., *Narrative of a Whaling Journey Around the Globe from the Year 1833–1836,* 2 vols. (London: R. Bentley, 1840).

Bingham, Hiram, *A Residence of Twenty-One Years in the Sandwich Islands* (Hartford, Conn.: H. Huntington, 1849).

Bishop, M. B., *Hawaiian Life of the Pre-European Period* (Portland, Maine: Southworth Anthoensen Press, 1940).
Bishop, Sereno Edwards, *Reminiscences of Old Hawaii* (Honolulu: Hawaiian Gazette Company, 1916).
Blackman, William F., *The Making of Hawaii* (New York: The Macmillan Company, 1899).
Bliss, W. R., *Paradise in the Pacific* (New York: Sheldon & Company, 1873).
Bloxam, Andrew, *Diary of Andrew Bloxam, Naturalist of the "Blonde," On Her Trip from England to the Hawaiian Islands,* 1824–25 (Honolulu: The Museum, 1925).
Bowden, Witt; Karpovich, Michael; and Usher, A. P., *Economic History of Europe Since 1750* (New York: American Book Company, 1937).
Brigham, W. T., *Hawaiian Feather Work* (Honolulu: Bishop Museum Press, 1903).
———, *The Ancient Hawaiian House* (Honolulu: Bishop Museum Press, 1908).
Broughton, W. R., *A Voyage of Discovery to the North Pacific Ocean* (London: Printed for Cadell and Davies, 1804).
Browne, George Waldo, *The New America and the Far East* (Boston: Marshall Jones Company, 1907).
Bryan, Edwin H., *Ancient Hawaiian Life* (Honolulu: Advertiser Publishing Company, 1938).
Byron, George Anson, Commander, *Voyage of H.M.S. Blonde . . . 1824–1825* (London: J. Murray, 1826).
Campbell, Archibald, *A Voyage Round the World, 1806 to 1812* (Edinburgh: Constable, 1816; Fourth American Edition, Roxbury, Massachusetts: 1825).
Carpenter, E. J., *America in Hawaii* (Boston: Small, Maynard and Company, 1899).
The Centennial Book: One Hundred Years of Christian Civilization in Hawaii, 1820–1920. A symposium published by the Central Committee of the Hawaiian Mission Centennial (Honolulu: 1920).
Chamberlin, E. H., *The Theory of Monopolistic Competition* (Cambridge: Harvard University Press, 1938).
Chambers, H. E., *Constitutional History of Hawaii* (Baltimore: Johns Hopkins Press, 1896).
Cheever, H. T., *The Island World of the Pacific* (New York: Harpers, 1851).
———, *The Sandwich or Hawaiian Islands* (New York: Biblical Repository, 1849).
Chittenden, H. M., *The American Fur Trade of the Far West* (New York: F. P. Harper, 1902).

Cleveland, R. J., *A Narrative of Voyages and Commercial Enterprises* (Cambridge: John Owen, 1843), 2 vols.
Coan, T. M., *Life in Hawaii* (New York: A. D. F. Randolph & Company, 1882).
———, *The Natives of Hawaii* (Philadelphia: American Academy of Political and Social Science, 1901).
Coman, Katherine, *The History of Contract Labor in the Hawaiian Islands* (New York: The Macmillan Company, 1903).
Cook, Captain James, *Voyages of Discovery* (London: W. and A. Strahan, 1784), 2 vols.
Corney, Peter, *Voyages in the Northern Pacific* (Honolulu: Thrum, 1896). Reprinted from the *London Literary Gazette* of 1821.
Coulter, J. W., *A Survey of Land Utilization in the Hawaiian Islands.* University of Hawaii Research Publications No. 8 (Honolulu: Printshop Company, 1933).
———, *Population and Utilization of Land and Sea in Hawaii, 1853* (Honolulu: Bishop Museum Press, 1931).
Cox, Ross, *Adventures on the Columbia River* (London: H. Colburn and R. Bentley, 1831).
Damon, Ethel M., *Father Bond of Kohala: A Chronicle of Pioneer Life in Hawaii* (Honolulu: *The Friend,* 1927).
———, *Koamalu; a Story of Pioneers on Kauai* (Honolulu: Honolulu *Star Bulletin,* 1931).
Delano, Amasa, *A Narrative of Voyages and Travels in the Northern and Southern Hemispheres* (Boston: 1817).
Dibble, Sheldon, *A History of the Sandwich Islands* (Honolulu: Thomas Thrum, 1909).
Dupuy, William, *Hawaii and Its Race Problem* (Washington: Department of the Interior, U. S. Government Printing Office, 1932).
Ellis, William, *A Journal of a Tour Around Hawaii* (Boston: Crocker and Brewster; New York: J. P. Haven, 1825).
———, *A Narrative of a Tour Through Hawaii* (London: H. Fisher, Son, and P. Jackson, 1826; Honolulu: *Hawaiian Gazette,* 1917).
———, *Polynesian Researches* (London: Fisher, Jackson and Son, 1832; New York: Harper, 1833).
Emerson, Nathaniel B., *Unwritten Literature of Hawaii* (Washington: U. S. Government Printing Office, 1909).
Emerson, O. P., *Pioneer Days in Hawaii* (New York: Doubleday, Doran & Company, 1928).
Eveleth, Rev. Ephraim, *History of the Sandwich Islands* (Philadelphia: American Sunday-School Union, 1831).
Fahys, Maria L., *Around the World.* (No place, publisher, or date.)
Fornander, Abraham, *The Polynesian Race* (Ludgate Hill: Truber & Company, 1880).

Frear, Walter F., *A Century of Achievement, 1820–1920* (Honolulu: 1920).

———, *Anti-Missionary Criticism* (Honolulu: *Honolulu Advertiser*, 1935).

Freeman, O. W., *The Economic Geography of Hawaii* (Honolulu: 1927). University of Hawaii, Research Publication No. 2.

Gilmore, A. B., *The Hawaii Sugar Manual* (New Orleans: 1931).

Golovnin, Captain V., *Tour Around the World of the Sloop of War Kamschatka, 1817–19,* partly translated in *The Friend* (July–August, 1894).

Gowen, H. H., *The Napoleon of the Pacific, Kamehameha the Great* (New York: Fleming H. Revell Company, 1919).

Gulick, Orramel H., *The Pilgrims of Hawaii* (New York: Fleming H. Revell Co., 1918).

Heine, Wilhelm, *Reis om de Wereld Naar Japan* (Rotterdam: 1856).

Henke, Louis A., *A Survey of Livestock in Hawaii,* "University of Hawaii Research Publication No. 5" (Honolulu: 1929).

Hill, S. S., *Travels in the Sandwich and Society Islands* (London: Chapman and Hall, 1856).

Hillebrand, W., *Flora of the Hawaiian Islands* (New York: Westermann, 1888).

Hobbs, J., *Hawaii: A Pageant of the Soil* (Stanford University: Stanford University Press, 1935).

Hohman, E. P., *The American Whaleman* (New York: Longmans, Green, 1928).

Hopkins, Manley, *Hawaii: the Past, Present, and Future of Its Island-Kingdom* (London: Longmans, Green & Company, 1866).

Hunnewell, James, *Journal of the Voyage of the "Missionary Packet," Boston to Honolulu* (Cambridge: University Press, 1880).

Hunt, T. D., *The Past and Present of the Sandwich Islands* (San Francisco: Whitton, Towne & Company, 1853).

Jarrett, Lorna H., *Hawaii and Its People* (Honolulu: *Honolulu Star Bulletin,* 1933).

Jarves, James Jackson, *History of the Hawaiian or Sandwich Islands* (Boston: Tappan and Dennett, 1843).

———, *Scenes and Scenery in the Sandwich Islands* (Boston: Monroe, 1843).

Jenkins, J. T., *A History of the Whale Fisheries* (London: H. F. & G. Witherby, 1921).

Judd, A. F., *An Essay on the Hawaiian Currency and the Silver Question* (Honolulu: Thrum, 1884).

Judd, Mrs. Laura Fish, *Honolulu: Sketches of Life, Social, Political, and Religious, in the Hawaiian Islands from 1828 to 1861* (New York: A. D. F. Randolph & Company, 1880).

King, N., vol. III of *Voyages of Discovery* by Captain James Cook (London: W. and A. Strahan, 1784).

Kinney, W. A., *Hawaii's Capacity for Self-Government All But Destroyed* (Salt Lake City: Jenson Press, *c.* 1927).

Kotzebue, Otto von, *A New Voyage Round the World* (London: H. Colburn and R. Bentley, 1830).

Kuykendall, Ralph S., *The Earliest Japanese Labor Immigration to Hawaii* (Honolulu: University of Hawaii, 1935).

———, *The Hawaiian Kingdom, 1778–1854* (Honolulu: University of Hawaii, 1938).

Lafond, Gabriel, *Voyages autour du Monde et Naufrages Célèbres* (Paris: Administration de Librairie, 1843–1844).

Lasker, B., *Filipino Immigration to Continental United States and to Hawaii* (Chicago: University of Chicago Press, 1931).

Laughlin, J. L., and Willis, H. P., *Reciprocity* (New York: Baker and Taylor, 1903).

Lawrence, Mary Stebbins, *Old Time Hawaiians and Their Work* (Boston: Ginn & Co., 1912).

Liliuokalani, Queen of Hawaii, *Hawaii's Story by Hawaii's Queen, Liliuokalani* (Boston: Lee & Shepard, 1898).

Lind, Andrew W., *Economic Succession and Racial Invasion of Hawaii.* Privately printed (Chicago: 1936); in *Race and Culture Contacts* (New York: McGraw Hill, 1934).

———, *An Island Community* (Chicago: University of Chicago Press, 1938).

Lisiansky, Urey, *A Voyage Round the World* (London: 1814).

Little, George, *Life on the Ocean* (Boston: Waite, Peirce & Co., 1845).

Logan, Daniel, ed., *History of the Hawaiian Islands* (New York: Lewis, 1907).

Lyman, C. S., *Around the Horn to the Sandwich Islands and California, 1845–1850* (New Haven: Yale University Press, 1924).

Lyman, H. M., *Hawaiian Yesterdays* (Chicago: McClurg, 1906).

Lyons, Curtis J., *A History of the Hawaiian Government Survey* (Honolulu: Hawaiian Gazette Co., 1903).

Macrae, James, *With Lord Byron at the Sandwich Islands in 1825, Being Extracts from the Diary of James Macrae* (Honolulu: 1922).

Macy, Obed, *History of Nantucket* (Boston: 1835).

Malo, David, *Hawaiian Antiquities* (Honolulu: Hawaiian Gazette Company, 1903).

Marques, A., *The Population of the Hawaiian Islands* (Honolulu: Hoomua Press, 1894).

Mathison, G. F., *A Visit to Brazil, Chile, Peru, and the Sandwich Islands . . . 1821 and 1822* (London: 1825). Printed for C. Knight.

Meares, (Captain) John, *Voyages* (London: Legographic Press, 1791), 2 vols.
Menzies, Archibald, *Hawaii Nei 128 Years Ago* (Honolulu: The New Freedom, 1920).
Monnier, Marcel, *Iles Hawaii* (Paris: Plon, Nourrit et Cie, 1888).
Musick, John Roy, *Hawaii: Our New Possessions* (New York: Funk and Wagnalls Company, 1898).
Newell, F. H., *Hawaii, Its Natural Resources and Opportunities for Home-making* (Washington: Government Printing Office, 1909).
Nicholson, H. W., *From Sword to Share* (London: W. H. Allen & Company, 1881).
Nicol, John, *Life and Adventures of John Nicol* (Edinburgh: William Blackwood, 1822).
Nordhoff, Charles, *Northern California, Oregon and the Sandwich Islands* (London: 1874).
Ogle and Aikman, *History of the Otaheitean Islands, with an Illustrated Sketch of the Sandwich Islands* (1800).
Olmsted, F. A., *Incidents of a Whaling Voyage* (New York: Appleton, 1841).
Orme, William, *A Defence of the Missions in the South Sea and Sandwich Islands* (London: Holdsworth, 1827).
Parke, William Cooper, *Personal Reminiscences* (Cambridge: The University Press, 1891).
Parker, Mrs. E. M. Wills, *The Sandwich Islands as They Are, Not as They Should Be* (San Francisco: Burgess, Gilbert & Still, 1852).
Parker, Samuel, *Journal of an Exploring Tour.* 3rd Edition (Ithaca: 1842).
Patterson, Samuel, *Narrative of the Adventures, Sufferings and Privations of Samuel Patterson* (Providence: 1825).
Perkins, Edward T., *Na Motu: or Reef-Rovings in the South Seas* (New York: Pudney & Russell, 1854).
Peron, Capitaine, *Memoires . . . sur Ses Voyages* (Paris: Brissot-Thivars, 1824).
Pettigrew, R. F., *The Course of Empire* (New York: Boni and Liveright, 1920).
Portlock, Captain Nathaniël, *A Voyage Round the World* (1785–1788) (London: 1789).
Quimpea Benito del Pino, Manuel, *Islas de Sandwich* (Madrid: 1822). Translated by Clark Lee (Honolulu: 1937).
Remy, Jules, *Récits d'un Vieux Sauvage pour Servir à l'Histoire Ancienne de Havaii* (Châlons-sur-Marne: E. Laurant, 1859).
Restarick, Henry Bond, *Hawaii, 1778–1920* (Honolulu: Paradise of the Pacific Press, 1924).

Reynolds, J. N., *Voyage of the United States Frigate Potomac* (1831–1834) (New York: Harper & Brothers, 1835).
Robbins, Lionel, *An Essay on the Nature and Significance of Economic Science* (London: Macmillan, 1935).
Robinson, Chalfant, *A History of Two Reciprocity Treaties* (New Haven, Connecticut: The Tuttle, Morehouse & Taylor Press, 1904).
Rushenberger, W. S. W., *Voyage Round the World, 1835–37* (London: Richard Bentley, 1838). 2 vols.
Shaw, William, *Golden Dreams and Waking Realities* (London: Smith, Elder and Company, 1851).
Simpson, Alexander, *The Sandwich Islands* (London: Smith, Elder & Company, 1843).
Simpson, Sir George, *Round the World (1841–2)* (London: H. Colburn, 1847). 2 vols.
Smucker, S. M., *Life of Dr. Elisha Kent Kane and of Other Distinguished American Explorers* (Philadelphia: G. G. Evans, 1860).
Starbuck, Alexander, *History of American Whale Fishery . . . to 1876* (published by the author, Waltham, Mass.: 1878).
Stewart, Charles Samuel, *Private Journal of a Voyage to the Pacific Ocean and Residence at the Sandwich Islands, in the years 1822, 1823, 1824 and 1825* (New York: Haven, 1828).
———, *The Hawaiian Islands in 1822* (Boston: Old South Association, 191–).
Stoddard, C. W., *Hawaiian Life* (Chicago: Neely Company, 1894).
———, *South Sea Idylls* (New York: Scribner's Sons, 1892).
Sullivan, Josephine, *A History of C. Brewer and Company, Ltd.* (Boston: Walton Advertising and Printing Company, 1926).
Taussig, F. W., *Some Aspects of the Tariff Question* (Cambridge, Mass.: Harvard University Press, 1915).
Taylor, Albert Pierce, *Under Hawaiian Skies* (Honolulu: Advertiser Publishing Company, 1922).
Thompson, J. E., *Our Pacific Possessions* (New York: Scribner's Sons, 1931).
Thurston, Lucy G., *Life and Times of Mrs. Lucy G. Thurston, wife of Rev. Asa Thurston, pioneer missionary to the Sandwich Islands* (Ann Arbor, Michigan: S. C. Andrews, 1882).
Tilton, Cecil G., *The History of Banking in Hawaii* (Honolulu: University of Hawaii Press, 1927).
Tower, W. S., *History of the American Whale Fishery* (Philadelphia: University of Pennsylvania Press, 1907).
Townsend, Ebenezer, *The Diary of Ebenezer Townsend* (Honolulu: Hawaiian Historical Society Reprint, 1921).
Townsend, J. K., *Narrative of a Journey Across the Rocky Mountains*

. . . *and a Visit to the Sandwich Islands* (Boston: Perkins and Marvin, 1839).

Turnbull, John, *A Voyage Round the World* (London: T. Gillet, 1805; Philadelphia: 1810).

Twain, Mark (S. L. Clemens), *Letters from the Sandwich Islands* (Stanford University: Stanford University Press, 1938).

Twombly, Alexander Stevenson, *Hawaii and Its People* (New York: Silver, Burdett & Company, 1899).

Tyerman, Daniel, and Bennet, George, *Voyages and Travels* (London: Frederick Westley and A. H. Davis, 1831).

Uttley, M. E., *The Geographic Basis of Hawaiian Commerce* (Chicago: University of Chicago Press, 1921).

Vancouver, Captain George, *A Voyage of Discovery* (London: G. G. & J. Robinson, 1798). 3 vols.

Varigny, Charles V. C., *Quartorze Ans aux Iles Sandwich* (Paris: Hachette et Cie, 1874).

Visger, Mrs. Jean Allen Owen, *The Story of Hawaii* (London: Harper, 1898).

Wadsworth, H. A., *A Historical Summary of Irrigation in Hawaii* (Honolulu, no date).

Wallace, A. R., *Island Life* (London: Macmillan, 1911).

Walpole, Frederick, *Four Years in the Pacific in Her Majesty's Ship Collingwood From 1844 to 1848* (Paris: A. and W. Galignani & Company, 1850).

Warriner, Francis, *Cruise of the United States Frigate Potomac* (New York: Leavitt, Lord & Company; Boston: Crocker & Brewster, 1835).

Whetham, J. W. B., *Pearls of the Pacific* (London: Hurst and Blackett, 1876).

Whitney, Caspar, *Hawaiian America* (New York and London: Harper & Brothers, 1899).

Whitney, H. M., *The Hawaiian Guide Book* (Honolulu: Published by the Author, 1875).

———, *The Tourists' Guide* (Honolulu: Hawaiian Gazette Company, 1890).

Wichman, Juliet R., *Hawaiian Planting Traditions* (Honolulu: Honolulu Star Bulletin Press, 1930).

Wilkes, Captain Charles, *Narrative of the United States Exploring Expedition,* 1838–1842 (Philadelphia: Lea & Blanchard, 1845). 5 vols.

Wise, H. A., *Los Gringos* (New York: Baker & Scribner, 1849).

Wright, Louis B. and Fry, Mary Isabel, *Puritans in the South Seas* (New York: Henry Holt, 1936).

Wyllie, R. C., *Answers to Questions Proposed by R. C. Wyllie . . . and*

Addressed to all the Missionaries in the Hawaiian Islands (Honolulu: 1848).
Young, Lucien, *The Real Hawaii: Its History and Present Condition* (New York: Doubleday & McClure, 1899).
Young, W. A., *Christianity and Civilization in the South Pacific* (London: Oxford, 1922).
Anonymous, *The Hawaiian Reciprocity Treaty* (Washington: Judd & Detweiler, 1884).
Anonymous, *The Hawaiian Treaty: A Review of Its Commercial Results* (Washington: Judd and Detweiler).
Anonymous, *History of the Catholic Religion in the Sandwich Islands* (Honolulu: R. J. Howard, 1840).
Anonymous, *History of the Otaheitan Islands* (Edinburgh: 1800).

2. Articles

Agee, H. P., "A Brief History of the HSPA [Hawaiian Sugar Planters' Association]." *Thrum's Annual* (1935), pp. 72–86.
———, "Hawaiian Agriculture Prior to 1860," *Hawaiian Planters' Record,* vol. 31, Quarter 2 (1927).
Alexander, W. D., *Appendix to the Surveyor General's Report* (1882).
Frear, W. F., "The Labor System of the Hawaiian Islands," *The Californian,* vol. 5, pp. 37–43 (1882).
"Great Britain, the United States and Hawaiian Independence, 1850–55," *Pacific Historical Review,* vol. 4 (March 1935).
Green, E., "Hawaii Ponoi, the Persistence of the Racial and Cultural Tradition," *Asia* (April 1935).
Green, J. A., "Female Education at the Sandwich Islands," *The Hawaiian Spectator,* p. 35 (January 1838).
Hall, E. O., "Common Schools at the Sandwich Islands," *The Hawaiian Spectator,* p. 352 (October 1838).
Hard, William, "American Empire," *Saturday Evening Post,* vol. 203 (October 11, 1930).
"Hawaii—Early Relations with England, France, and Russia," *Official Papers Read at the Captain Cook Sesquicentennial Celebration* (August 17, 1928).
Howay, F. W., "Early Hawaiians on the Northwest Coast." In Taylor and Kuykendall's *The Hawaiian Islands,* pp. 11–21.
Hughes, Rupert, "Bligh's Notes on Cook's Last Voyage," *Mariner's Mirror* (London, October 1928).
Jones, Maud, "Whaling in Hawaiian Waters," *Paradise of the Pacific* (April 1938).
Jones, S. M., "Economic Adjustment of the Hawaiians to European Culture," *Pacific Affairs,* vol. 4 (November 1931).
Krause, F. G., "Cotton Culture in Hawaii," *Hawaiian Annual* (1911).

Kuns, F., "Crude Sugar: Refined Politics," *Nation*, vol. 121 (September 9, 1925).

Kuykendall, R. S., "Early Hawaiian Commercial Development," *Pacific Historical Review* (December 1934).

Ladd, W., "Remarks Upon the Natural Resources of the Sandwich Islands," *The Hawaiian Spectator*, vol. 1, No. 2, pp. 68–79 (April 1838).

Lyons, C. J., "Land Matters in Hawaii," *The Islander* (July 2, 9, and 16, 1875).

Porter, K. W., "J. J. Astor and the Sandalwood Trade of the Hawaiian Islands (1816–28)," *Journal of Economics and Business History* (May 1930).

Rowland, D., "United States and the Contract Labor Question in Hawaii, 1862–1900," *Pacific Historical Review* (September 1933).

"Statistics of Schools," *Hawaiian Spectator*, p. 427 (October 1838).

Taggard, G., "Chapters from Unwritten Autobiographies: A Haole Scrapbook," *Bookman*, vol. 59 (June 1924).

Thrum, T. G., "Fifty Years of Hawaiian Commercial Development," *The Friend*, pp. 66–67 (September 1893).

———, "Hawaiian Commercial Development," *Hawaiian Annual*, pp. 87–106 (1896).

———, "Notes on the History of Coffee Culture in the Hawaiian Islands," *Hawaiian Annual*, pp. 46–52 (1876).

———, "Notes on the History of Rice Culture in the Hawaiian Islands," *Hawaiian Annual*, pp. 45–49 (1877).

———, "Notes on the History of the Sugar Industry," *Hawaiian Annual* (1875).

———, "The Sandalwood Trade of Early Hawaii, as Told by the Pioneer Traders, Voyagers, and Others," *Hawaiian Annual* (1905), pp. 43–74.

Whitney, S., "Account of the Russians on Kauai," *The Hawaiian Spectator*, 1, No. k, p. 48 (January 1838).

Willfong, G. W., "Twenty Years' Experience in Cane Culture," *Planters' Monthly*, I.

Williams, J. N. S., "Some of the Factors in the Industrial Development of the Hawaiian Islands," *Journal of the Royal Society of Arts*, vol. 67, no. 3479 (July 25, 1919).

3. Hawaiian Historical Society Papers

Alexander, W. D., "Early Trading in Hawaii," *Hawaiian Historical Society Papers*, No. 11 (1904).

Bailey, E., "Historical Notes," *Hawaiian Historical Society Papers*, No. 3 (1895), pp. 13–15.

Blue, G. V., "Early Relations Between Hawaii and the Northwest

Coast," *Hawaiian Historical Society Reports*, No. 33, p. 16 (Honolulu: Paradise of the Pacific Press, 1925).

Colcord, John N., "Journal" (MS.), Hawaiian Historical Society Library.

Dole, Sanford B., "Evolution of Land Tenure in Hawaii," *Hawaiian Historical Society Papers,* December 5, 1892.

Emerson, Dr., "Long Voyages of the Ancient Hawaiians," *Hawaiian Historical Society Papers,* No. 5.

Hunnewell, James, "Honolulu in 1817 and 1818," *Hawaiian Historical Society Papers,* No. 8.

Ingraham, Joseph, "The Log of the Brig Hope, May 20, Oct. 12, 1791," *Hawaiian Historical Society Reprint,* No. 3 (Honolulu: 1918).

Judd, Laura Fish, "A Suppressed Chapter of Hawaiian History," *Hawaiian Historical Society* (1902), pp. 7–12.

Kuykendall, Ralph S., "American Interests and American Influence in Hawaii in 1842," *Hawaiian Historical Society Papers,* No. 39 (1930), pp. 48–67.

M'Konochie, Alexander, "Considerations on the Propriety of Establishing a Colony on One of the Sandwich Islands," *Hawaiian Historical Society* (1906), pp. 29–43.

"Sandalwood," *Hawaiian Historical Society Papers,* No. 8.

Smith, S. Percy, "Origins and Migrations of the Polynesians," *Hawaiian Historical Society Papers,* No. 5.

Stoddard, Francis R., "Annexation Scheme of 1854 that Failed," *Hawaiian Historical Society Papers,* No. 17 (1930), pp. 39–52.

Taylor, Albert P., "Intrigues, Conspiracies and Accomplishments in the Era of Kamehameha IV and V and Robert Crychton Wyllie," *Hawaiian Historical Society Papers,* No. 16 (1929), pp. 16–32.

4. Hawaiian Periodicals

The Friend (monthly, began as *The Temperance Advocate and Seamen's Friend,* January 1843 to date).

1849—June, July, and August, not published.
1851—January and February were the only numbers published.
1852—Publication began in May.
1853—August not published.
1854—August not published.
1861—June, July and August not published.
1885—July and August not published.

Hawaiian Annual, T. G. Thrum, editor or compiler (1875 to date).

Hawaiian Spectator, vols. 1 and 2 (January 1838 to October 1839).

The Islander (weekly, March 5, 1875 through October 29, 1875).

Paradise of the Pacific (monthly, January 1, 1888 to date).

Planter's Monthly (1883 to date).
Social Process in Hawaii (Sociology Club, University of Hawaii, Vol. 1, May 1935; Vol. 2, May 1936; Vol. 3, 1937).
The Temperance Advocate and Seamen's Friend (Forerunner of *The Friend*).

5. Hawaiian Newspapers

Daily Bulletin (February 1, 1882 to May 15, 1895, when name was changed to *Evening Bulletin,* a predecessor of the *Honolulu Star-Bulletin*).
Evening Bulletin (daily, May 16, 1895 through June 30, 1912; a predecessor of the *Honolulu Star-Bulletin.*
The Hawaiian Gazette (weekly, January 2, 1865 through December 1893, also daily August 3, 1887 to December 31, 1887, daily January 2, 1888 through May 26, 1888, also semiweekly January 3, 1894 to November 29, 1918, successor to *Polynesian*).
The Hawaiian Star (daily April 1, 1893 to July 1, 1912; one of the predecessors of the *Honolulu Star-Bulletin*).
Honolulu Advertiser (daily since March 31, 1921; forerunners—*The Pacific Commercial Advertiser, The Daily Pacific Commercial Advertiser*).
Honolulu Star-Bulletin (daily since July 1, 1912; a merger of the daily *Evening Bulletin,* whose forerunner was the *Daily Bulletin,* and *The Hawaiian Star*).
Independent (daily May 1, 1895 through October 31, 1905).
The Pacific Commercial Advertiser (weekly July 2, 1856 through May 21, 1888, daily May 1, 1882 in addition to weekly until May 21, 1888, then weekly ceased; *The Daily Pacific Commercial Advertiser* continued 1882 till March 31, 1921 when name changed to *Honolulu Advertiser*).
Polynesian (weekly, June 6, 1840 through February 1864).
Sandwich Islands Gazette (weekly, July 30, 1836 to July 27, 1839).
Sandwich Island News (weekly, September 2, 1846 through August 25, 1847; no issues printed August 25, 1847 to November 4, 1847; then November 4, 1847 through April 14, 1849).

6. U. S. Government Publications

Boutwell, G. S. and Allen, E. H., *Remarks before Committee on Foreign Affairs, House of Representatives* (Washington: Government Printing Office, 1882).
Chapman, Emmett A., *Hawaii: Its Resources and Trade.* Division of Regional Information (Washington: Government Printing Office, 1927).

Commerce of the United States with the Hawaiian Islands from 1871 to 1892. Prepared by the Chief of the Bureau of Statistics. (Washington: Government Printing Office, 1893.)

Dole, Sanford B., *Report of Committee of Senate on Foreign Relations for 1894* (Washington: Government Printing Office, 1894).

International Bureau of the American Republics, Washington, D. C. *Commercial Directory of the American Republics,* comprising the manufacturers, merchants, shippers, and banks and bankers engaged in foreign trade; together with the names of officials, maps, commercial statistics, industrial data, and other information concerning the countries of the international union of American Republics, the American Colonies, and Hawaii. Compiled by the Bureau of the American Republics. (Washington: Government Printing Office, 1897–98). 2 vols.

Hawaii, Its Natural Resources and Opportunities for Home Making (F. H. Newell), Document 668 (Government Printing Office, 1909).

Hawaiian Islands—*Report of the Committee on Foreign Relations, United States Senate, January 1, 1893 to March 10, 1894,* 2 vols. (Government Printing Office, 1894).

Papers and Documents Relating to the Hawaiian Islands. In Senate executive documents No. 45, 57, 75, and 77, 52nd Congress, second session (1892–93).

Refined Sugar: Costs, Prices and Profits. Tariff Information Series No. 16 (Washington: Government Printing Office, 1920).

Report of Commission appointed by the Secretary of the Treasury to Investigate Alleged Frauds under the Hawaiian Reciprocity Treaty (Washington: Government Printing Office, 1883).

Report of the Commissioner of Labor on Hawaii, 1901, 1902, 1905, 1910, 1915.

Report of the Secretary of State on the Subject of the Cod and Whaling Fisheries (Washington: 1791).

Stubbs, William C., *Agricultural Resources and Capabilities of Hawaii, Report on the;* U.S.D.A. (Washington: 1901).

Tariff Commission Report (1882).

7. Hawaiian Government Publications

Full Statement of Applications Made for Government Lands to the Interior Department, from 1882 to date. Department of the Interior. (Honolulu: 1884.)

Hawaiian Historical Commission Report, vol. 1, No. 2 (1924). Appendix A, *An American Diplomat in Hawaii* (*Gregg*); Appendix B, *The Policy of Great Britain toward the Hawaiian Islands* (*1824–1854*).

Interior, Department of the, *Index to all Grants Issued by the Hawaiian Government Previous to March 31, 1886.* (*Honolulu Advertiser,* 1887.)

Inventory of the Resources of the Territory of Hawaii. Territorial Planning Board (Honolulu: 1939).

Ministerial Reports, Vol. 1. *Report of the Minister of Finance.* House of Nobles (1846, 1848).

Ministerial Reports, Vol. 1. *Report of the Minister of the Interior, 1846, 1848, 1849.*

Treaties and Conventions Concluded between the Hawaiian Kingdom and Other Powers, since 1825. (Honolulu: 1887.)

8. Miscellaneous

Bell's Journal, Manuscript copy in Archives of Hawaii.

Memoirs of the Bernice P. Bishop Museum,

Vol. 1, No. 1, W. T. Brigham, *Featherwork.*

Vol. 1, No. 4, W. T. Brigham, *Stone Implements.*

Vol. 2, No. 1, W. T. Brigham, *Mat and Basket Weaving.*

Vol. 2, No. 3, W. T. Brigham, *The Ancient Hawaiian House.*

Vol. 3, W. T. Brigham, *Bark Cloth in Hawaii.*

Vols. 4, 5, 6, A. Fornander, *Collection of Hawaiian Antiquities and Folklore.*

Bernice P. Bishop Museum Bulletin, C. D. Miller, *Food Values of Poi, Taro, and Lima* (Honolulu: 1927).

Boit, Article in *Journal of the Union* (MS., in Archives of Hawaii).

Gregory, Dr. Herbert, *Official Papers of the Captain Cook Sesquicentennial Celebration* (Honolulu: 1928).

Howay, Frederick, *Papers of Captain Cook Sesquicentennial Celebration* (Honolulu: 1928).

———, *The Hawaiian Islands, Early Relations with the Pacific Northwest, etc.* Publication No. 5, Archives of Hawaii. (Honolulu: 1930.)

Richards, William, *Letter of William Richards to Commander Charles Wilkes, Esq., Commander of the U. S. A. Exploring Expedition.* (March 15, 1841.)

Spaulding, T. M., *The Crown Lands of Hawaii.* University of Hawaii Occasional Papers No. 1 (Honolulu).

Taylor, William H., "The Hawaiian Sugar Industry," MS. dissertation in Library of University of California at Berkeley.

Wadsworth, H. A., *Historical Summary of Irrigation in Hawaii.* University of Hawaii Miscellaneous Publications.

Wood, R. W., "The Manufacture of Sugar," Royal Agricultural Society *Transactions* (1850).

INDEX

Bei Fragen zur Produktsicherheit wenden Sie sich bitte an:
If you have any questions regarding product safety,
please contact:

Walter de Gruyter GmbH
Genthiner Straße 13
10785 Berlin
productsafety@degruyterbrill.com